INDEPENDENCE DAY
DARK FATHOM

TITAN
COMICS

INDEPENDENCE DAY

INDEPENDENCE DAY: DARK FATHOM

ISBN: 9781785851803

Published by Titan Comics, a division of Titan Publishing Group, Ltd. 144 Southwark Street, London, SE1 0UP.

Contains material originally published in Independence Day (2016) #1-5.

A CIP catalogue record for this title is available from the British Library. First edition: July 2016.

10 9 8 7 6 5 4 3 2 1

Printed in the U.S.A. TC1564.

WWW.TITAN-COMICS.COM

TITAN COMICS

COLLECTION EDITOR
Tom Williams

SENIOR COMICS EDITOR
Andrew James

ASSISTANT COLLECTION EDITOR
Jessica Burton

COLLECTION DESIGNER
Rob Farmer

TITAN COMICS EDITORIAL
Lizzie Kaye, Amoona Saohin

PRODUCTION ASSISTANT
Peter James

PRODUCTION SUPERVISORS
Maria Pearson, Jackie Flook

PRODUCTION MANAGER
Obi Onuora

SENIOR SALES MANAGER
Steve Tothill

BRAND MANAGER, MARKETING
Lucy Ripper

PRESS OFFICER
William O'Mullane

SENIOR MARKETING & PRESS OFFICER
Owen Johnson

DIRECT SALES & MARKETING MANAGER
Ricky Claydon

COMMERCIAL MANAGER
Michelle Fairlamb

PUBLISHING MANAGER
Darryl Tothill

PUBLISHING DIRECTOR
Chris Teather

OPERATIONS DIRECTOR
Leigh Baulch

EXECUTIVE DIRECTOR
Vivian Cheung

PUBLISHER
Nick Landau

TITAN COMICS

20th CENTURY FOX CONSUMER PRODUCTS

CENTROPOLIS ENTERTAINMENT

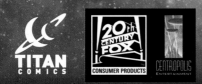

INDEPENDENCE DAY
DARK FATHOM

WRITTEN BY
VICTOR GISCHLER

ART BY
**STEVE SCOTT · RODNEY RAMOS
ALEX SHIBAO · TAZIO BETTIN
IVAN RODRIGUEZ**

ART ASSISTS BY
RUI WOBERTO · RENARTO ARLEM

INKS BY
**RODNEY RAMOS · GIORGIA SPOSITO
JED DOUGHERTY**

LETTERS BY
ROB STEEN

COLORED BY:
STEFANI RENNEE
THIAGO RIBEIRO · MARCIO MENYZ
MAX FLAN · RODRIGO FERNANDES
ARISON AGUIAR · MANNY CLARK

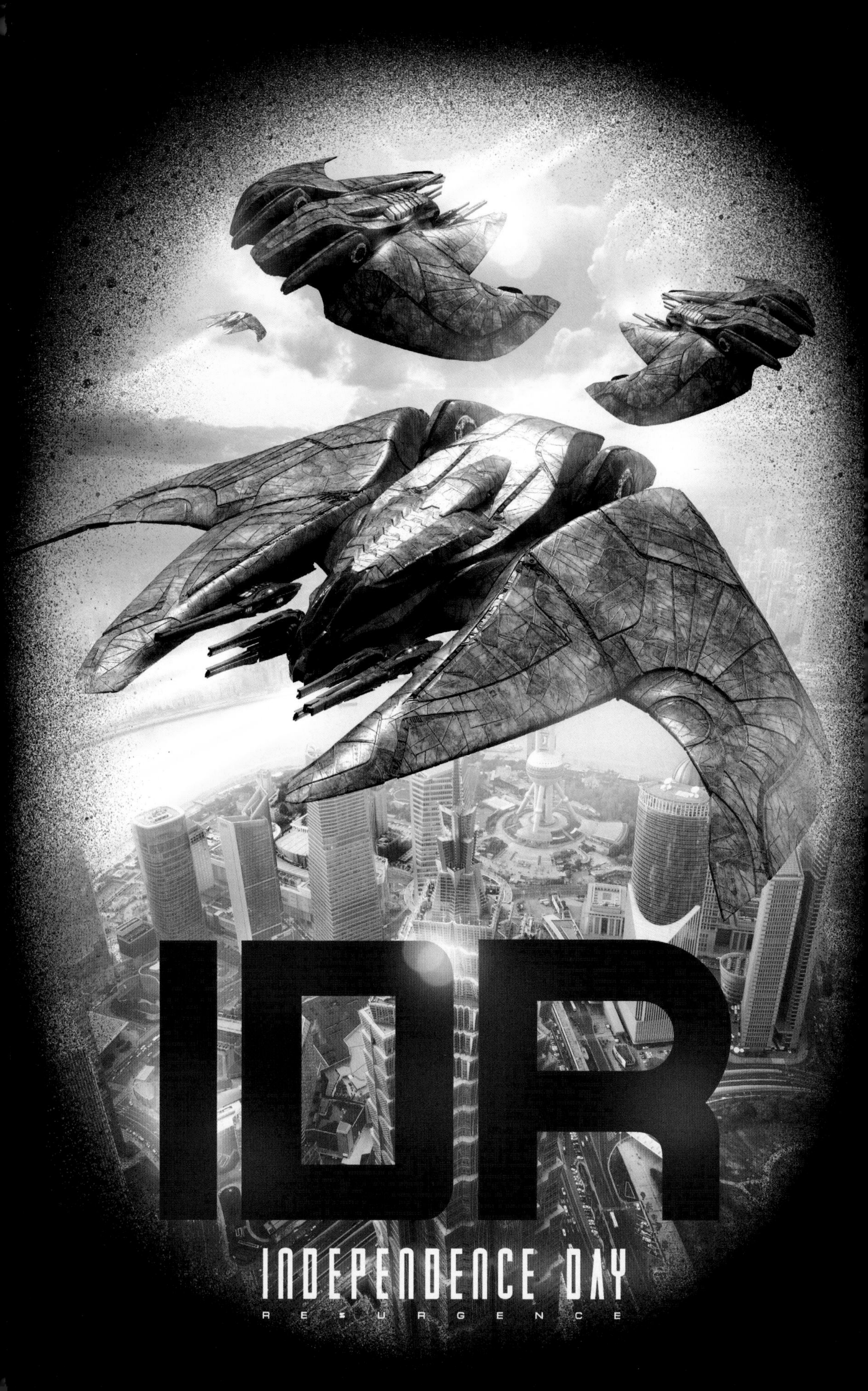
IDR
INDEPENDENCE DAY
RESURGENCE

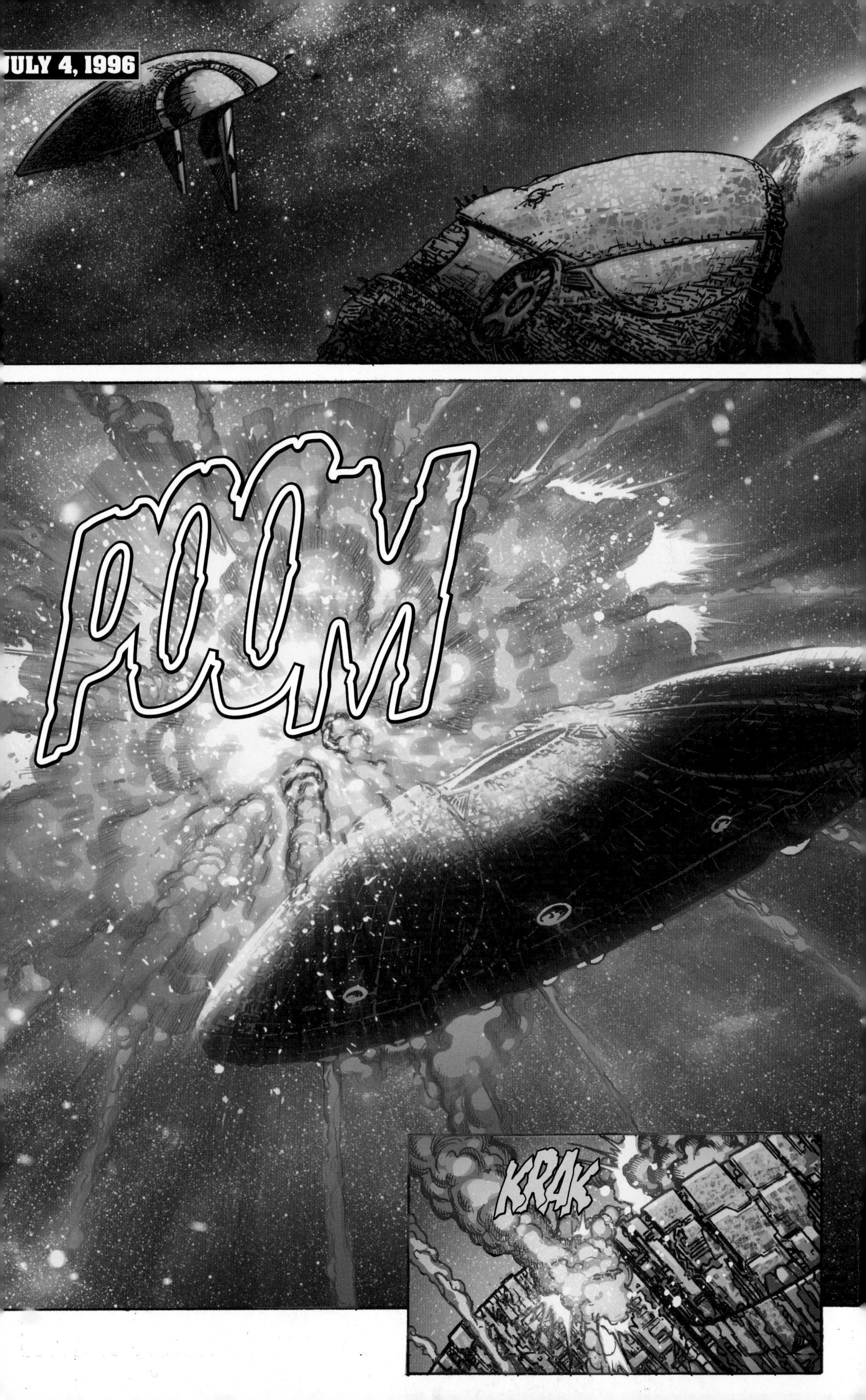
ULY 4, 1996
BOOM
KRAK

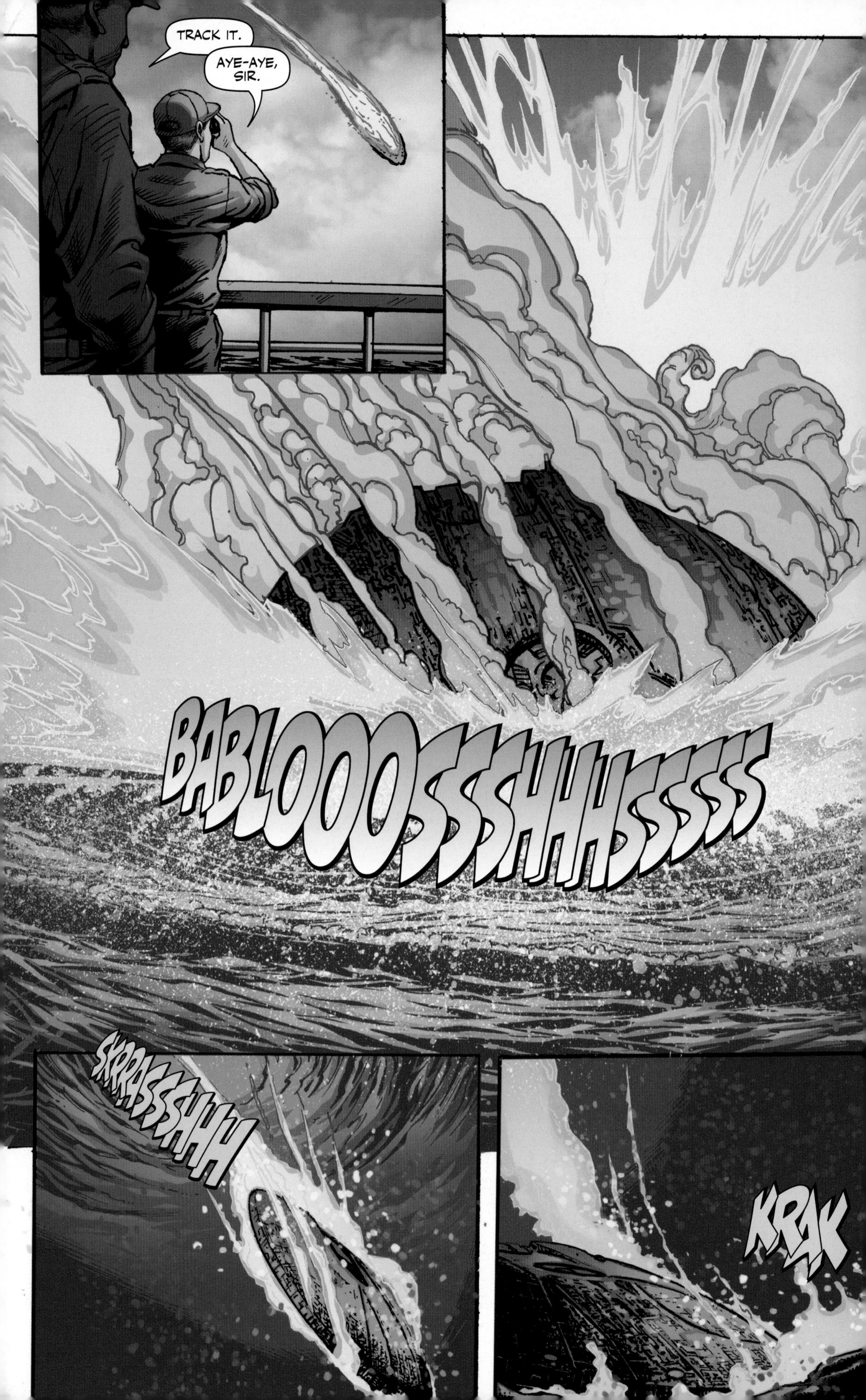
TRACK IT.
AYE-AYE, SIR.
BABLOOOSSSHHSSSSS
SKRASSSHHH
KRAK

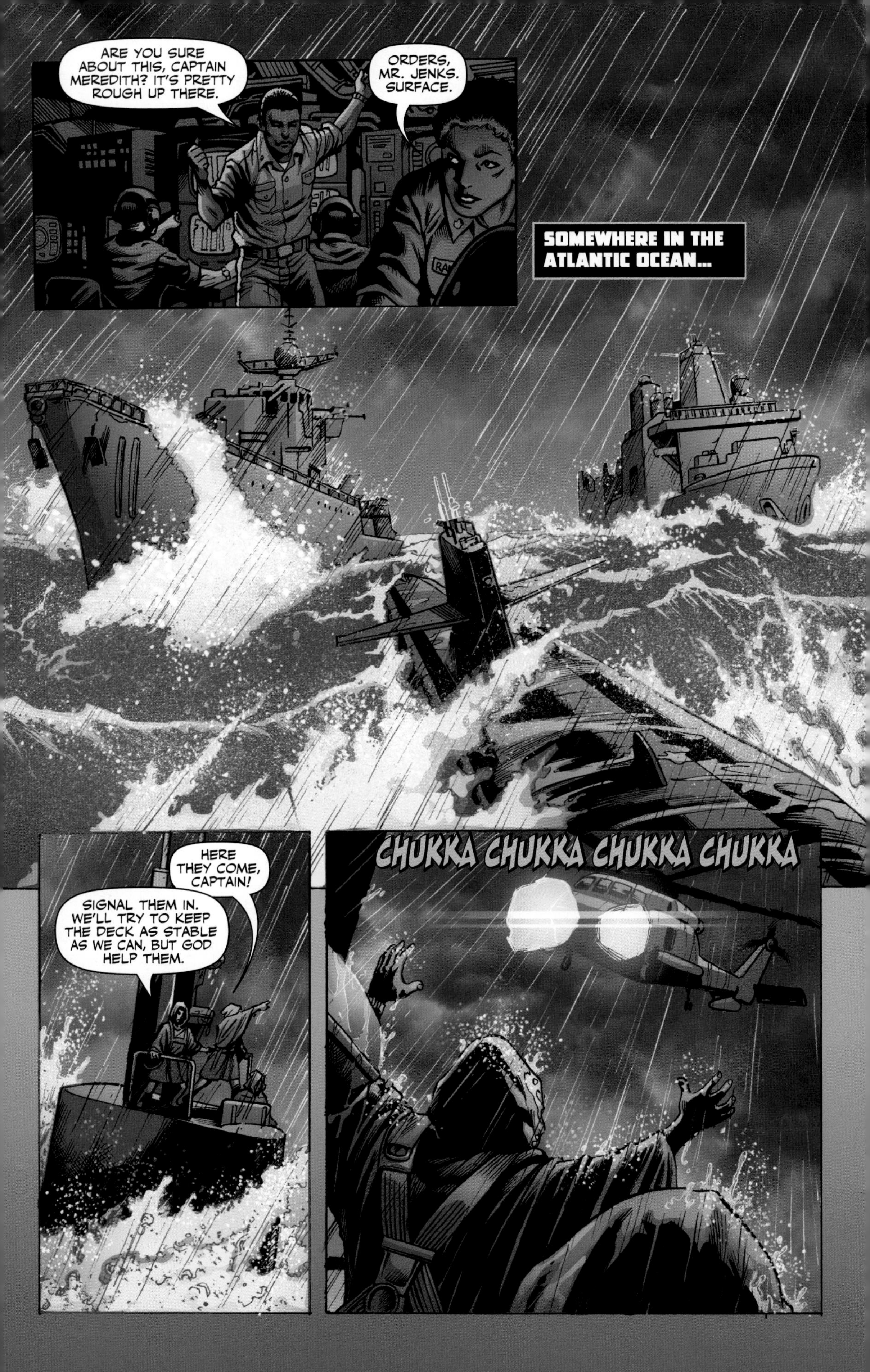
ARE YOU SURE ABOUT THIS, CAPTAIN MEREDITH? IT'S PRETTY ROUGH UP THERE.
ORDERS, MR. JENKS. SURFACE.
SOMEWHERE IN THE ATLANTIC OCEAN...
HERE THEY COME, CAPTAIN!
SIGNAL THEM IN. WE'LL TRY TO KEEP THE DECK AS STABLE AS WE CAN, BUT GOD HELP THEM.
CHUKKA CHUKKA CHUKKA CHUKKA

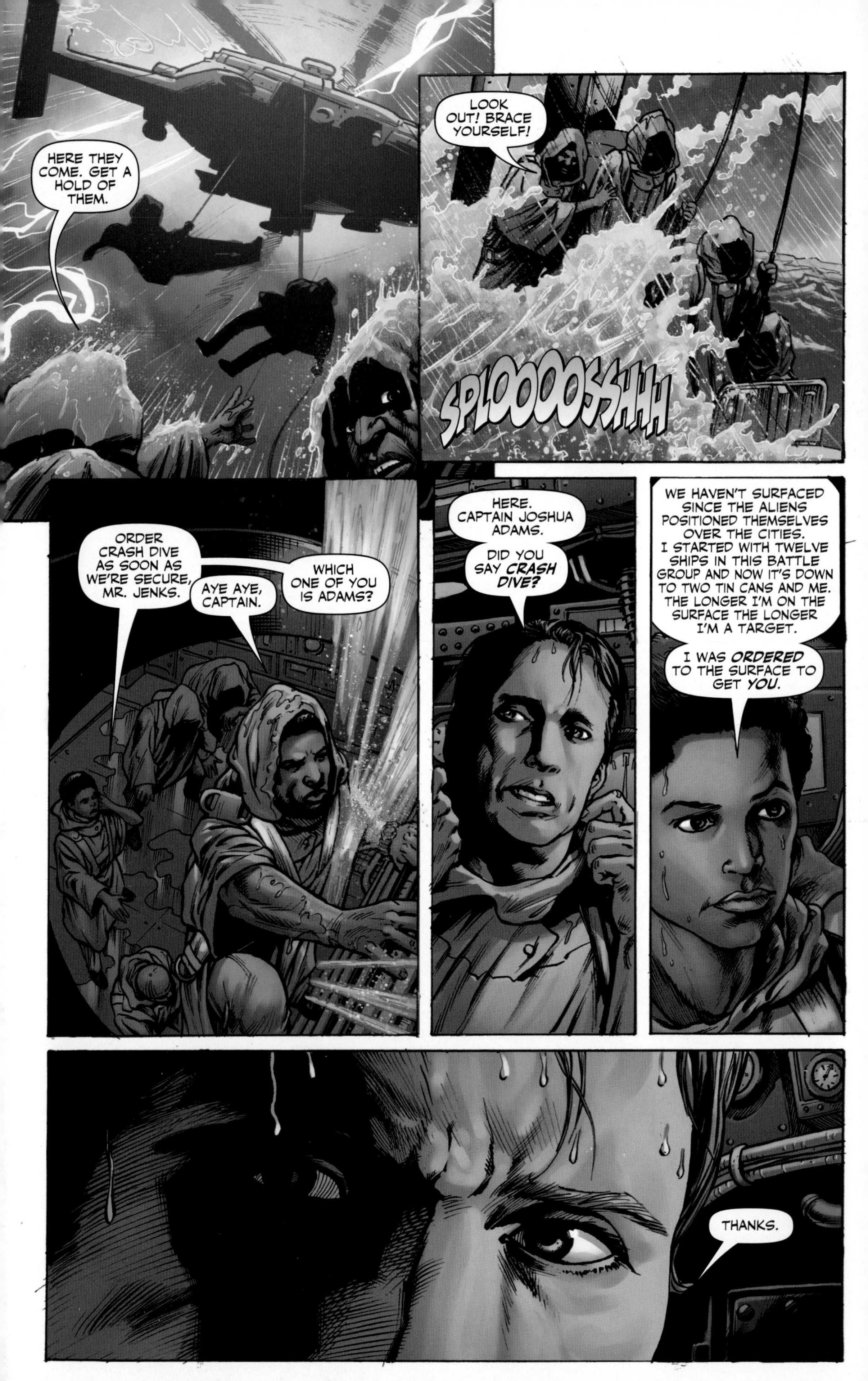
HERE THEY COME. GET A HOLD OF THEM.
LOOK OUT! BRACE YOURSELF!
SPLOOOOSSHHH
ORDER CRASH DIVE AS SOON AS WE'RE SECURE, MR. JENKS.
AYE AYE, CAPTAIN.
WHICH ONE OF YOU IS ADAMS?
HERE. CAPTAIN JOSHUA ADAMS.
DID YOU SAY *CRASH DIVE?*
WE HAVEN'T SURFACED SINCE THE ALIENS POSITIONED THEMSELVES OVER THE CITIES. I STARTED WITH TWELVE SHIPS IN THIS BATTLE GROUP AND NOW IT'S DOWN TO TWO TIN CANS AND ME. THE LONGER I'M ON THE SURFACE THE LONGER I'M A TARGET.
I WAS *ORDERED* TO THE SURFACE TO GET *YOU*.
THANKS.

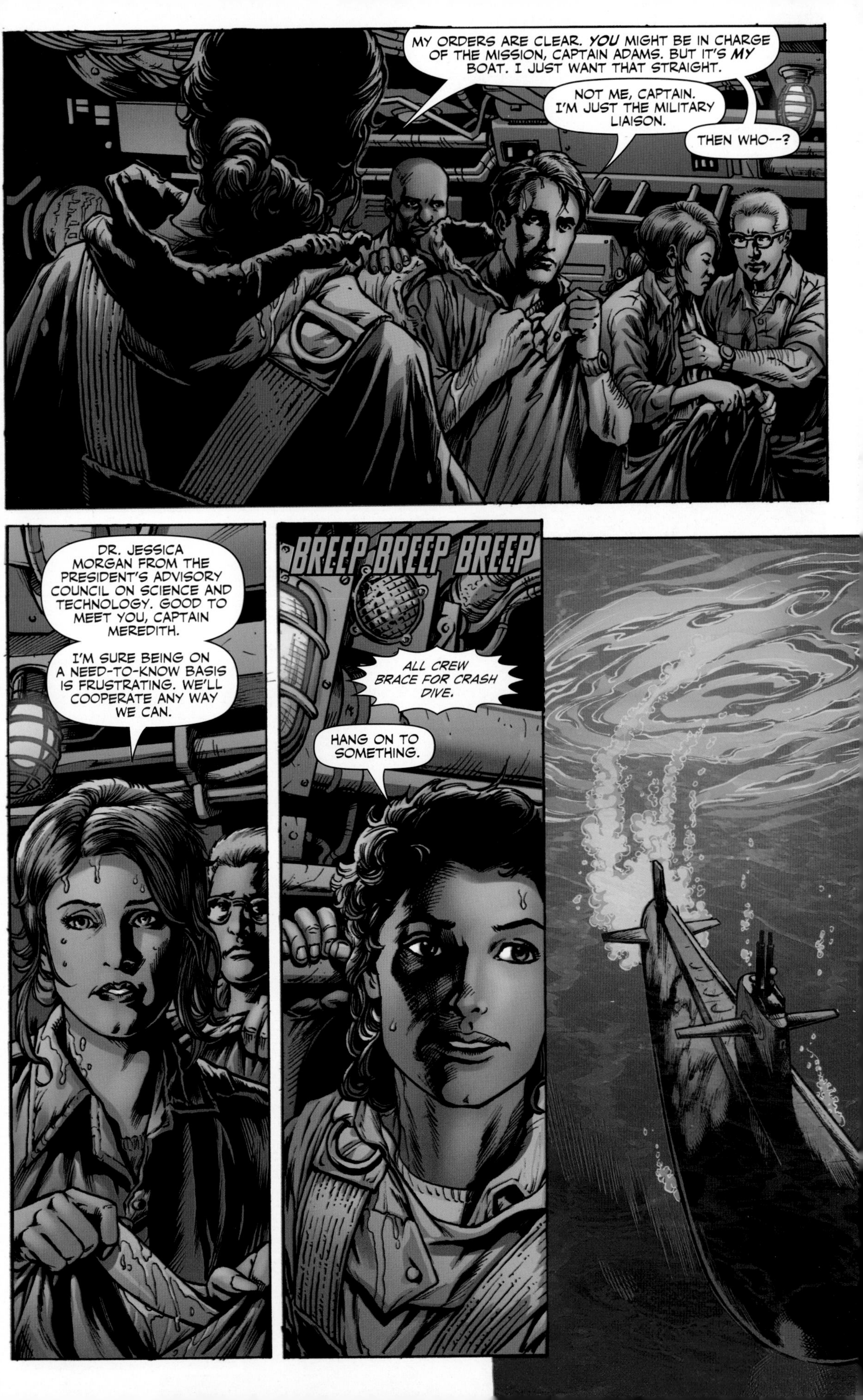
MY ORDERS ARE CLEAR. YOU MIGHT BE IN CHARGE OF THE MISSION, CAPTAIN ADAMS. BUT IT'S MY BOAT. I JUST WANT THAT STRAIGHT.
NOT ME, CAPTAIN. I'M JUST THE MILITARY LIAISON.
THEN WHO--?
DR. JESSICA MORGAN FROM THE PRESIDENT'S ADVISORY COUNCIL ON SCIENCE AND TECHNOLOGY. GOOD TO MEET YOU, CAPTAIN MEREDITH.
I'M SURE BEING ON A NEED-TO-KNOW BASIS IS FRUSTRATING. WE'LL COOPERATE ANY WAY WE CAN.
BREEP BREEP BREEP
ALL CREW BRACE FOR CRASH DIVE.
HANG ON TO SOMETHING.

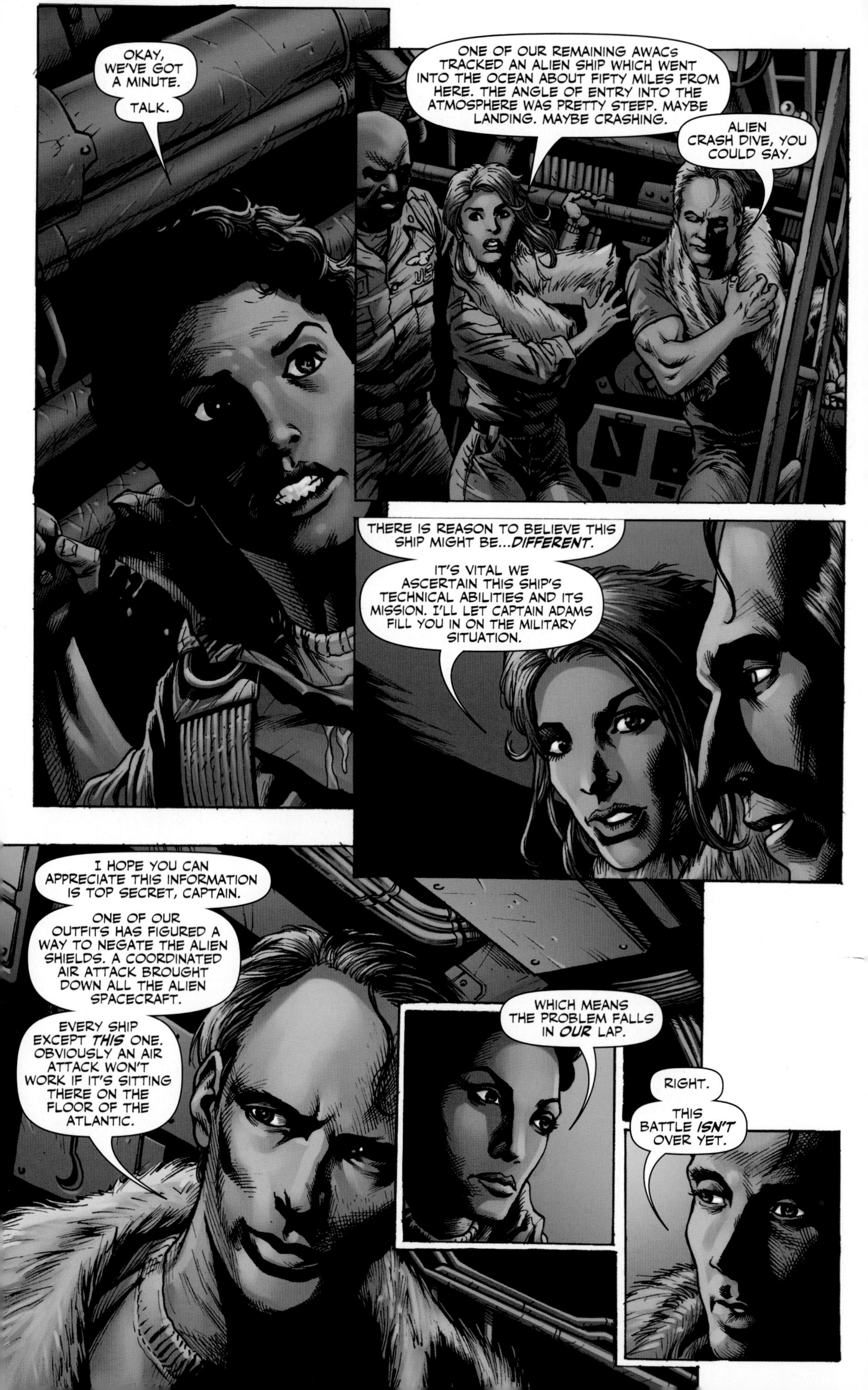
OKAY, WE'VE GOT A MINUTE.
TALK.
ONE OF OUR REMAINING AWACs TRACKED AN ALIEN SHIP WHICH WENT INTO THE OCEAN ABOUT FIFTY MILES FROM HERE. THE ANGLE OF ENTRY INTO THE ATMOSPHERE WAS PRETTY STEEP. MAYBE LANDING. MAYBE CRASHING.
ALIEN CRASH DIVE, YOU COULD SAY.
THERE IS REASON TO BELIEVE THIS SHIP MIGHT BE...*DIFFERENT*.
IT'S VITAL WE ASCERTAIN THIS SHIP'S TECHNICAL ABILITIES AND ITS MISSION. I'LL LET CAPTAIN ADAMS FILL YOU IN ON THE MILITARY SITUATION.
I HOPE YOU CAN APPRECIATE THIS INFORMATION IS TOP SECRET, CAPTAIN.
ONE OF OUR OUTFITS HAS FIGURED A WAY TO NEGATE THE ALIEN SHIELDS. A COORDINATED AIR ATTACK BROUGHT DOWN ALL THE ALIEN SPACECRAFT.
EVERY SHIP EXCEPT ***THIS*** ONE. OBVIOUSLY AN AIR ATTACK WON'T WORK IF IT'S SITTING THERE ON THE FLOOR OF THE ATLANTIC.
WHICH MEANS THE PROBLEM FALLS IN ***OUR*** LAP.
RIGHT.
THIS BATTLE *ISN'T* OVER YET.

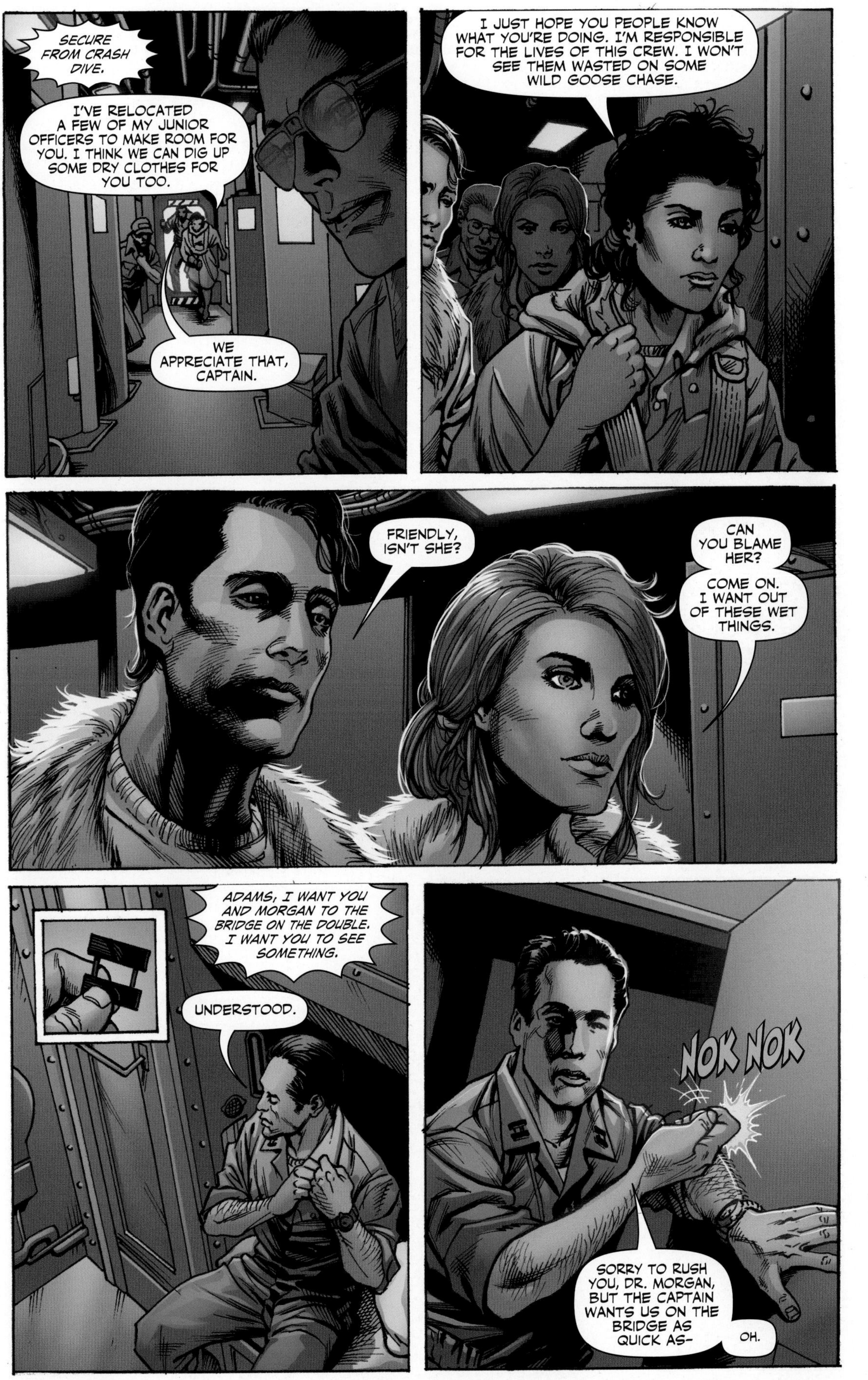
SECURE FROM CRASH DIVE.
I'VE RELOCATED A FEW OF MY JUNIOR OFFICERS TO MAKE ROOM FOR YOU. I THINK WE CAN DIG UP SOME DRY CLOTHES FOR YOU TOO.
WE APPRECIATE THAT, CAPTAIN.
I JUST HOPE YOU PEOPLE KNOW WHAT YOU'RE DOING. I'M RESPONSIBLE FOR THE LIVES OF THIS CREW. I WON'T SEE THEM WASTED ON SOME WILD GOOSE CHASE.
FRIENDLY, ISN'T SHE?
CAN YOU BLAME HER?
COME ON. I WANT OUT OF THESE WET THINGS.
ADAMS, I WANT YOU AND MORGAN TO THE BRIDGE ON THE DOUBLE. I WANT YOU TO SEE SOMETHING.
UNDERSTOOD.
NOK NOK
SORRY TO RUSH YOU, DR. MORGAN, BUT THE CAPTAIN WANTS US ON THE BRIDGE AS QUICK AS-
OH.

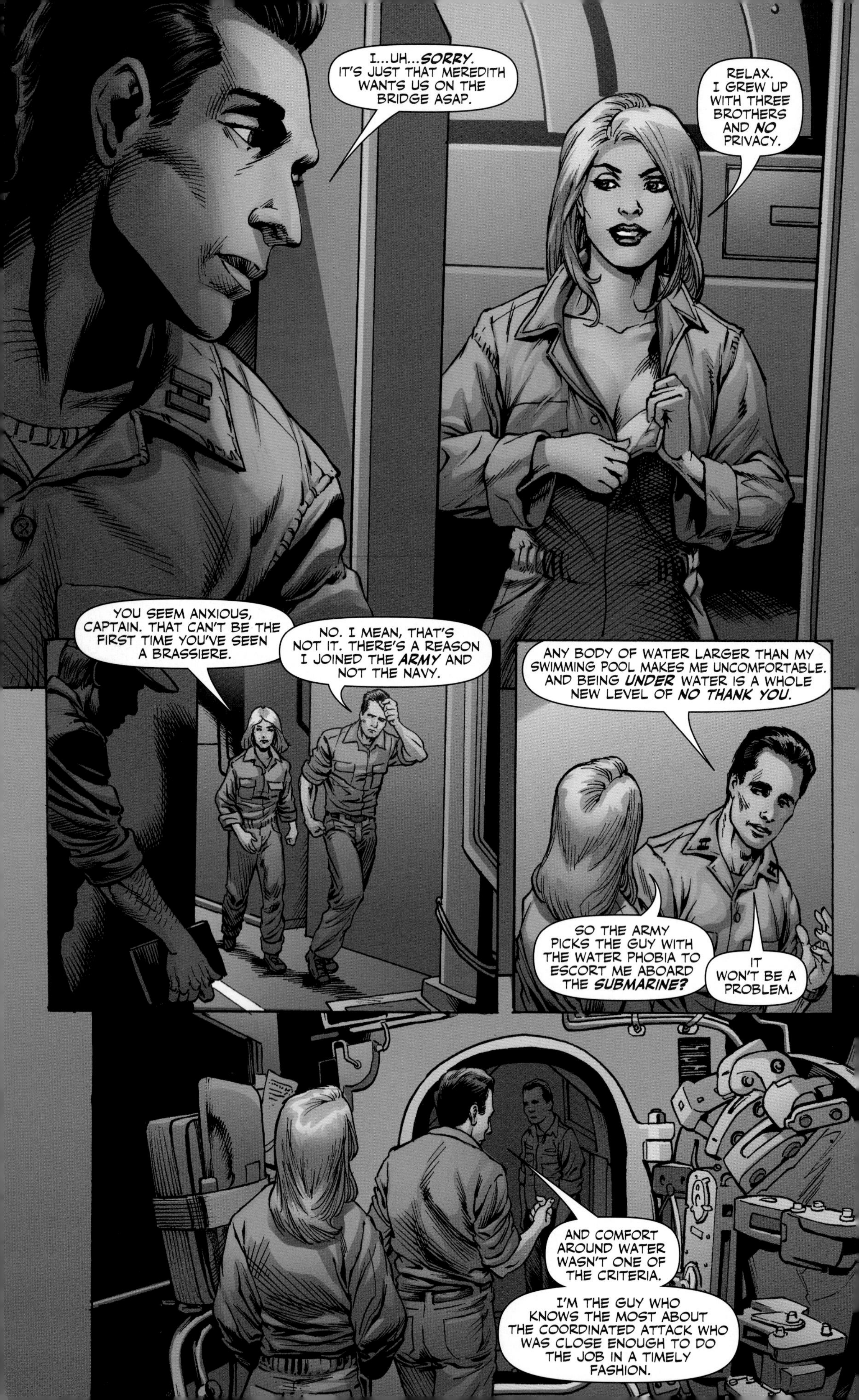
I...UH...SORRY. IT'S JUST THAT MEREDITH WANTS US ON THE BRIDGE ASAP.
RELAX. I GREW UP WITH THREE BROTHERS AND NO PRIVACY.
YOU SEEM ANXIOUS, CAPTAIN. THAT CAN'T BE THE FIRST TIME YOU'VE SEEN A BRASSIERE.
NO. I MEAN, THAT'S NOT IT. THERE'S A REASON I JOINED THE ARMY AND NOT THE NAVY.
ANY BODY OF WATER LARGER THAN MY SWIMMING POOL MAKES ME UNCOMFORTABLE. AND BEING UNDER WATER IS A WHOLE NEW LEVEL OF NO THANK YOU.
SO THE ARMY PICKS THE GUY WITH THE WATER PHOBIA TO ESCORT ME ABOARD THE SUBMARINE?
IT WON'T BE A PROBLEM.
AND COMFORT AROUND WATER WASN'T ONE OF THE CRITERIA.
I'M THE GUY WHO KNOWS THE MOST ABOUT THE COORDINATED ATTACK WHO WAS CLOSE ENOUGH TO DO THE JOB IN A TIMELY FASHION.

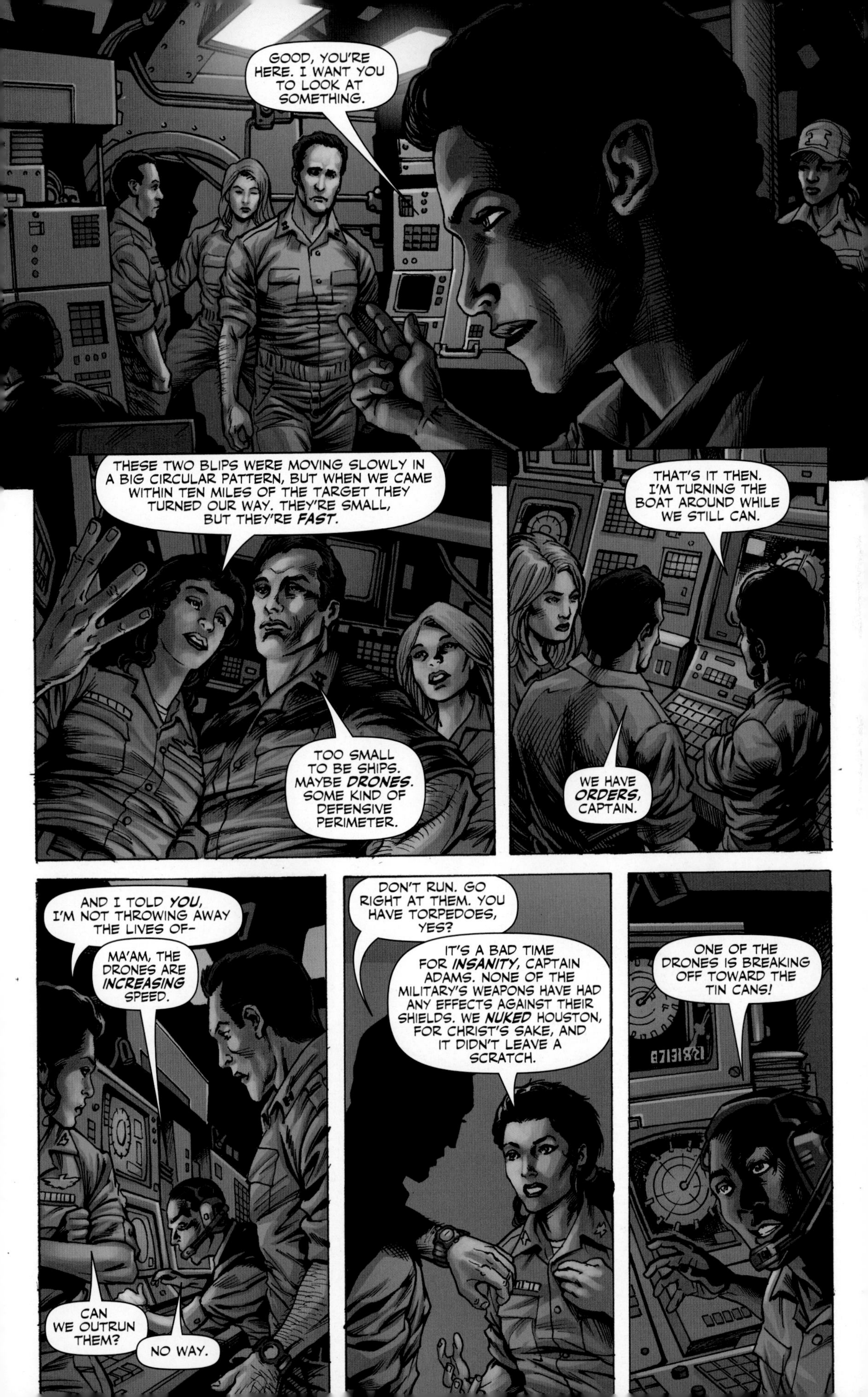
GOOD, YOU'RE HERE. I WANT YOU TO LOOK AT SOMETHING.
THESE TWO BLIPS WERE MOVING SLOWLY IN A BIG CIRCULAR PATTERN, BUT WHEN WE CAME WITHIN TEN MILES OF THE TARGET THEY TURNED OUR WAY. THEY'RE SMALL, BUT THEY'RE FAST.
TOO SMALL TO BE SHIPS. MAYBE DRONES. SOME KIND OF DEFENSIVE PERIMETER.
THAT'S IT THEN. I'M TURNING THE BOAT AROUND WHILE WE STILL CAN.
WE HAVE ORDERS, CAPTAIN.
AND I TOLD YOU, I'M NOT THROWING AWAY THE LIVES OF-
MA'AM, THE DRONES ARE INCREASING SPEED.
CAN WE OUTRUN THEM?
NO WAY.
DON'T RUN. GO RIGHT AT THEM. YOU HAVE TORPEDOES, YES?
IT'S A BAD TIME FOR INSANITY, CAPTAIN ADAMS. NONE OF THE MILITARY'S WEAPONS HAVE HAD ANY EFFECTS AGAINST THEIR SHIELDS. WE NUKED HOUSTON, FOR CHRIST'S SAKE, AND IT DIDN'T LEAVE A SCRATCH.
ONE OF THE DRONES IS BREAKING OFF TOWARD THE TIN CANS!

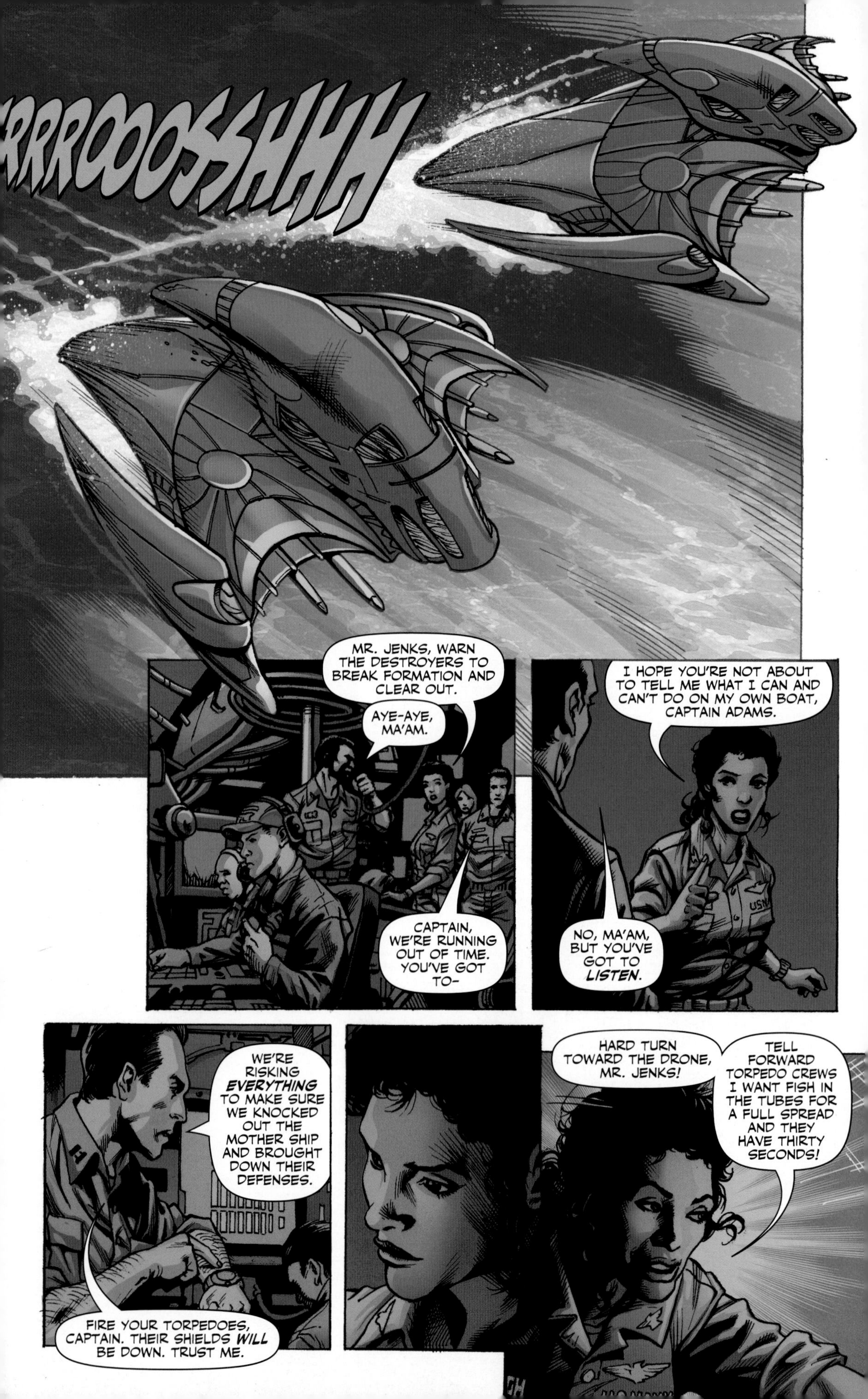

RRROOOSSHHH
MR. JENKS, WARN THE DESTROYERS TO BREAK FORMATION AND CLEAR OUT.
AYE-AYE, MA'AM.
CAPTAIN, WE'RE RUNNING OUT OF TIME. YOU'VE GOT TO-
I HOPE YOU'RE NOT ABOUT TO TELL ME WHAT I CAN AND CAN'T DO ON MY OWN BOAT, CAPTAIN ADAMS.
NO, MA'AM, BUT YOU'VE GOT TO *LISTEN*.
WE'RE RISKING *EVERYTHING* TO MAKE SURE WE KNOCKED OUT THE MOTHER SHIP AND BROUGHT DOWN THEIR DEFENSES.
FIRE YOUR TORPEDOES, CAPTAIN. THEIR SHIELDS *WILL* BE DOWN. TRUST ME.
HARD TURN TOWARD THE DRONE, MR. JENKS!
TELL FORWARD TORPEDO CREWS I WANT FISH IN THE TUBES FOR A FULL SPREAD AND THEY HAVE THIRTY SECONDS!

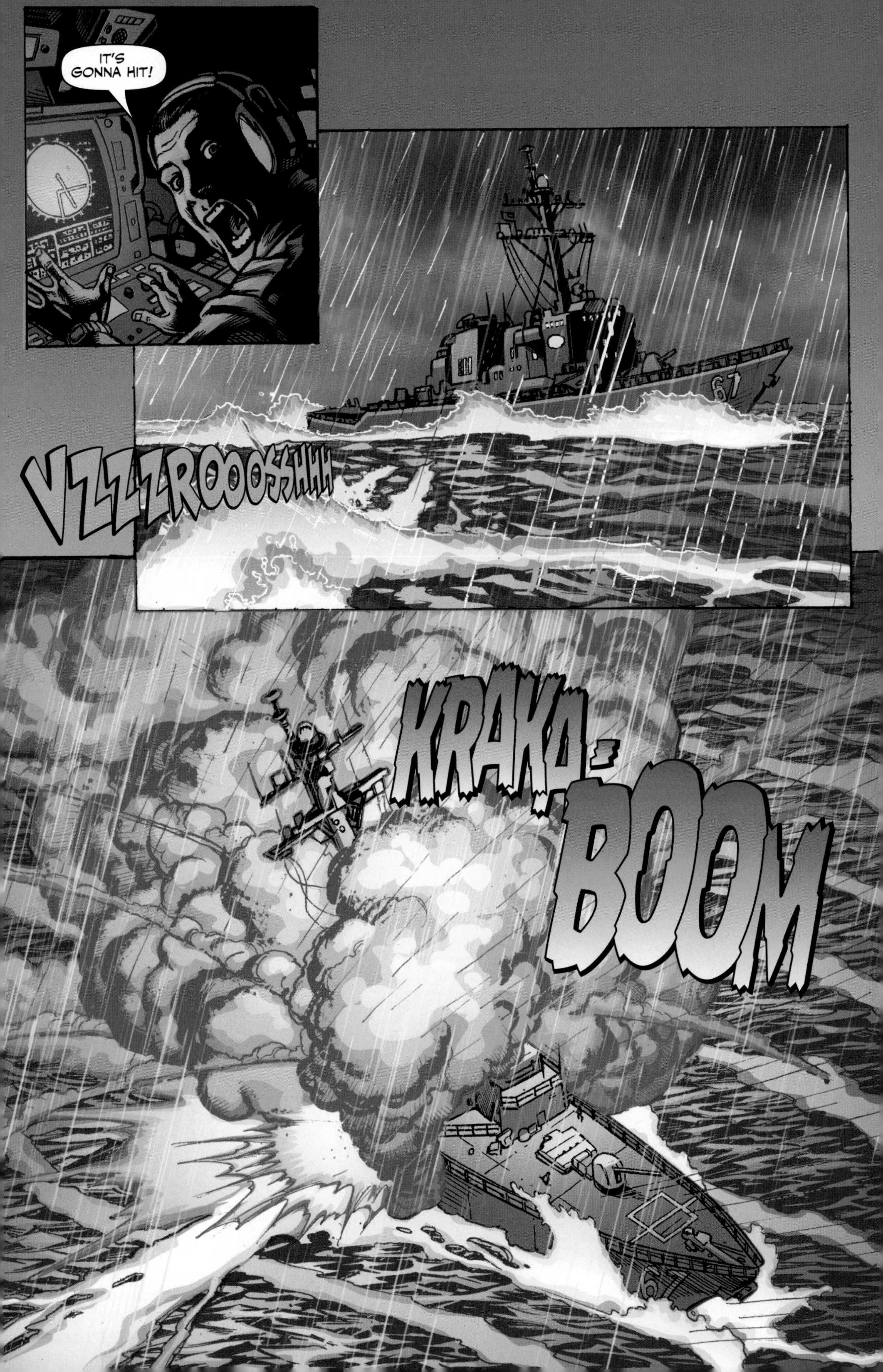
IT'S GONNA HIT!
VZZZROOOSHHH
KRAKA-BOOM

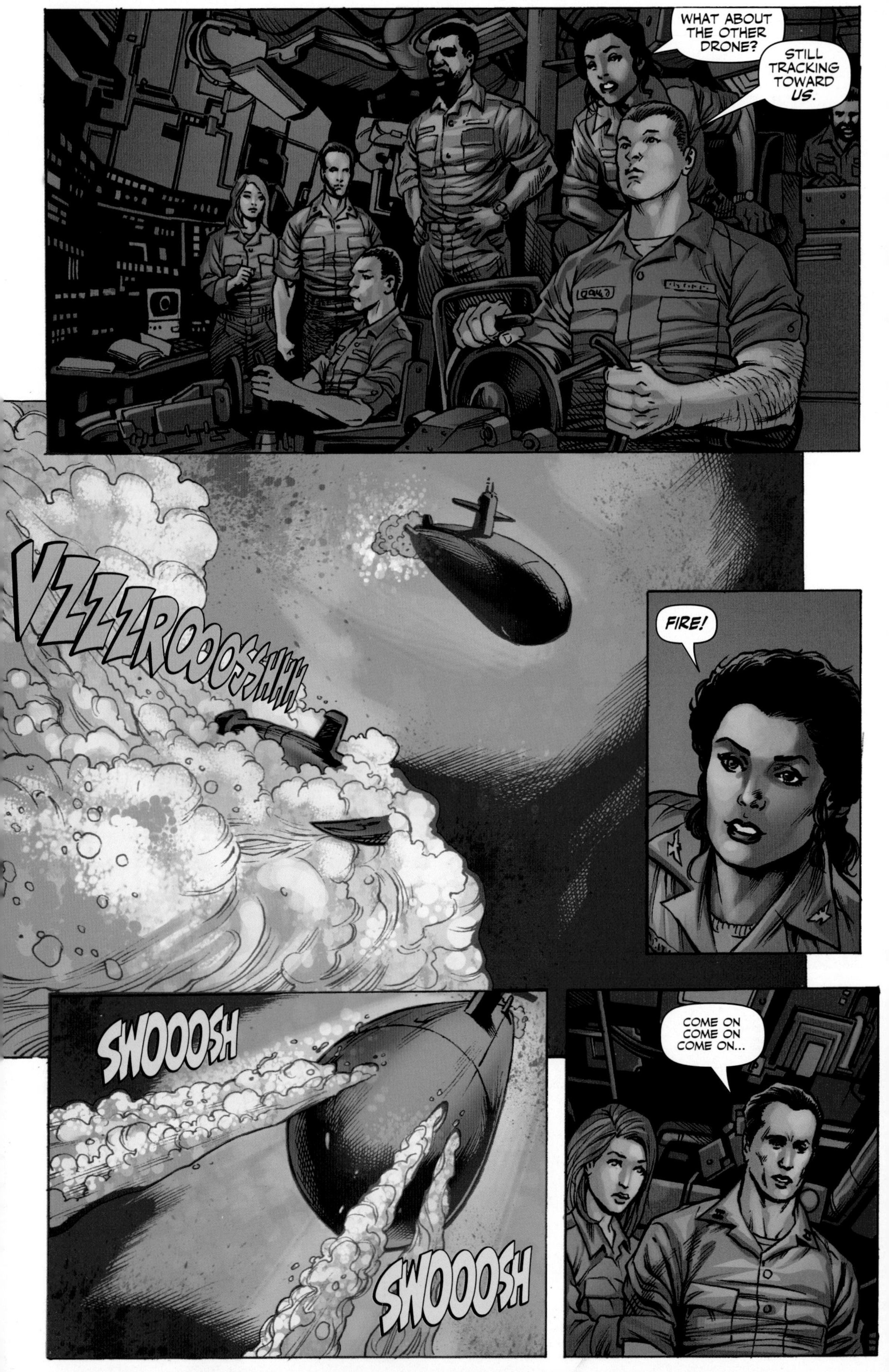
WHAT ABOUT THE OTHER DRONE?
STILL TRACKING TOWARD US.
VZZZROOOSHHH
FIRE!
SWOOOSH
SWOOOSH
COME ON COME ON COME ON...

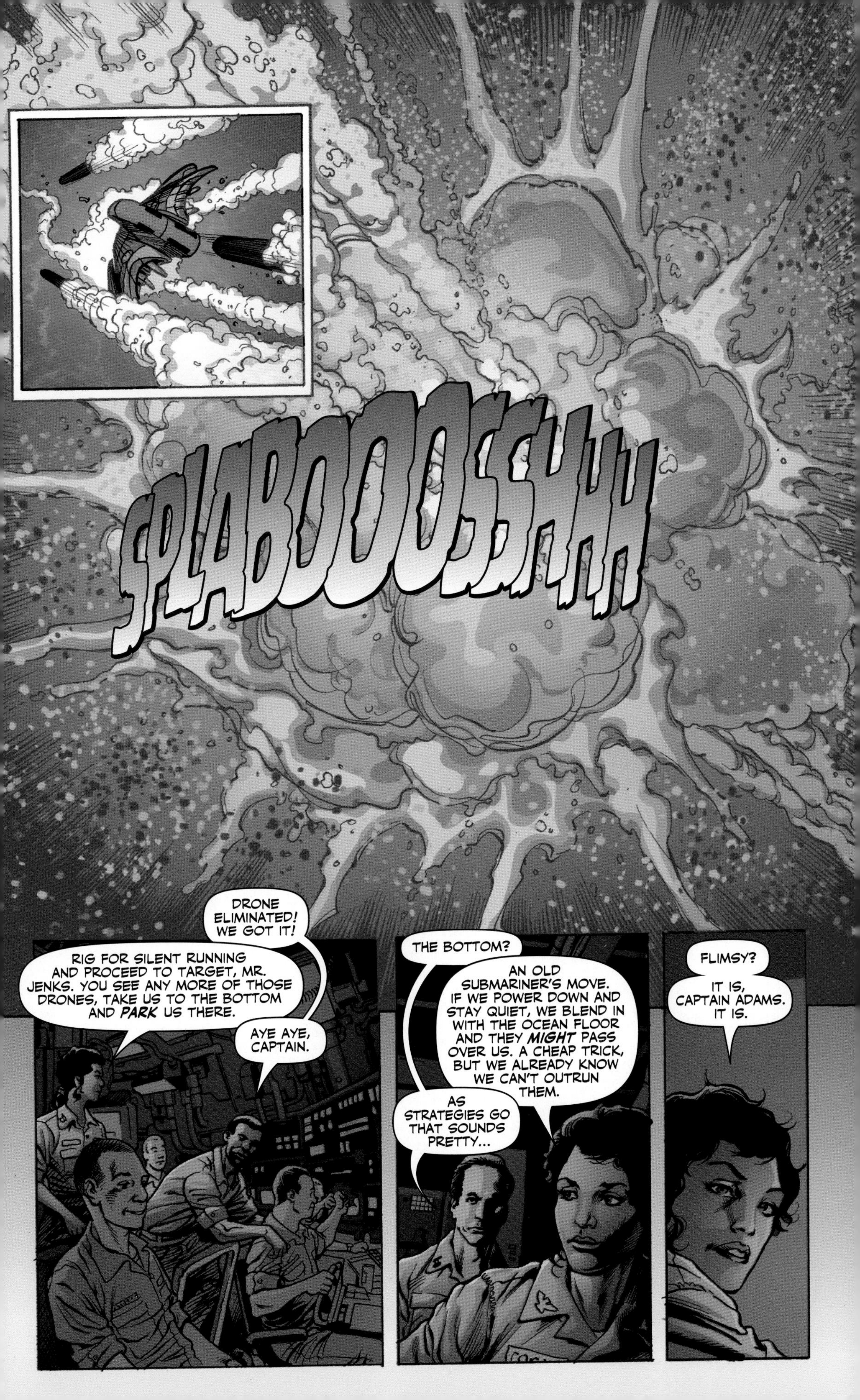
SPLABOOOSHHH
DRONE ELIMINATED! WE GOT IT!
RIG FOR SILENT RUNNING AND PROCEED TO TARGET, MR. JENKS. YOU SEE ANY MORE OF THOSE DRONES, TAKE US TO THE BOTTOM AND PARK US THERE.
AYE AYE, CAPTAIN.
THE BOTTOM?
AN OLD SUBMARINER'S MOVE. IF WE POWER DOWN AND STAY QUIET, WE BLEND IN WITH THE OCEAN FLOOR AND THEY MIGHT PASS OVER US. A CHEAP TRICK, BUT WE ALREADY KNOW WE CAN'T OUTRUN THEM.
AS STRATEGIES GO THAT SOUNDS PRETTY...
FLIMSY?
IT IS, CAPTAIN ADAMS. IT IS.

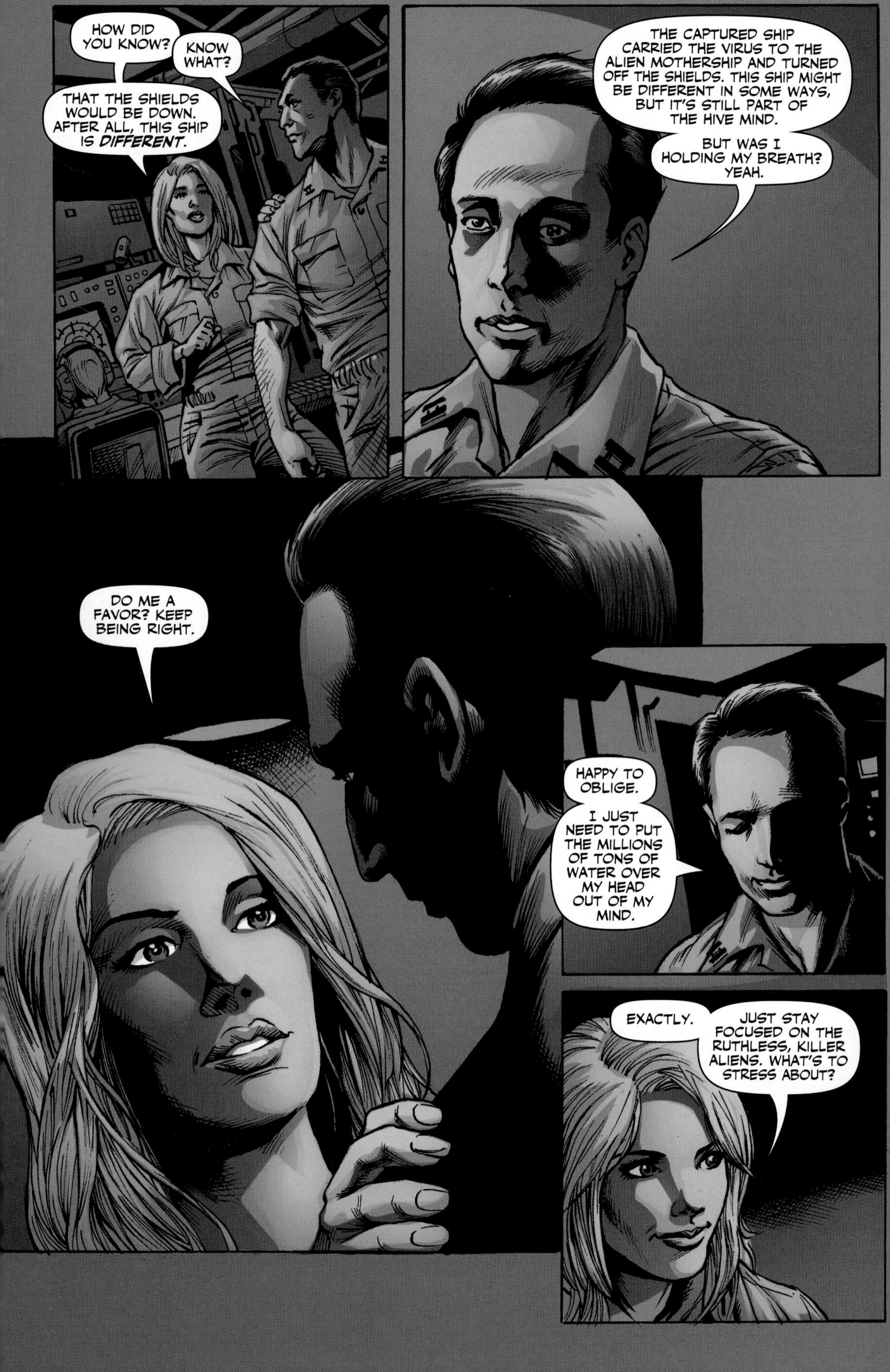
HOW DID YOU KNOW?
KNOW WHAT?
THAT THE SHIELDS WOULD BE DOWN. AFTER ALL, THIS SHIP IS *DIFFERENT*.
THE CAPTURED SHIP CARRIED THE VIRUS TO THE ALIEN MOTHERSHIP AND TURNED OFF THE SHIELDS. THIS SHIP MIGHT BE DIFFERENT IN SOME WAYS, BUT IT'S STILL PART OF THE HIVE MIND.
BUT WAS I HOLDING MY BREATH? YEAH.
DO ME A FAVOR? KEEP BEING RIGHT.
HAPPY TO OBLIGE.
I JUST NEED TO PUT THE MILLIONS OF TONS OF WATER OVER MY HEAD OUT OF MY MIND.
EXACTLY.
JUST STAY FOCUSED ON THE RUTHLESS, KILLER ALIENS. WHAT'S TO STRESS ABOUT?

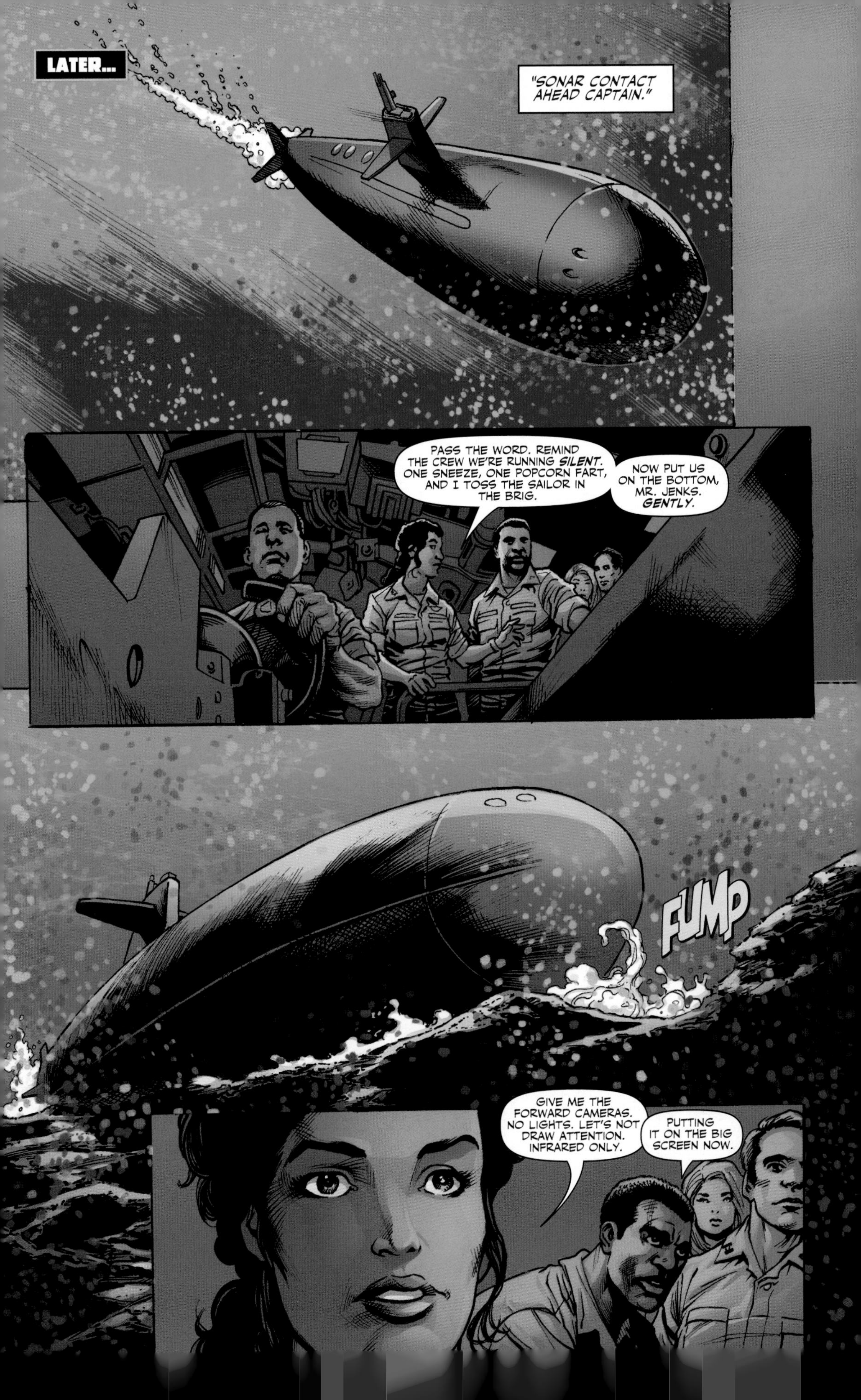
LATER...
"SONAR CONTACT AHEAD CAPTAIN."
PASS THE WORD. REMIND THE CREW WE'RE RUNNING SILENT. ONE SNEEZE, ONE POPCORN FART, AND I TOSS THE SAILOR IN THE BRIG.
NOW PUT US ON THE BOTTOM, MR. JENKS. GENTLY.
FUMP
GIVE ME THE FORWARD CAMERAS. NO LIGHTS. LET'S NOT DRAW ATTENTION. INFRARED ONLY.
PUTTING IT ON THE BIG SCREEN NOW.

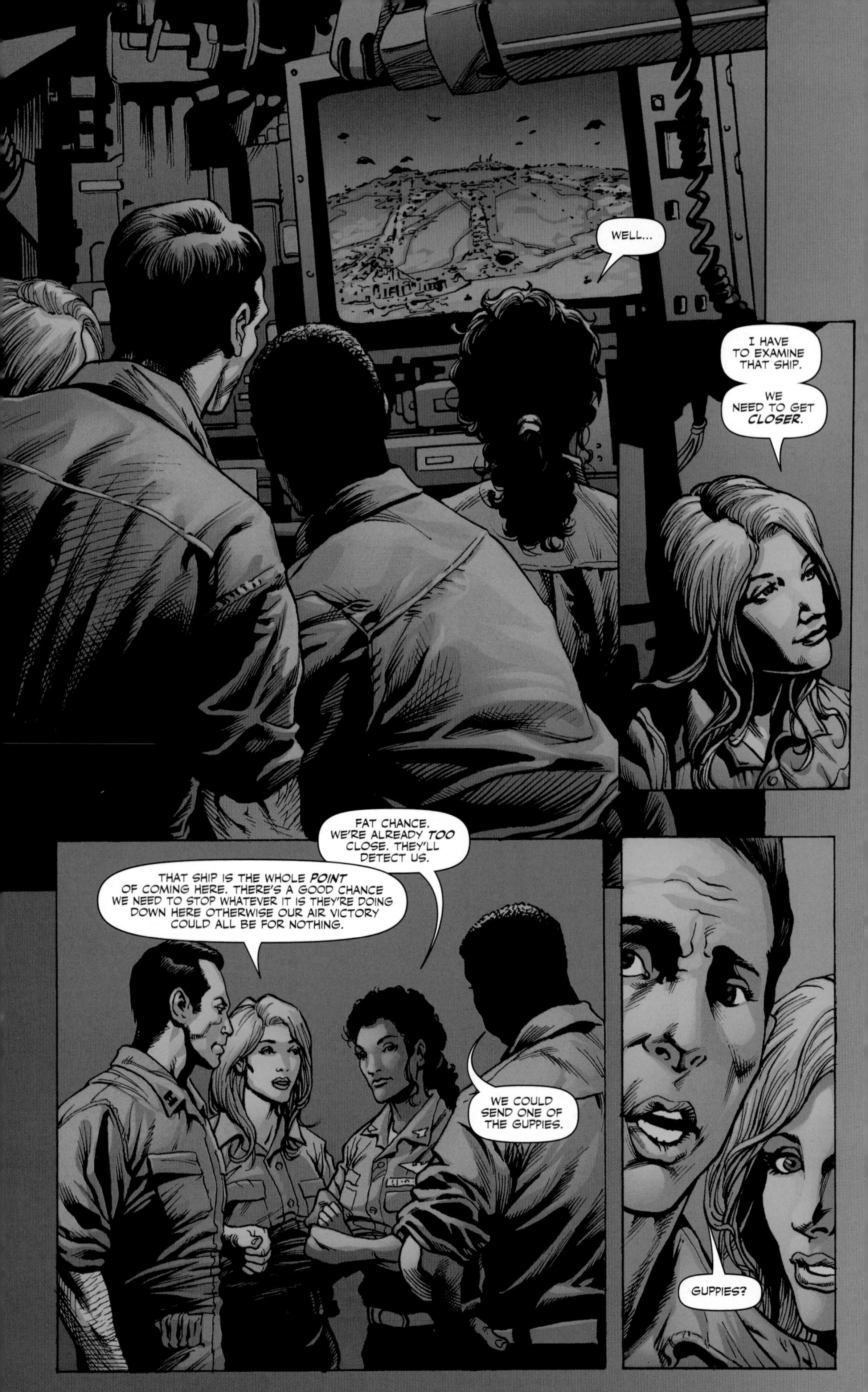
WELL...
I HAVE TO EXAMINE THAT SHIP.
WE NEED TO GET *CLOSER*.
THAT SHIP IS THE WHOLE *POINT* OF COMING HERE. THERE'S A GOOD CHANCE WE NEED TO STOP WHATEVER IT IS THEY'RE DOING DOWN HERE OTHERWISE OUR AIR VICTORY COULD ALL BE FOR NOTHING.
FAT CHANCE. WE'RE ALREADY *TOO* CLOSE. THEY'LL DETECT US.
WE COULD SEND ONE OF THE GUPPIES.
GUPPIES?

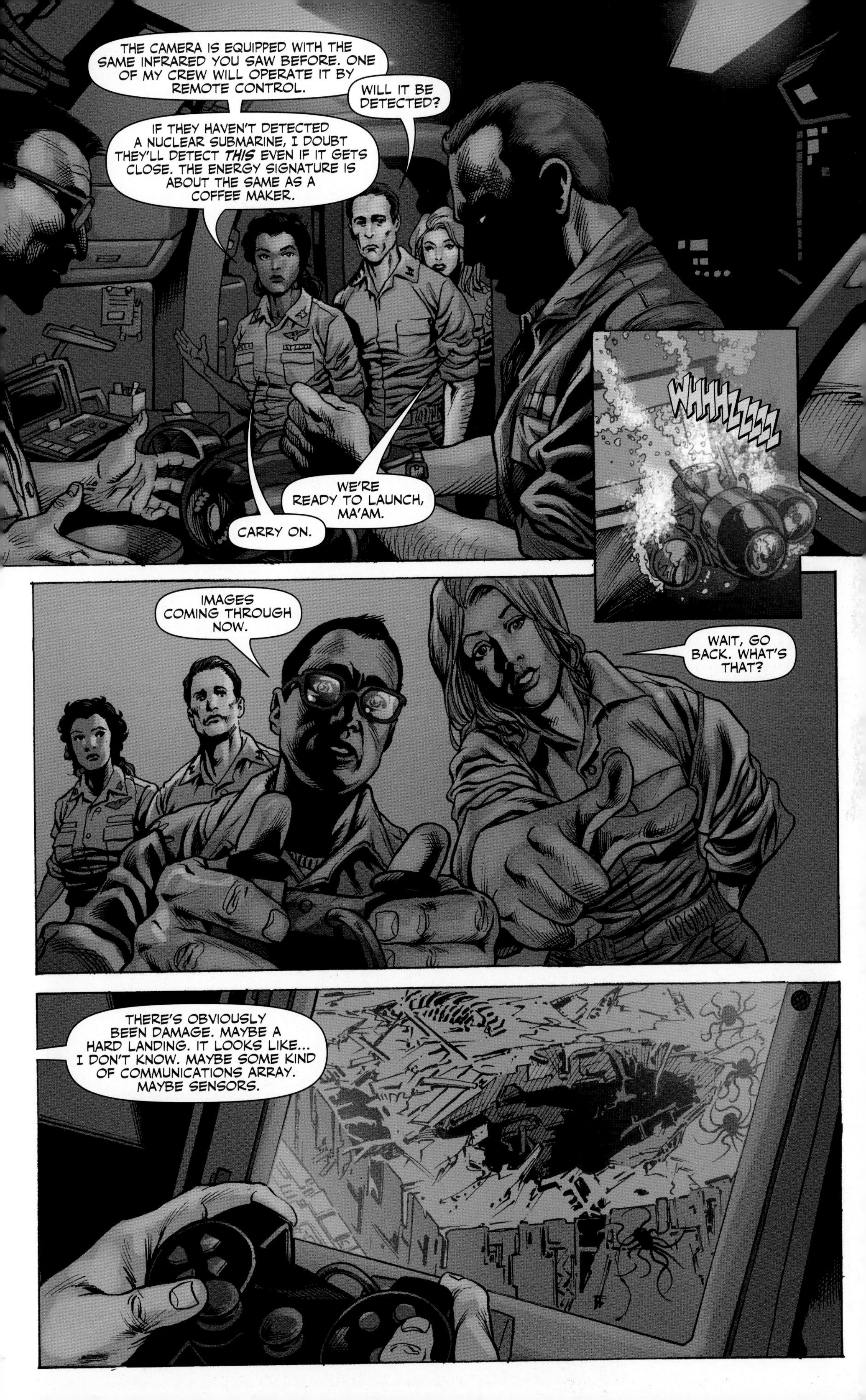
THE CAMERA IS EQUIPPED WITH THE SAME INFRARED YOU SAW BEFORE. ONE OF MY CREW WILL OPERATE IT BY REMOTE CONTROL.
WILL IT BE DETECTED?
IF THEY HAVEN'T DETECTED A NUCLEAR SUBMARINE, I DOUBT THEY'LL DETECT *THIS* EVEN IF IT GETS CLOSE. THE ENERGY SIGNATURE IS ABOUT THE SAME AS A COFFEE MAKER.
WE'RE READY TO LAUNCH, MA'AM.
CARRY ON.
WHHHZZZZZ
IMAGES COMING THROUGH NOW.
WAIT, GO BACK. WHAT'S THAT?
THERE'S OBVIOUSLY BEEN DAMAGE. MAYBE A HARD LANDING. IT LOOKS LIKE... I DON'T KNOW. MAYBE SOME KIND OF COMMUNICATIONS ARRAY. MAYBE SENSORS.

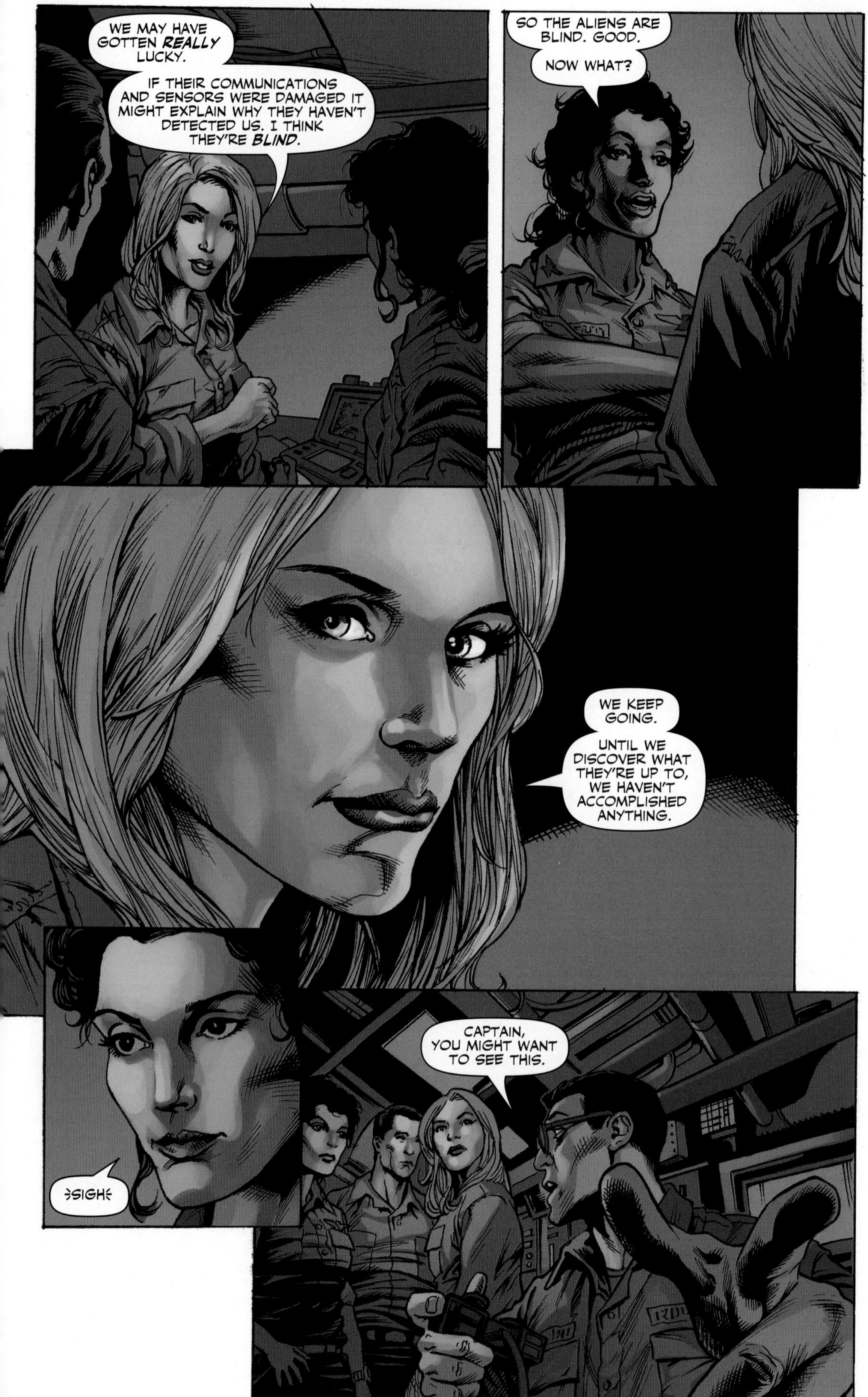

WE MAY HAVE GOTTEN *REALLY* LUCKY.
IF THEIR COMMUNICATIONS AND SENSORS WERE DAMAGED IT MIGHT EXPLAIN WHY THEY HAVEN'T DETECTED US. I THINK THEY'RE *BLIND*.
SO THE ALIENS ARE BLIND. GOOD.
NOW WHAT?
WE KEEP GOING.
UNTIL WE DISCOVER WHAT THEY'RE UP TO, WE HAVEN'T ACCOMPLISHED ANYTHING.
SIGH
CAPTAIN, YOU MIGHT WANT TO SEE THIS.

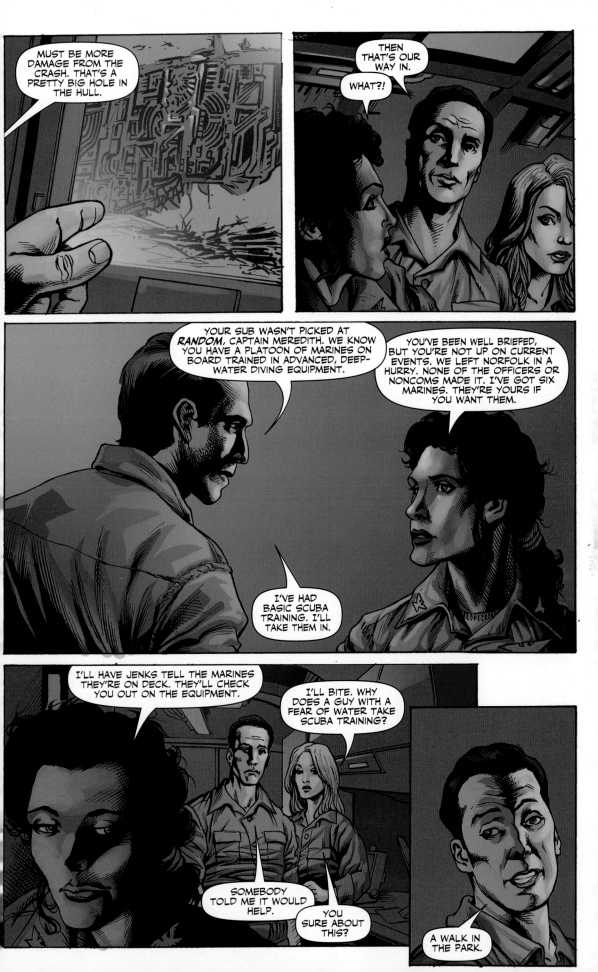

MUST BE MORE DAMAGE FROM THE CRASH. THAT'S A PRETTY BIG HOLE IN THE HULL.

THEN THAT'S OUR WAY IN.

WHAT?!

YOUR SUB WASN'T PICKED AT *RANDOM*, CAPTAIN MEREDITH. WE KNOW YOU HAVE A PLATOON OF MARINES ON BOARD TRAINED IN ADVANCED, DEEP-WATER DIVING EQUIPMENT.

YOU'VE BEEN WELL BRIEFED, BUT YOU'RE NOT UP ON CURRENT EVENTS. WE LEFT NORFOLK IN A HURRY. NONE OF THE OFFICERS OR NONCOMS MADE IT. I'VE GOT SIX MARINES. THEY'RE YOURS IF YOU WANT THEM.

I'VE HAD BASIC SCUBA TRAINING. I'LL TAKE THEM IN.

I'LL HAVE JENKS TELL THE MARINES THEY'RE ON DECK. THEY'LL CHECK YOU OUT ON THE EQUIPMENT.

I'LL BITE. WHY DOES A GUY WITH A FEAR OF WATER TAKE SCUBA TRAINING?

SOMEBODY TOLD ME IT WOULD HELP.

YOU SURE ABOUT THIS?

A WALK IN THE PARK.

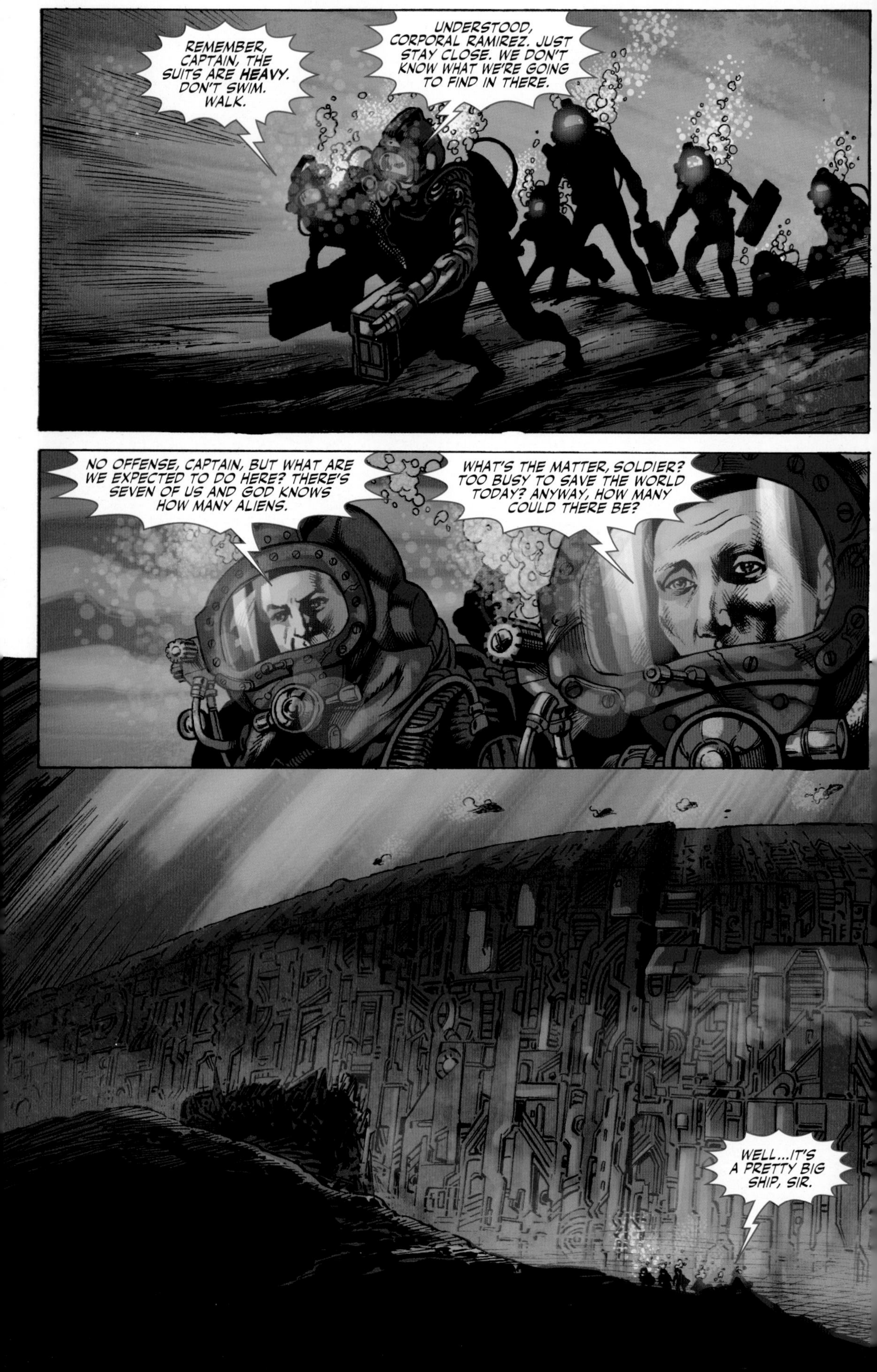
REMEMBER, CAPTAIN, THE SUITS ARE HEAVY. DON'T SWIM. WALK.
UNDERSTOOD, CORPORAL RAMIREZ. JUST STAY CLOSE. WE DON'T KNOW WHAT WE'RE GOING TO FIND IN THERE.
NO OFFENSE, CAPTAIN, BUT WHAT ARE WE EXPECTED TO DO HERE? THERE'S SEVEN OF US AND GOD KNOWS HOW MANY ALIENS.
WHAT'S THE MATTER, SOLDIER? TOO BUSY TO SAVE THE WORLD TODAY? ANYWAY, HOW MANY COULD THERE BE?
WELL...IT'S A PRETTY BIG SHIP, SIR.

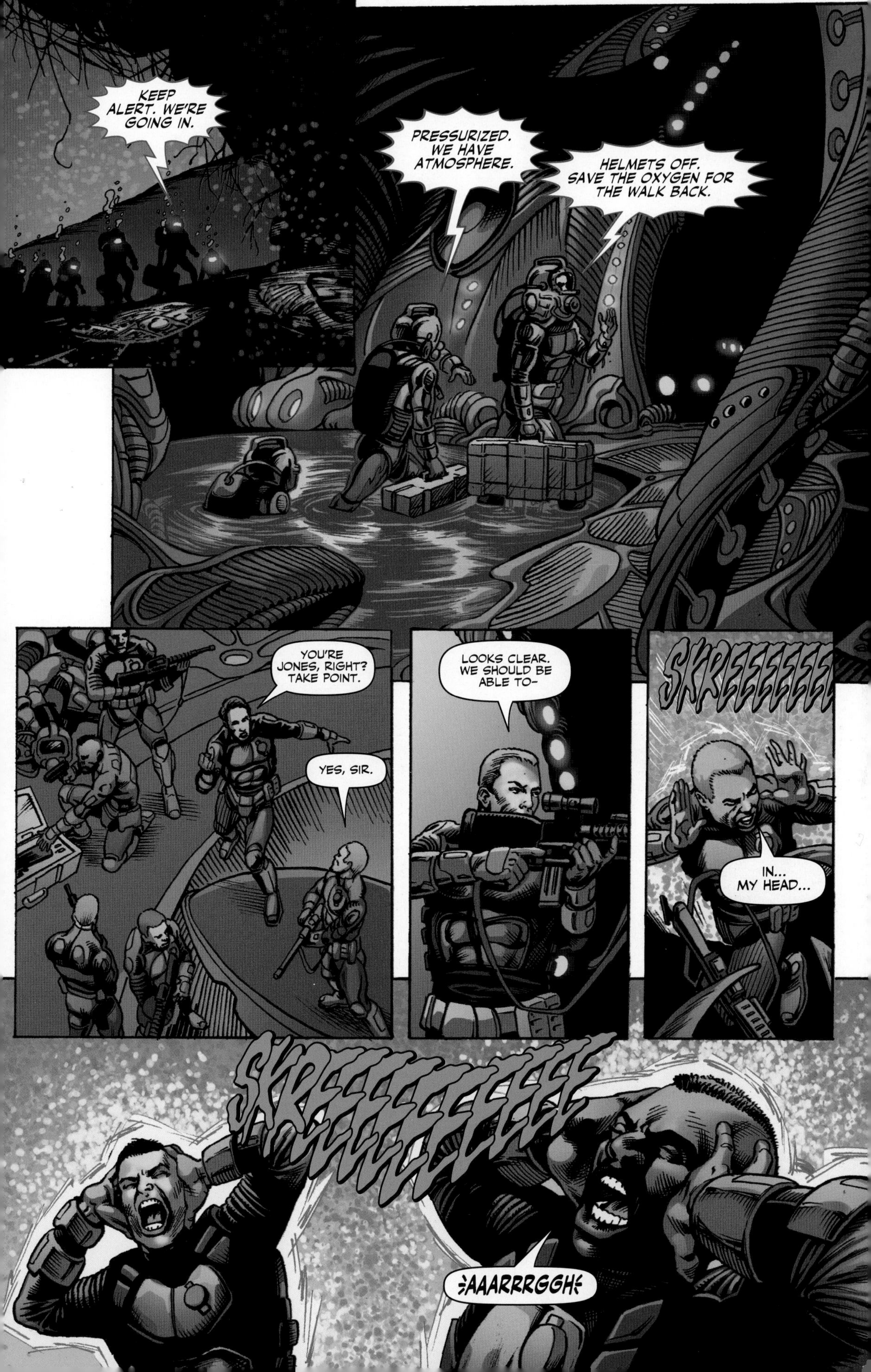
KEEP ALERT. WE'RE GOING IN.
PRESSURIZED. WE HAVE ATMOSPHERE.
HELMETS OFF. SAVE THE OXYGEN FOR THE WALK BACK.
YOU'RE JONES, RIGHT? TAKE POINT.
YES, SIR.
LOOKS CLEAR. WE SHOULD BE ABLE TO-
SKREEEEEEEE
IN... MY HEAD...
SKREEEEEEEEEEEEEEEEE
AAARRRGGH

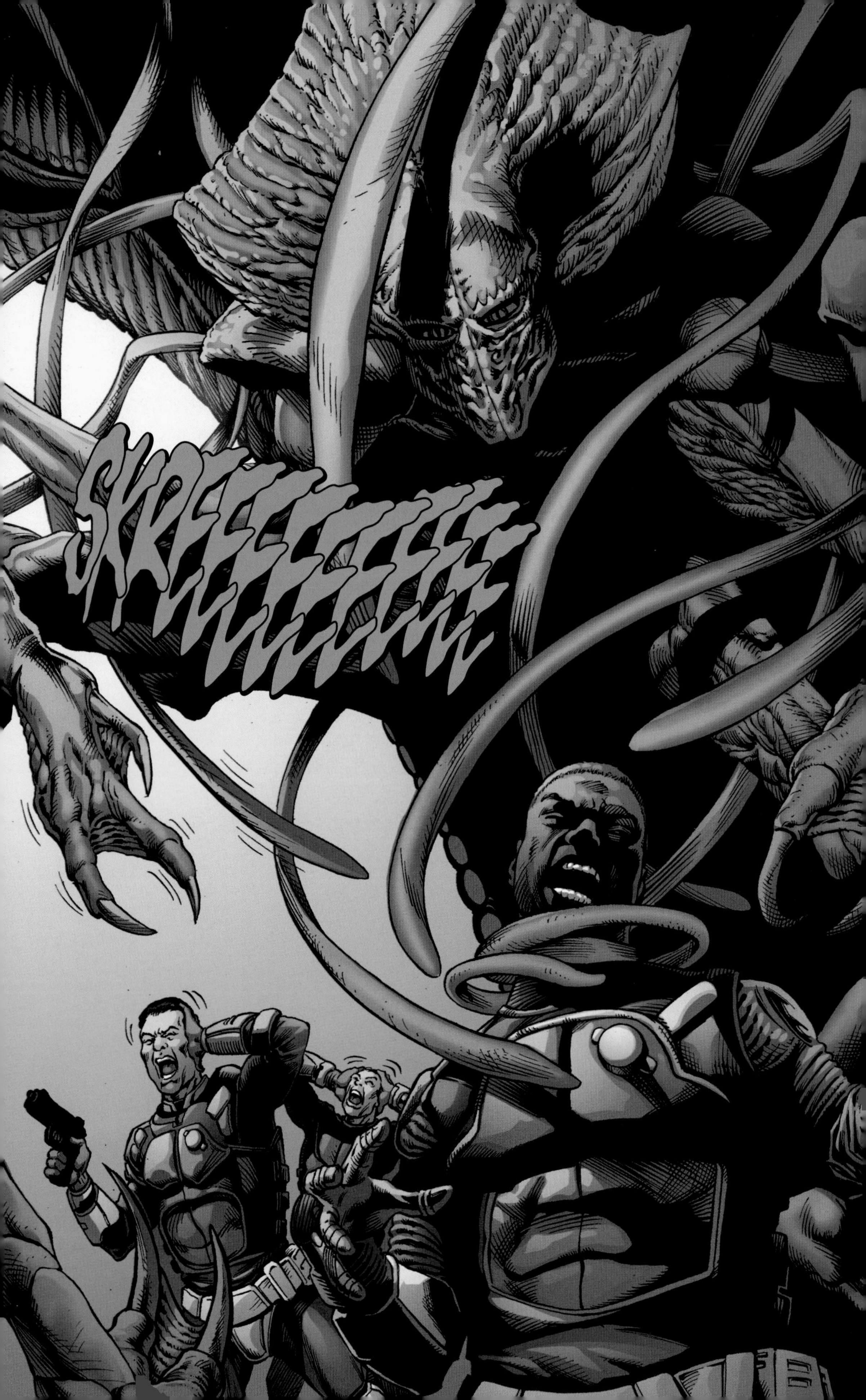
SKREEEEEEEEE

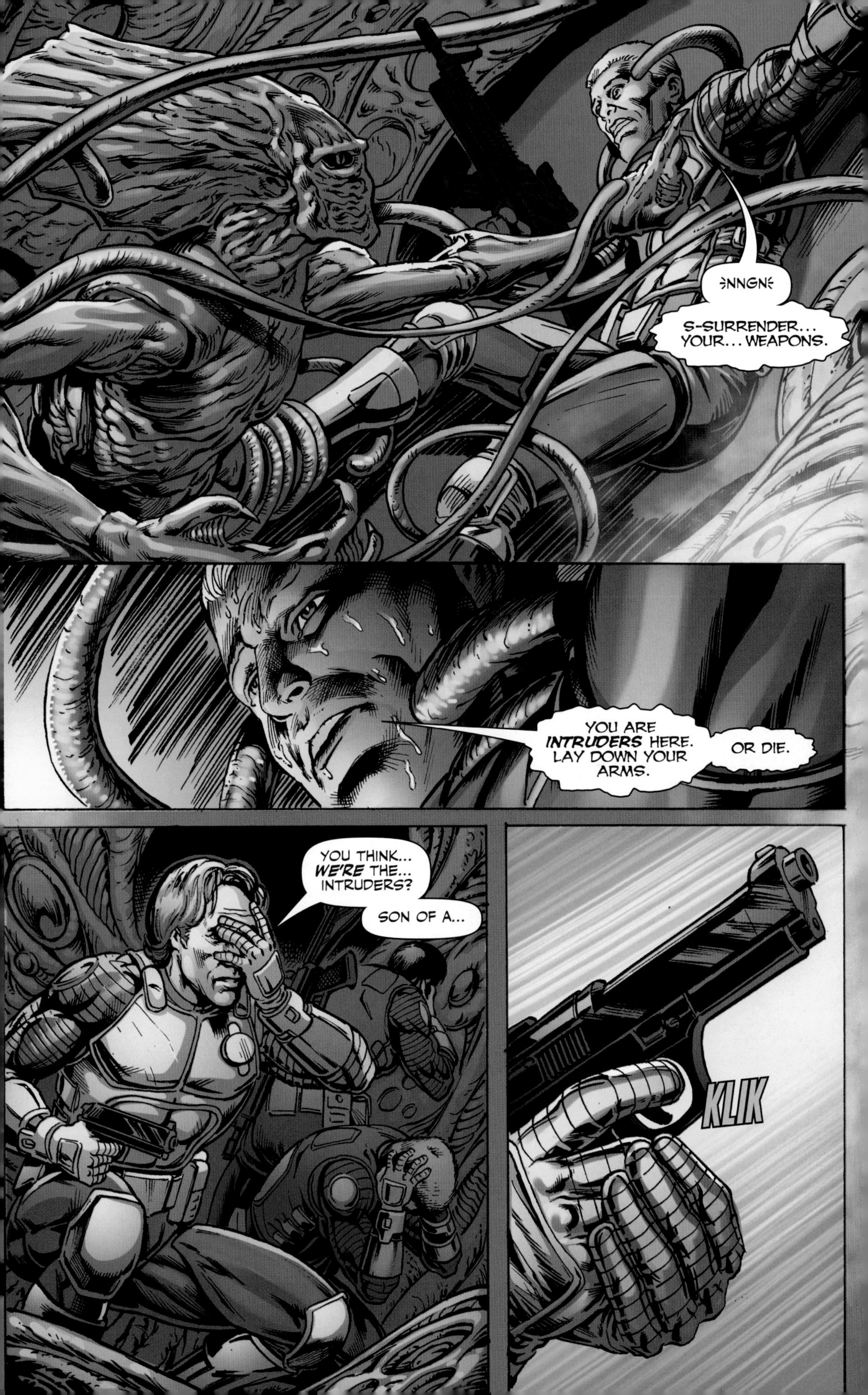

NNGN
S-SURRENDER... YOUR... WEAPONS.
YOU ARE INTRUDERS HERE. LAY DOWN YOUR ARMS.
OR DIE.
YOU THINK... WE'RE THE... INTRUDERS?
SON OF A...
KLIK

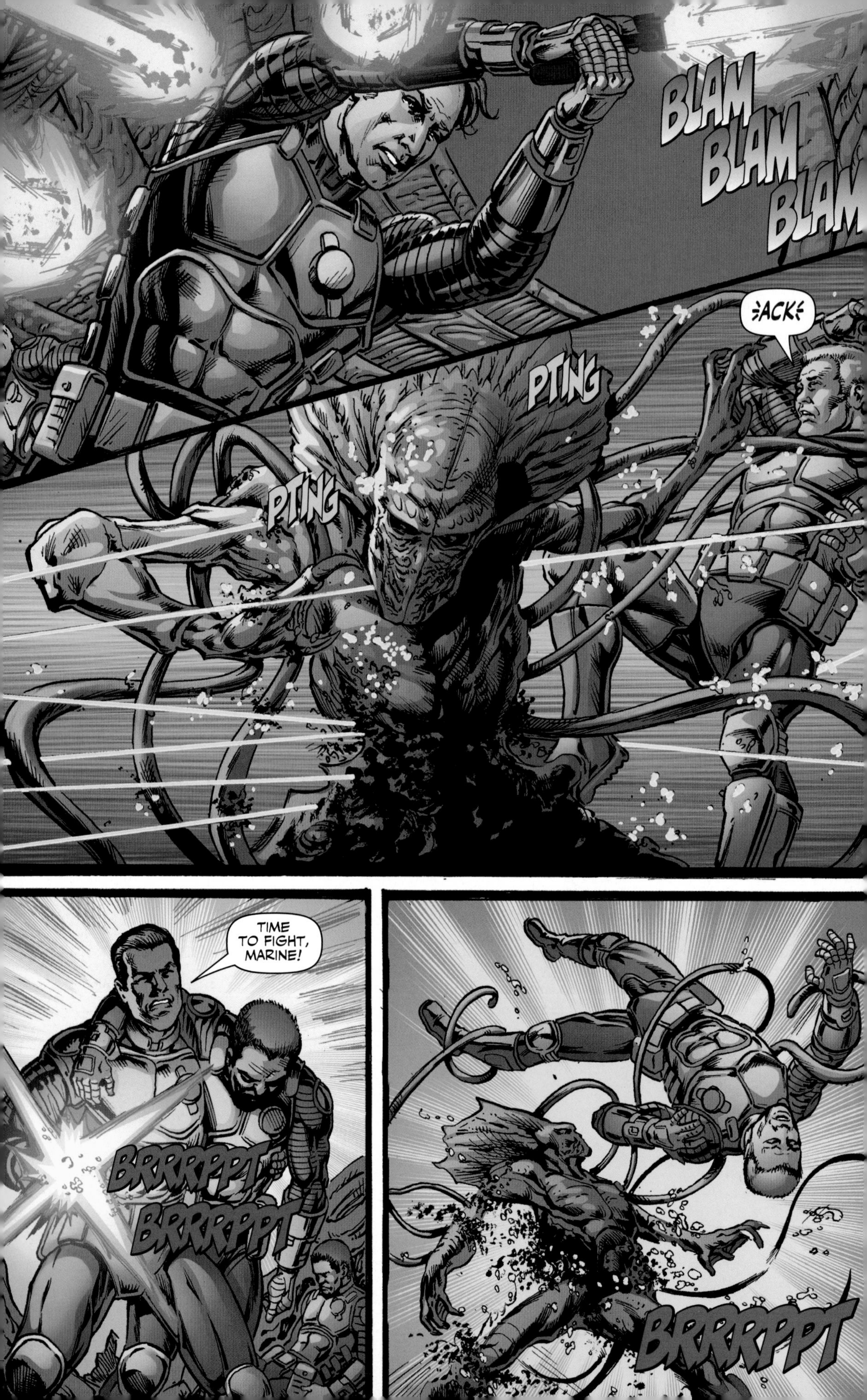
BLAM
BLAM
BLAM
ACK
PTING
PTING
TIME TO FIGHT, MARINE!
BRRRPPT
BRRRPPT
BRRRPPT

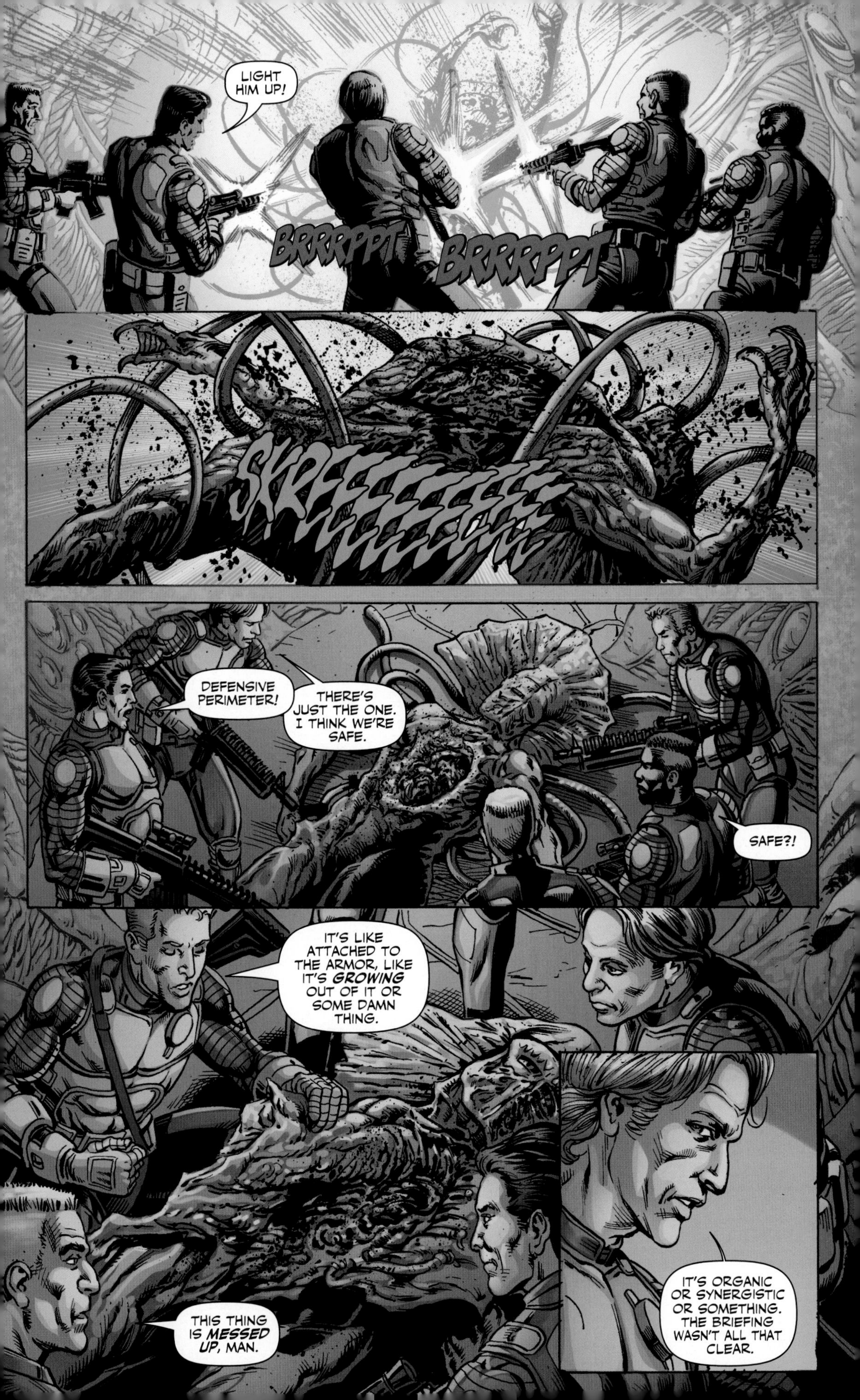
LIGHT HIM UP!
BRRRRPPT
BRRRRPPT
SKREEEEEEEEEEEEEE
DEFENSIVE PERIMETER!
THERE'S JUST THE ONE. I THINK WE'RE SAFE.
SAFE?!
IT'S LIKE ATTACHED TO THE ARMOR, LIKE IT'S GROWING OUT OF IT OR SOME DAMN THING.
THIS THING IS MESSED UP, MAN.
IT'S ORGANIC OR SYNERGISTIC OR SOMETHING. THE BRIEFING WASN'T ALL THAT CLEAR.

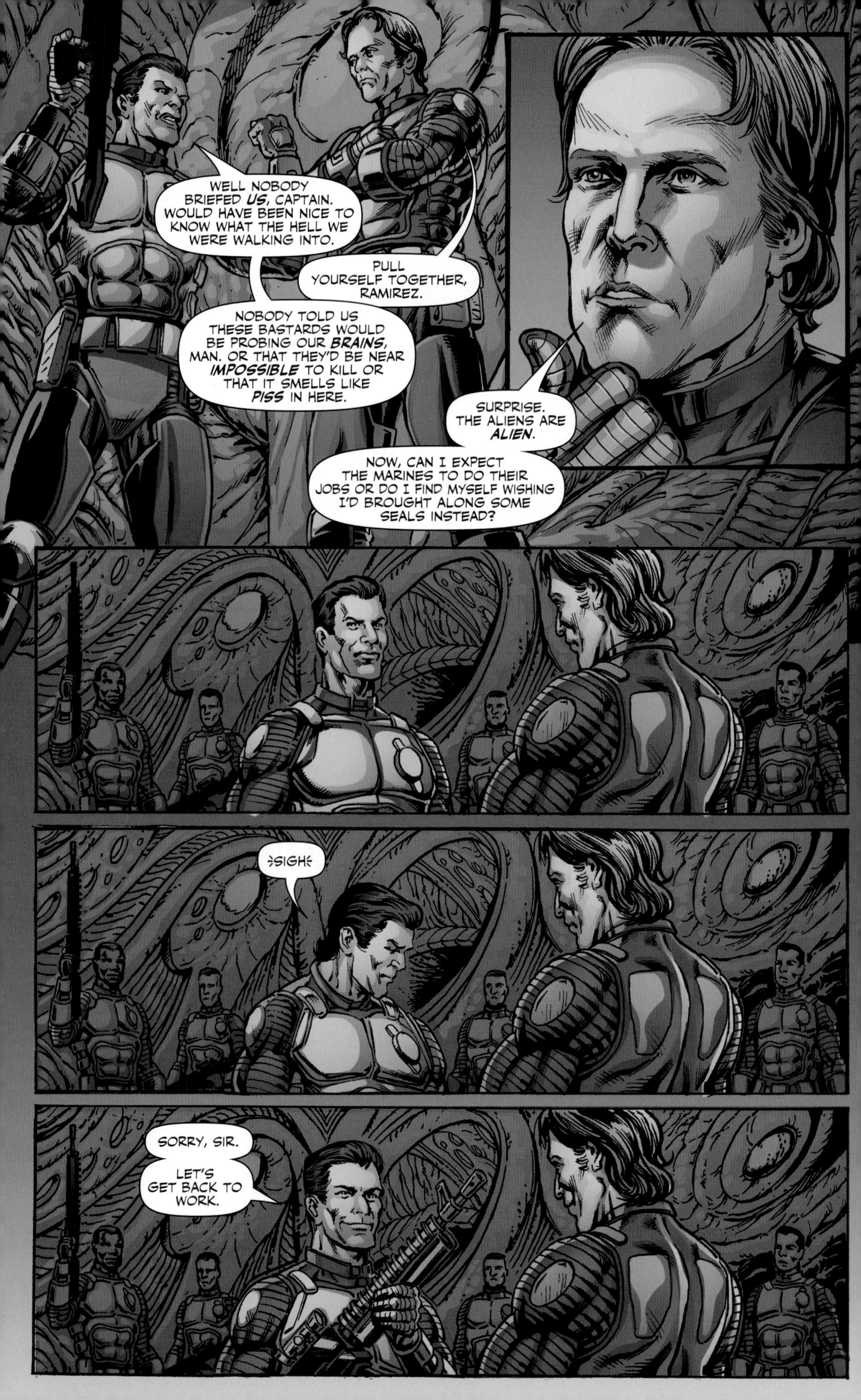
WELL NOBODY BRIEFED US, CAPTAIN. WOULD HAVE BEEN NICE TO KNOW WHAT THE HELL WE WERE WALKING INTO.
PULL YOURSELF TOGETHER, RAMIREZ.
NOBODY TOLD US THESE BASTARDS WOULD BE PROBING OUR BRAINS, MAN. OR THAT THEY'D BE NEAR IMPOSSIBLE TO KILL OR THAT IT SMELLS LIKE PISS IN HERE.
SURPRISE. THE ALIENS ARE ALIEN.
NOW, CAN I EXPECT THE MARINES TO DO THEIR JOBS OR DO I FIND MYSELF WISHING I'D BROUGHT ALONG SOME SEALS INSTEAD?
SIGH
SORRY, SIR.
LET'S GET BACK TO WORK.

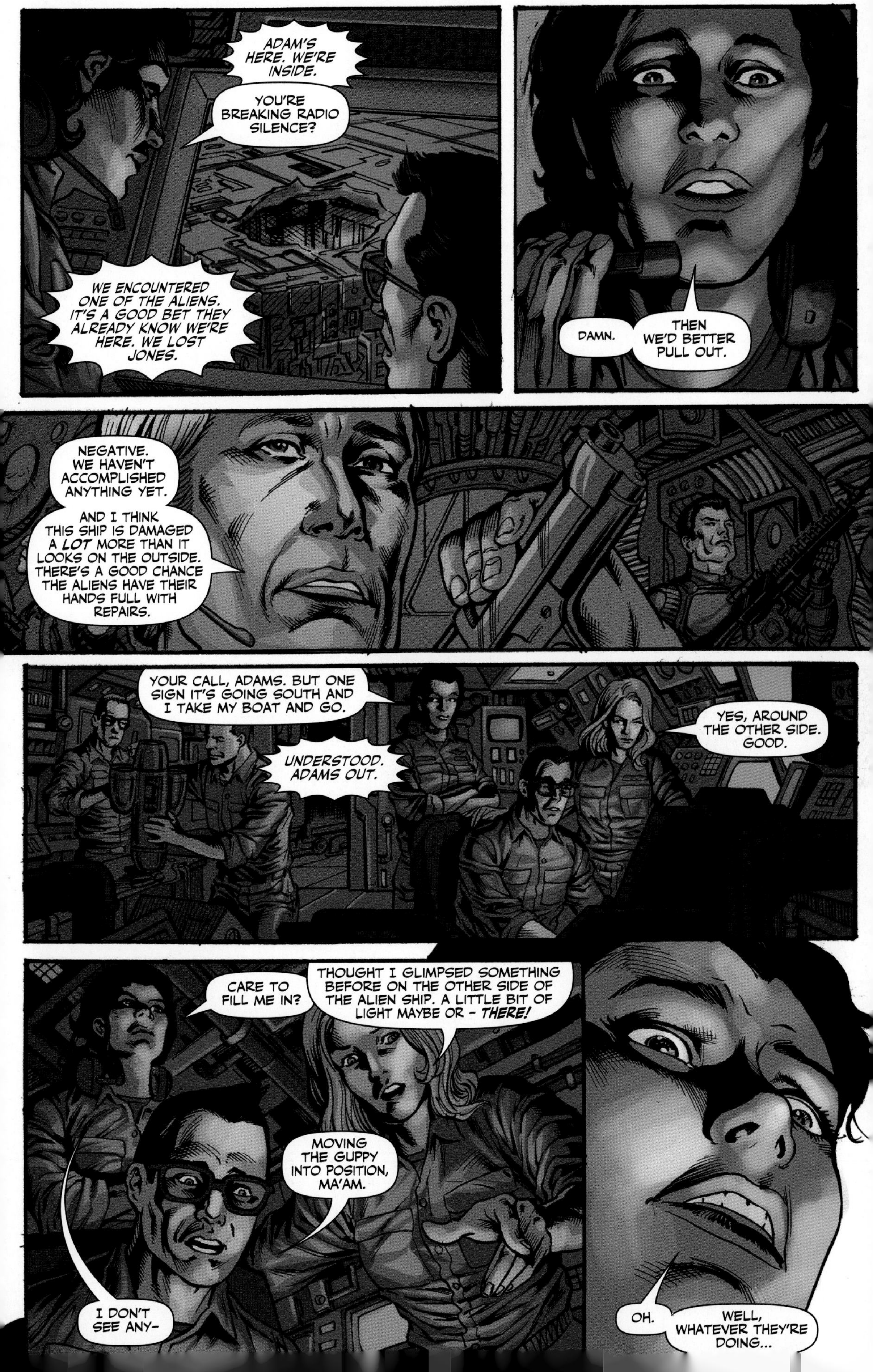
ADAM'S HERE. WE'RE INSIDE.
YOU'RE BREAKING RADIO SILENCE?
WE ENCOUNTERED ONE OF THE ALIENS. IT'S A GOOD BET THEY ALREADY KNOW WE'RE HERE. WE LOST JONES.
DAMN.
THEN WE'D BETTER PULL OUT.
NEGATIVE. WE HAVEN'T ACCOMPLISHED ANYTHING YET.
AND I THINK THIS SHIP IS DAMAGED A LOT MORE THAN IT LOOKS ON THE OUTSIDE. THERE'S A GOOD CHANCE THE ALIENS HAVE THEIR HANDS FULL WITH REPAIRS.
YOUR CALL, ADAMS. BUT ONE SIGN IT'S GOING SOUTH AND I TAKE MY BOAT AND GO.
UNDERSTOOD. ADAMS OUT.
YES, AROUND THE OTHER SIDE. GOOD.
CARE TO FILL ME IN?
THOUGHT I GLIMPSED SOMETHING BEFORE ON THE OTHER SIDE OF THE ALIEN SHIP. A LITTLE BIT OF LIGHT MAYBE OR - THERE!
MOVING THE GUPPY INTO POSITION, MA'AM.
I DON'T SEE ANY-
OH.
WELL, WHATEVER THEY'RE DOING...

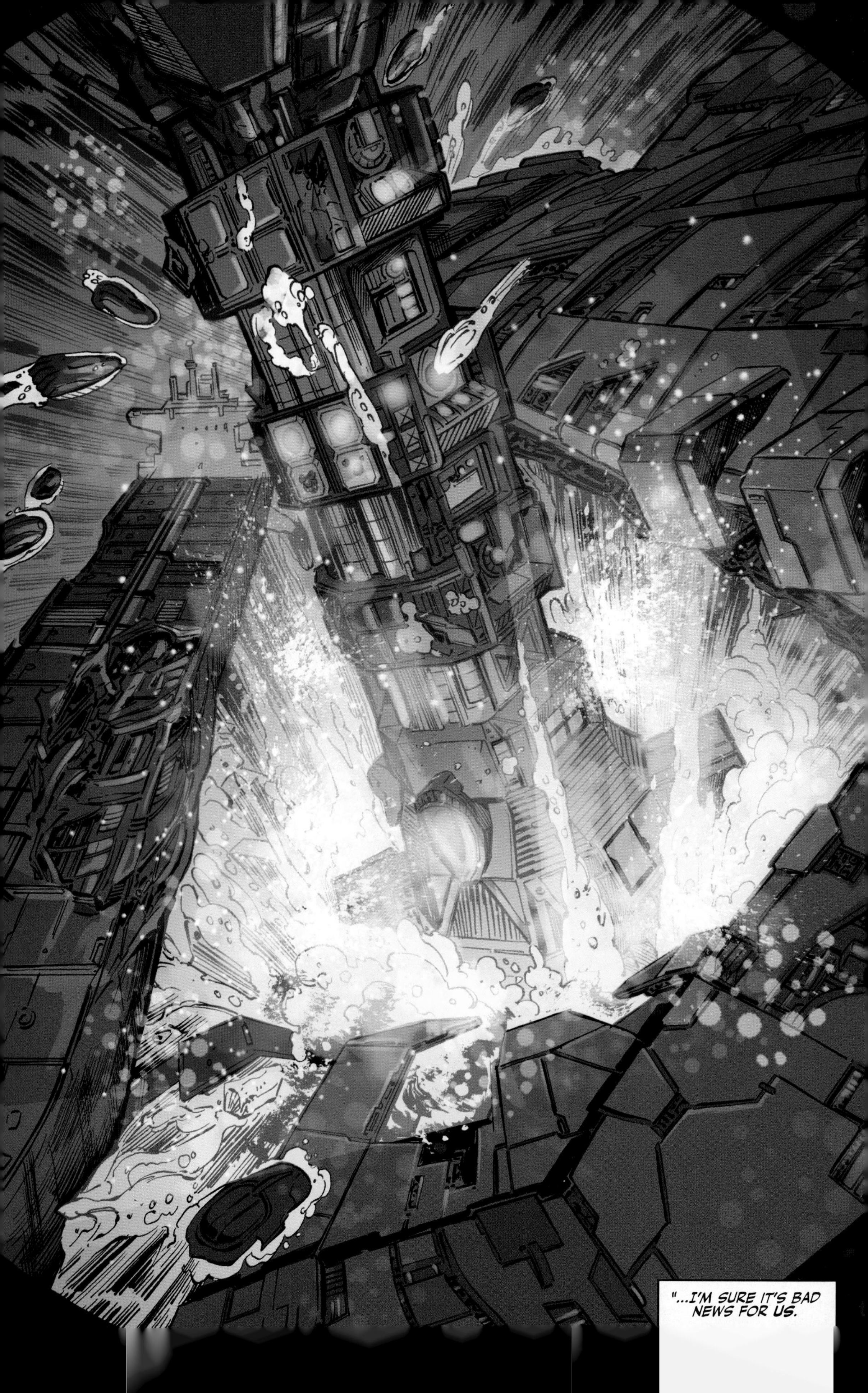
"...I'M SURE IT'S BAD NEWS FOR US.

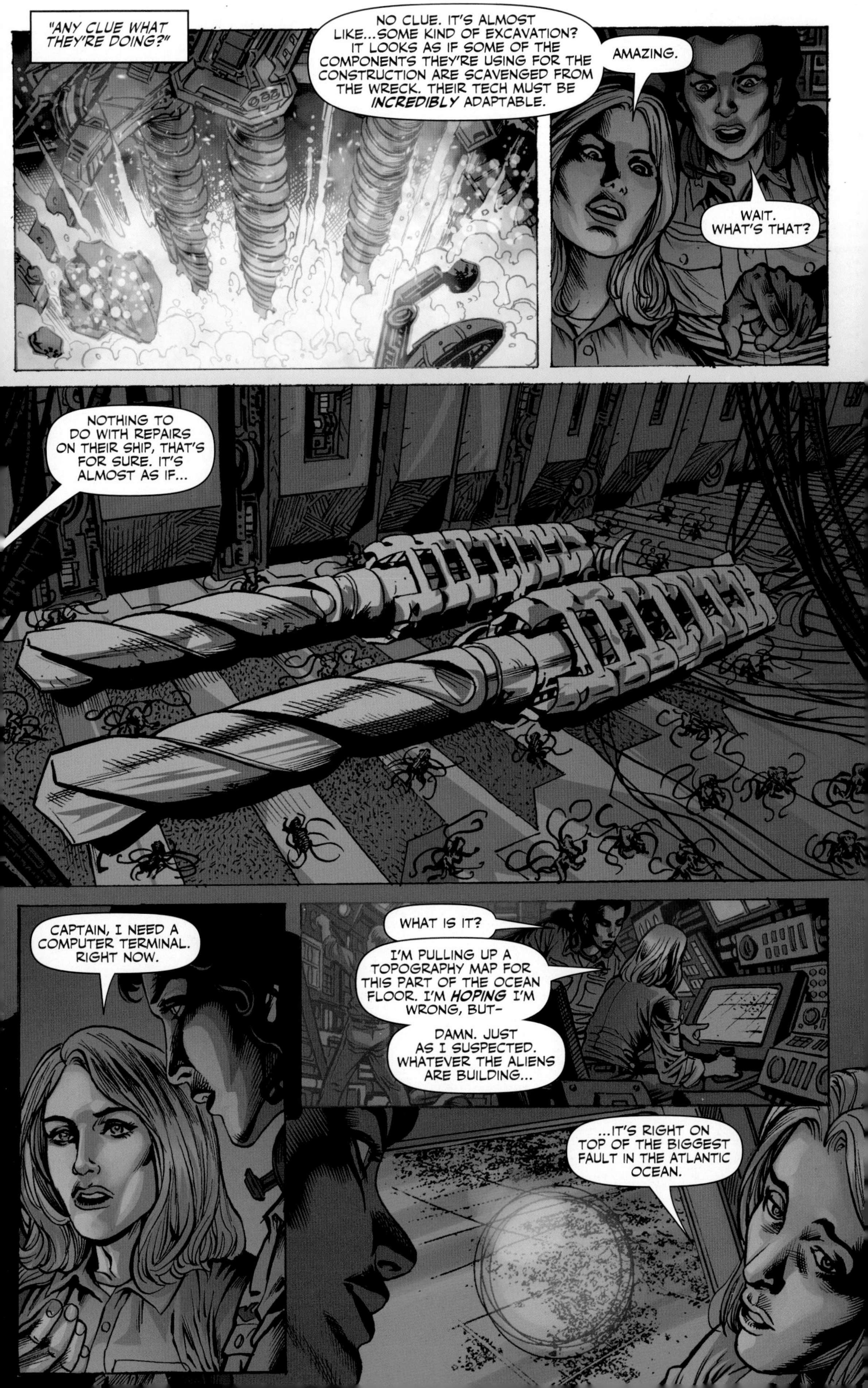
"ANY CLUE WHAT THEY'RE DOING?"
NO CLUE. IT'S ALMOST LIKE...SOME KIND OF EXCAVATION? IT LOOKS AS IF SOME OF THE COMPONENTS THEY'RE USING FOR THE CONSTRUCTION ARE SCAVENGED FROM THE WRECK. THEIR TECH MUST BE *INCREDIBLY* ADAPTABLE.
AMAZING.
WAIT. WHAT'S THAT?
NOTHING TO DO WITH REPAIRS ON THEIR SHIP, THAT'S FOR SURE. IT'S ALMOST AS IF...
CAPTAIN, I NEED A COMPUTER TERMINAL. RIGHT NOW.
WHAT IS IT?
I'M PULLING UP A TOPOGRAPHY MAP FOR THIS PART OF THE OCEAN FLOOR. I'M *HOPING* I'M WRONG, BUT-
DAMN. JUST AS I SUSPECTED. WHATEVER THE ALIENS ARE BUILDING...
...IT'S RIGHT ON TOP OF THE BIGGEST FAULT IN THE ATLANTIC OCEAN.

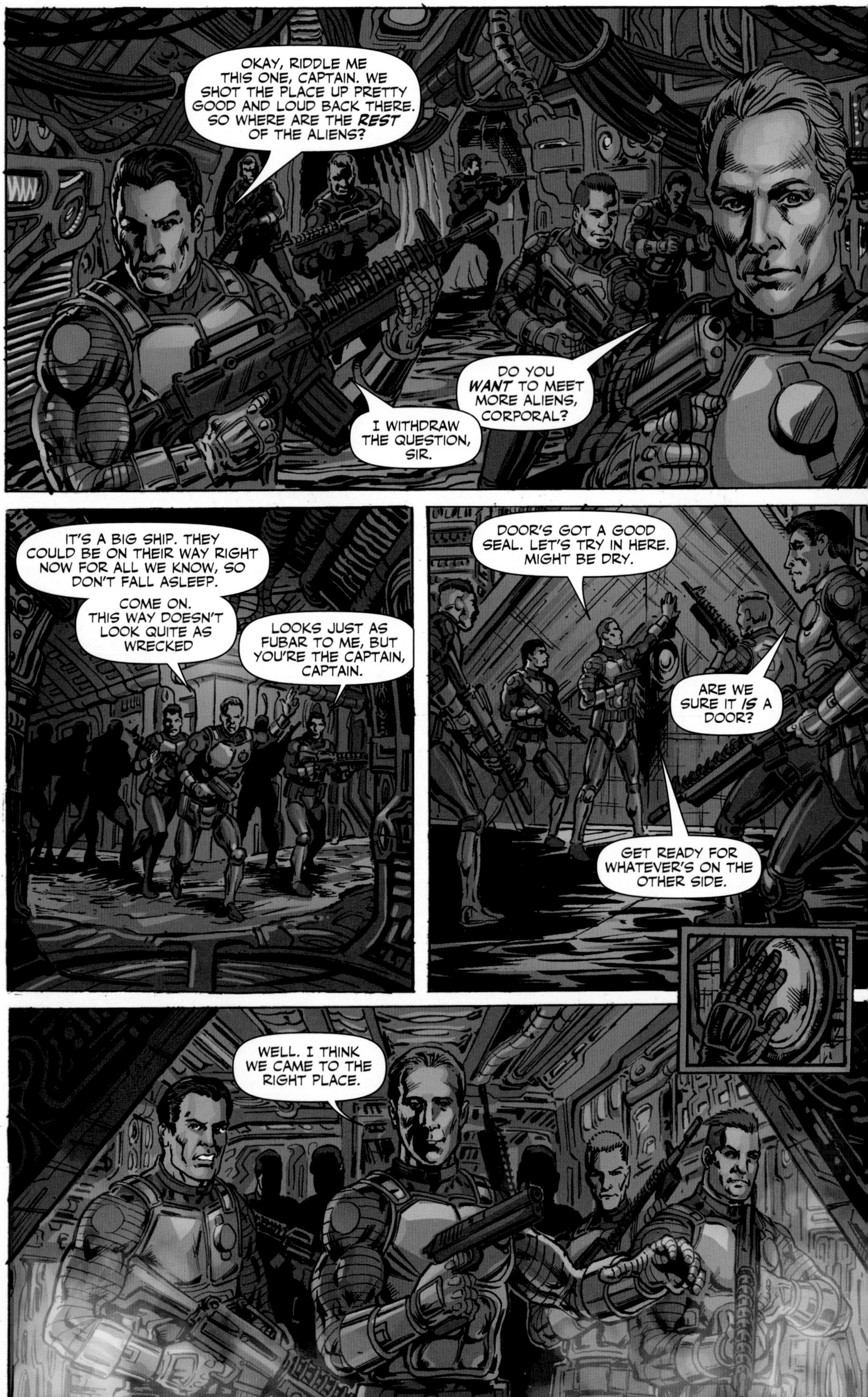
OKAY, RIDDLE ME THIS ONE, CAPTAIN. WE SHOT THE PLACE UP PRETTY GOOD AND LOUD BACK THERE. SO WHERE ARE THE REST OF THE ALIENS?
DO YOU WANT TO MEET MORE ALIENS, CORPORAL?
I WITHDRAW THE QUESTION, SIR.
IT'S A BIG SHIP. THEY COULD BE ON THEIR WAY RIGHT NOW FOR ALL WE KNOW, SO DON'T FALL ASLEEP.
COME ON. THIS WAY DOESN'T LOOK QUITE AS WRECKED
LOOKS JUST AS FUBAR TO ME, BUT YOU'RE THE CAPTAIN, CAPTAIN.
DOOR'S GOT A GOOD SEAL. LET'S TRY IN HERE. MIGHT BE DRY.
ARE WE SURE IT IS A DOOR?
GET READY FOR WHATEVER'S ON THE OTHER SIDE.
WELL. I THINK WE CAME TO THE RIGHT PLACE.

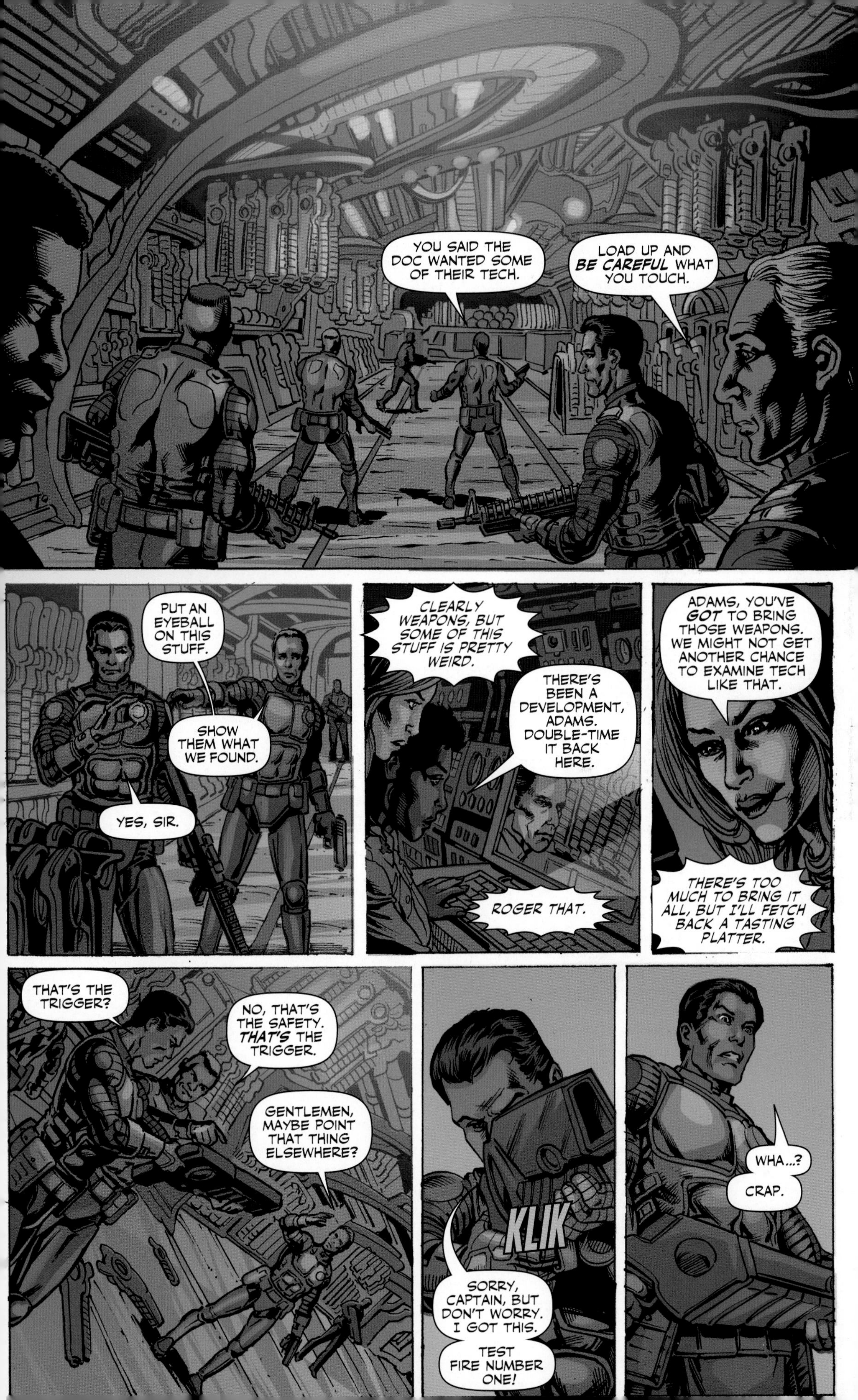

YOU SAID THE DOC WANTED SOME OF THEIR TECH.
LOAD UP AND *BE CAREFUL* WHAT YOU TOUCH.
PUT AN EYEBALL ON THIS STUFF.
SHOW THEM WHAT WE FOUND.
YES, SIR.
CLEARLY WEAPONS, BUT SOME OF THIS STUFF IS PRETTY WEIRD.
THERE'S BEEN A DEVELOPMENT, ADAMS. DOUBLE-TIME IT BACK HERE.
ROGER THAT.
ADAMS, YOU'VE *GOT* TO BRING THOSE WEAPONS. WE MIGHT NOT GET ANOTHER CHANCE TO EXAMINE TECH LIKE THAT.
THERE'S TOO MUCH TO BRING IT ALL, BUT I'LL FETCH BACK A TASTING PLATTER.
THAT'S THE TRIGGER?
NO, THAT'S THE SAFETY. *THAT'S* THE TRIGGER.
GENTLEMEN, MAYBE POINT THAT THING ELSEWHERE?
KLIK
SORRY, CAPTAIN, BUT DON'T WORRY. I GOT THIS.
TEST FIRE NUMBER ONE!
WHA...?
CRAP.

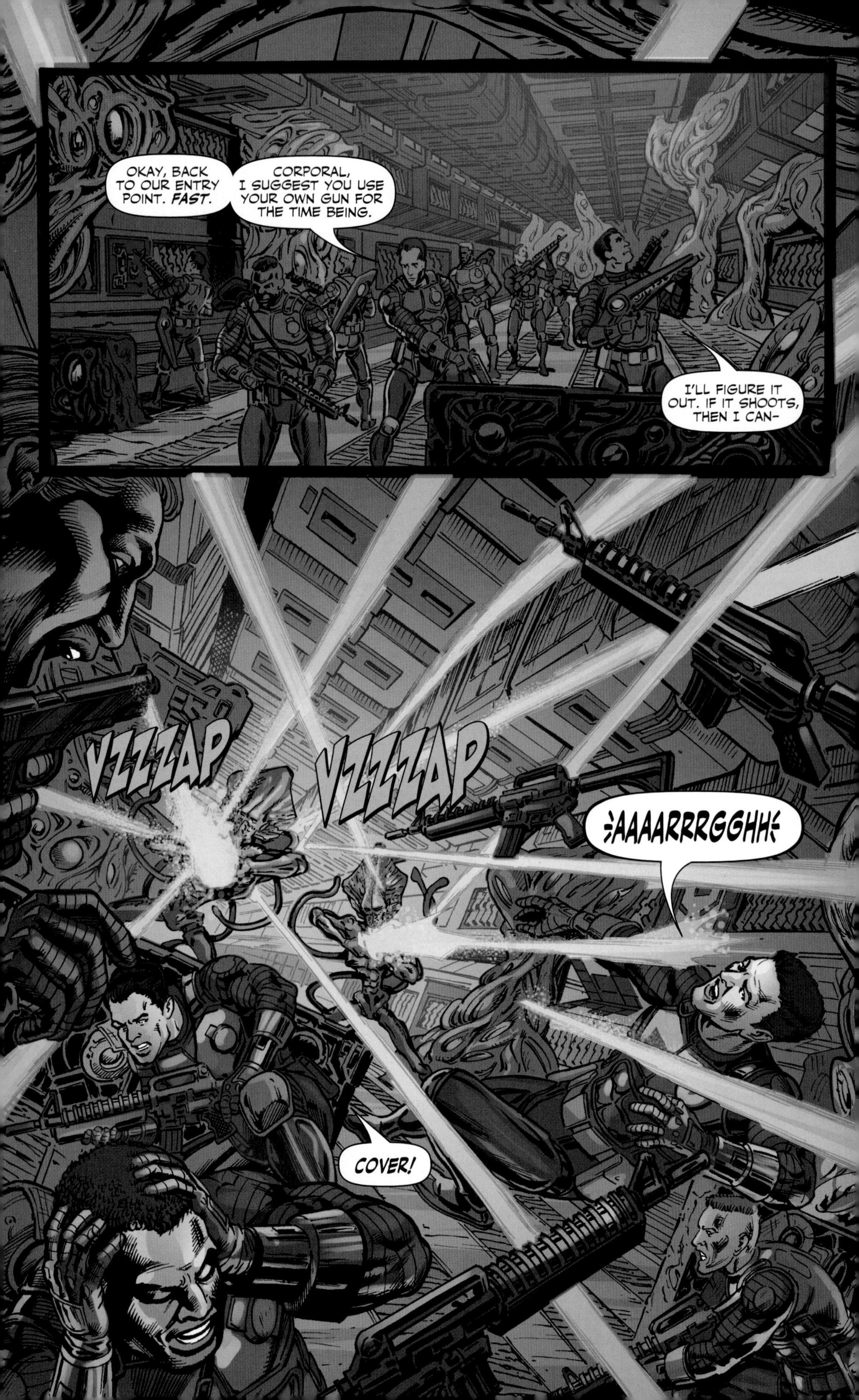
OKAY, BACK TO OUR ENTRY POINT. *FAST*.
CORPORAL, I SUGGEST YOU USE YOUR OWN GUN FOR THE TIME BEING.
I'LL FIGURE IT OUT. IF IT SHOOTS, THEN I CAN–
VZZZAP
VZZZAP
AAAARRRGGHH
COVER!

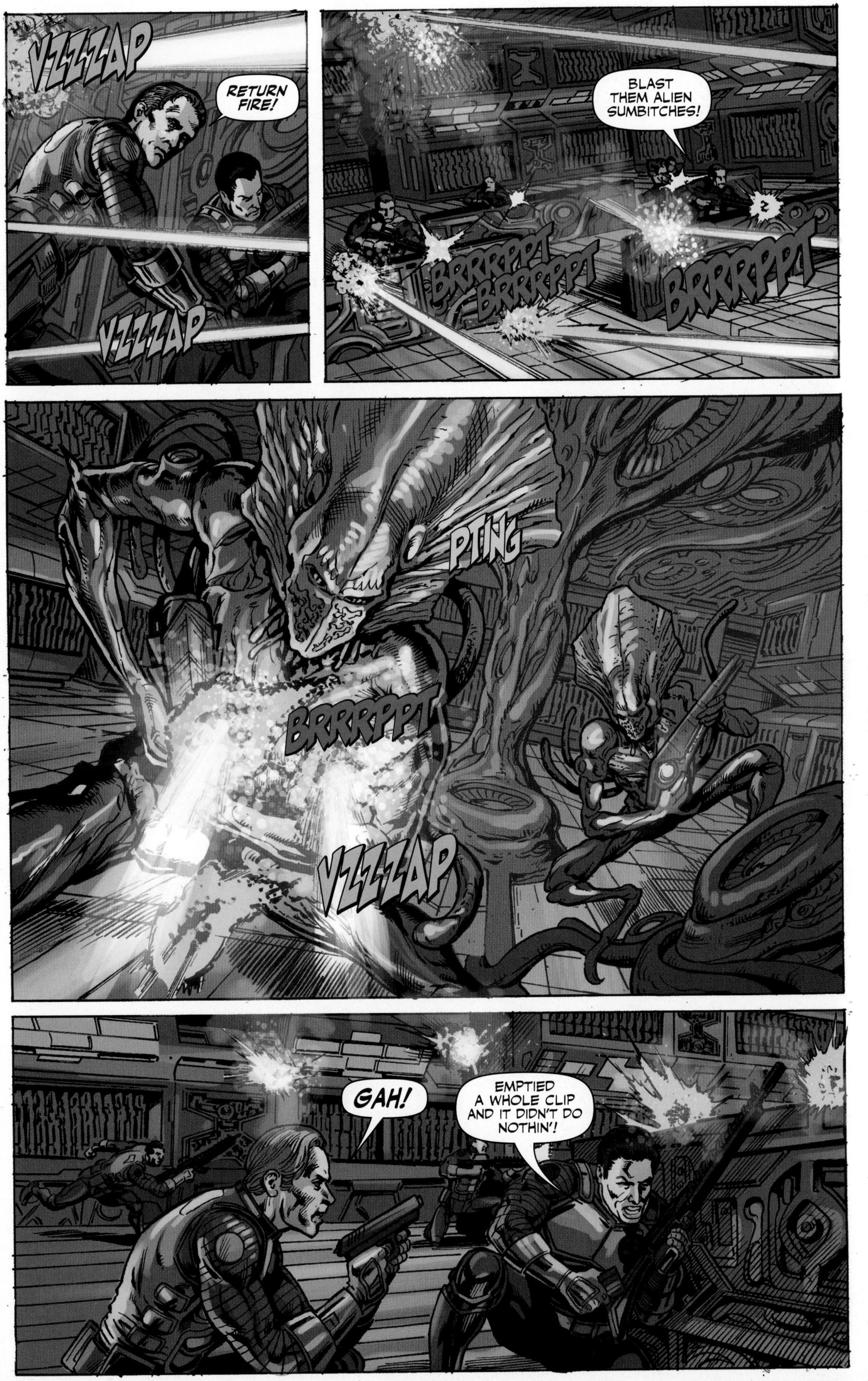
VZZZAP
RETURN FIRE!
VZZZAP
BLAST THEM ALIEN SUMBITCHES!
BRRRPPT
BRRRPPT
BRRRPPT
PTING
BRRRPPT
VZZZAP
GAH!
EMPTIED A WHOLE CLIP AND IT DIDN'T DO NOTHIN'!

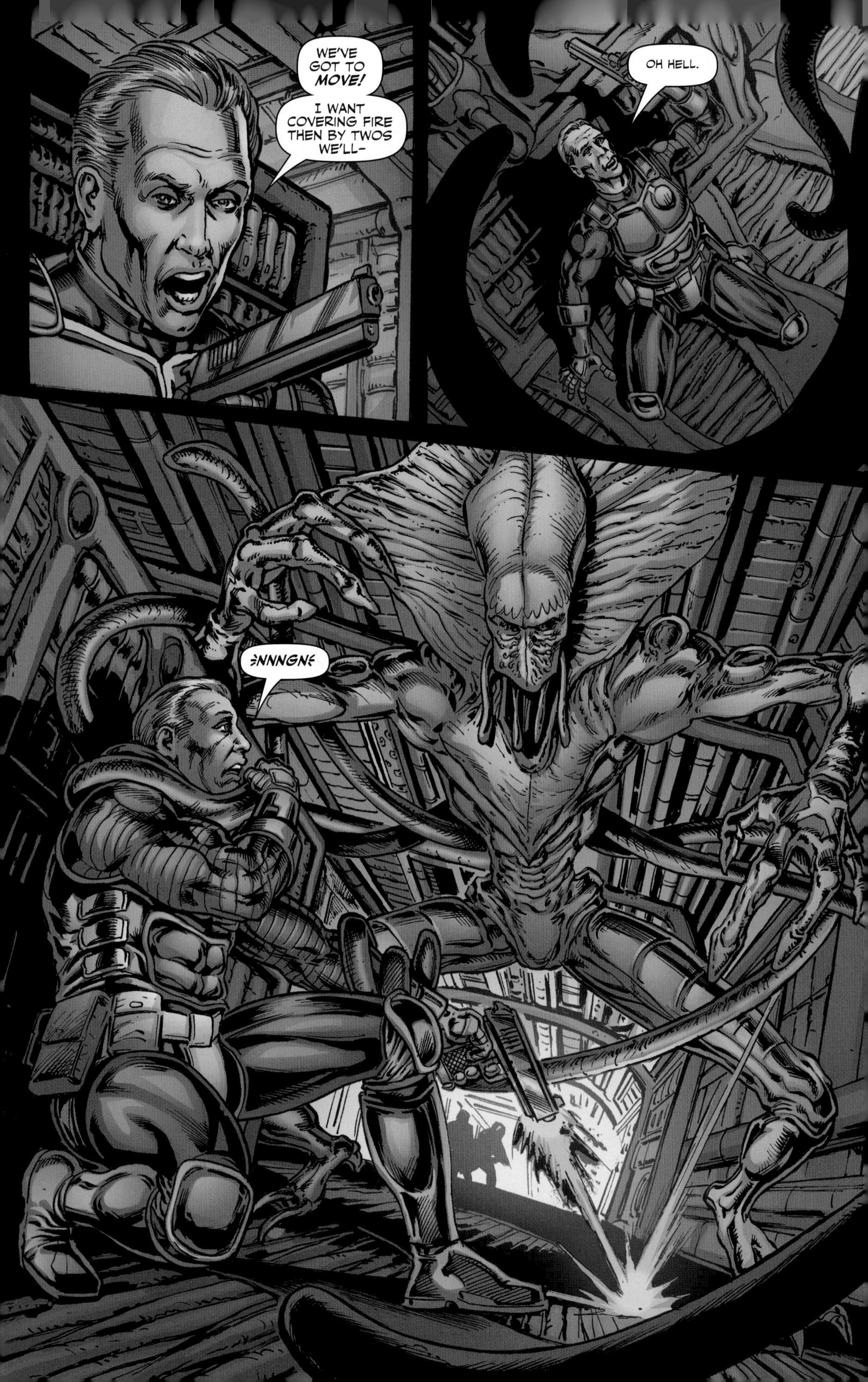
WE'VE GOT TO MOVE!
I WANT COVERING FIRE THEN BY TWOS WE'LL-
OH HELL.
NNNGN

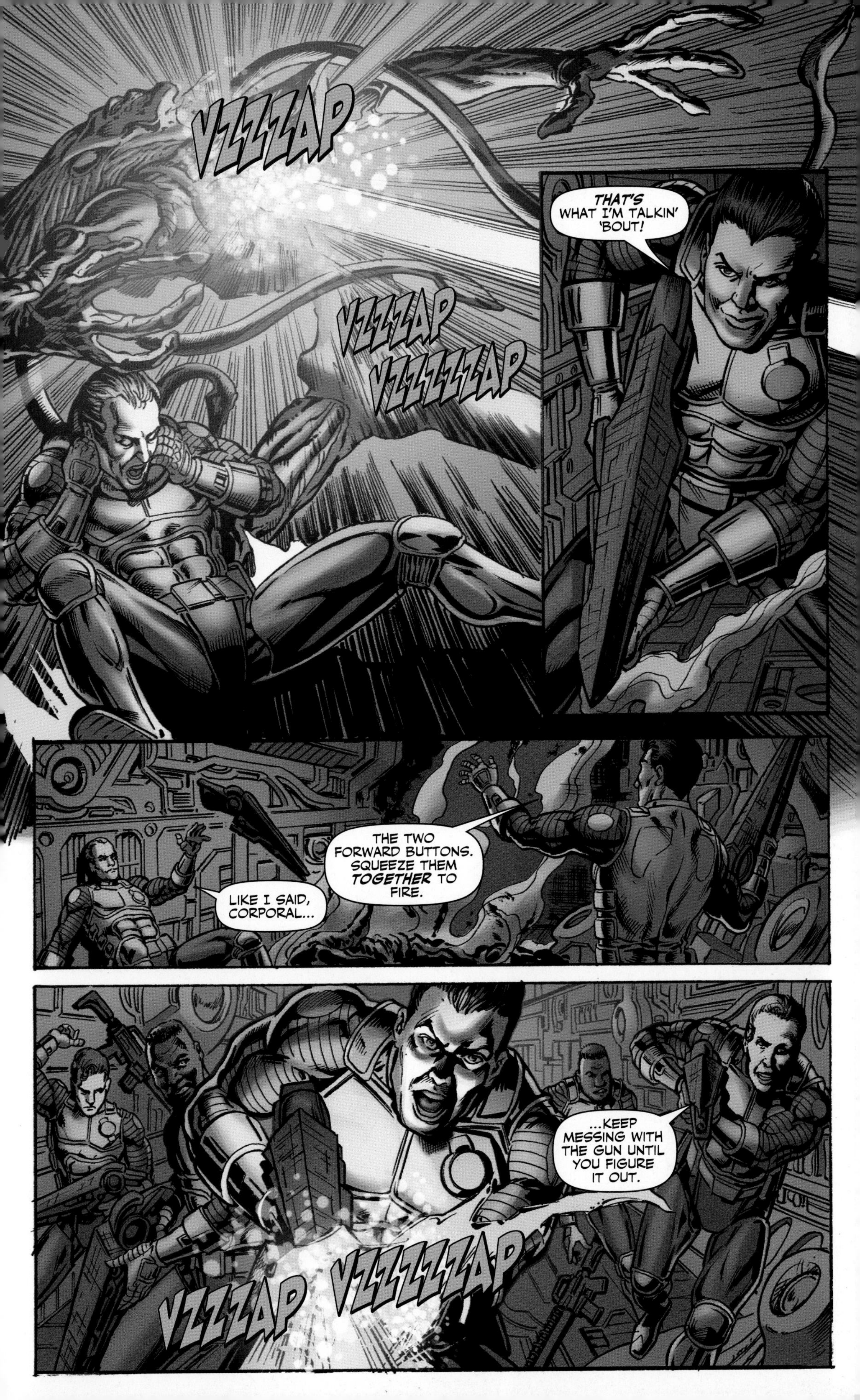

VZZZAP
VZZZAP
VZZZZZAP
THAT'S WHAT I'M TALKIN' 'BOUT!
LIKE I SAID, CORPORAL...
THE TWO FORWARD BUTTONS. SQUEEZE THEM TOGETHER TO FIRE.
...KEEP MESSING WITH THE GUN UNTIL YOU FIGURE IT OUT.
VZZZAP
VZZZZZAP

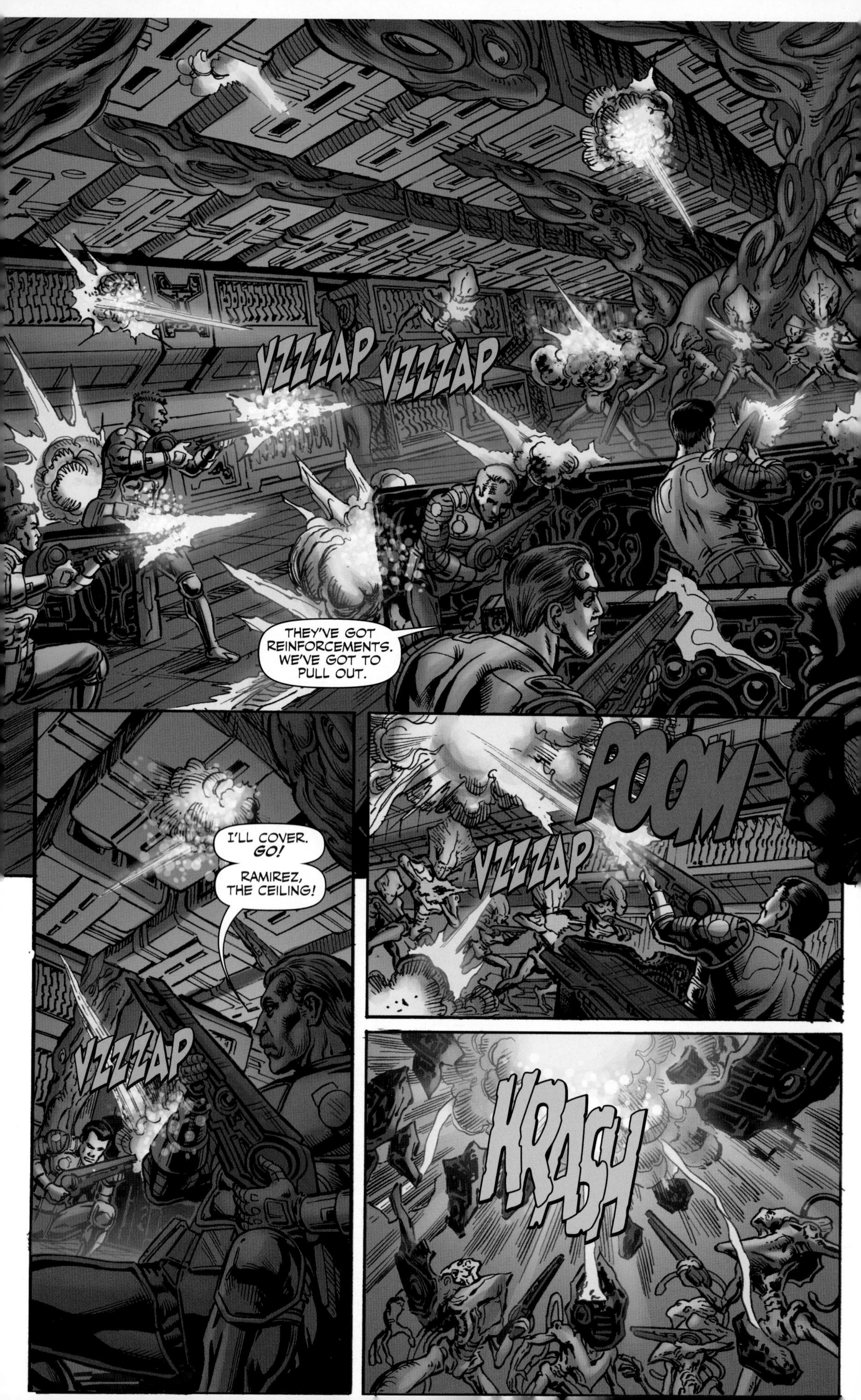
VZZZAP
VZZZAP
THEY'VE GOT REINFORCEMENTS. WE'VE GOT TO PULL OUT.
I'LL COVER. GO!
RAMIREZ, THE CEILING!
VZZZAP
POOM
VZZZAP
KRASH

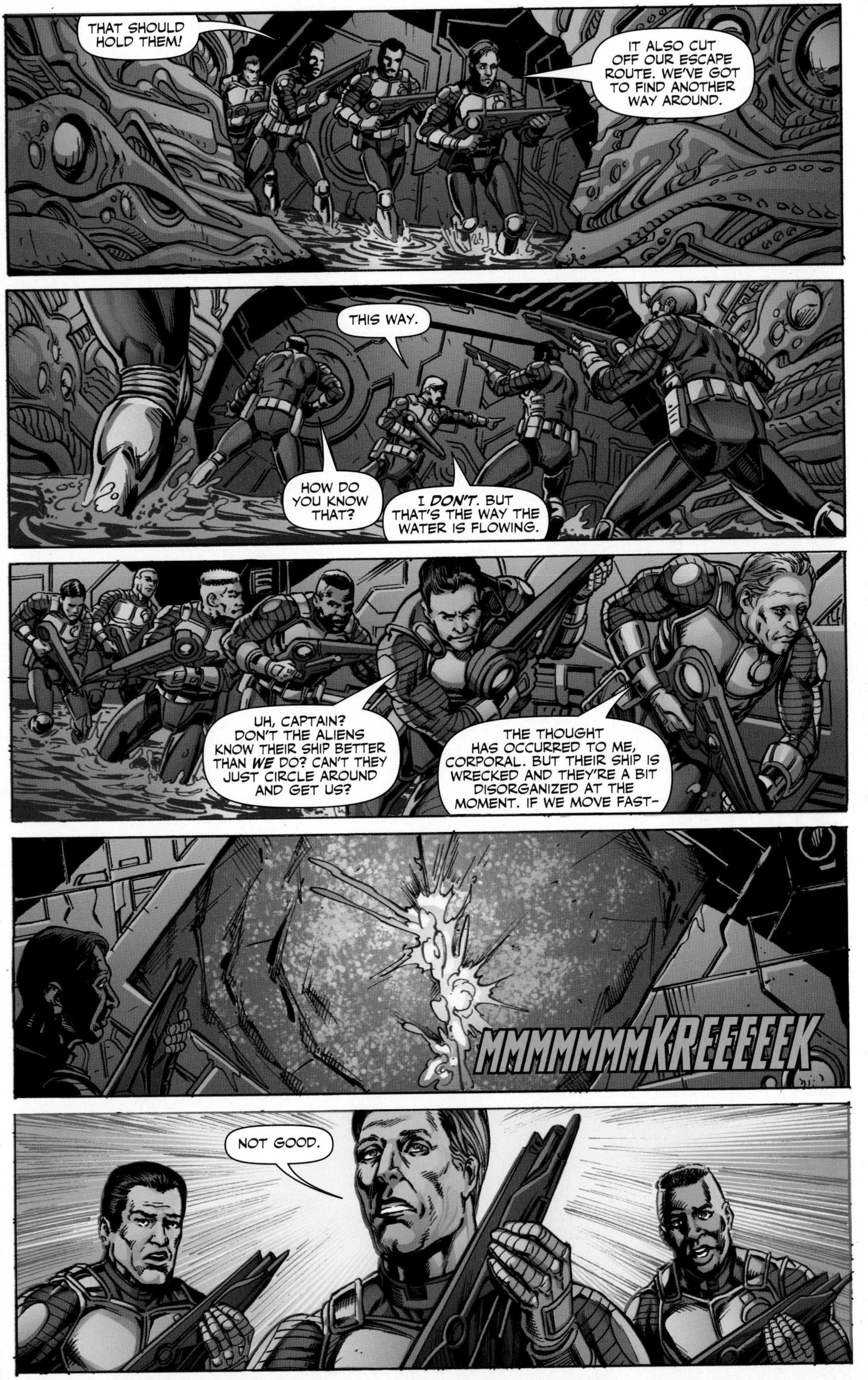
THAT SHOULD HOLD THEM!
IT ALSO CUT OFF OUR ESCAPE ROUTE. WE'VE GOT TO FIND ANOTHER WAY AROUND.
THIS WAY.
HOW DO YOU KNOW THAT?
I *DON'T*. BUT THAT'S THE WAY THE WATER IS FLOWING.
UH, CAPTAIN? DON'T THE ALIENS KNOW THEIR SHIP BETTER THAN *WE* DO? CAN'T THEY JUST CIRCLE AROUND AND GET US?
THE THOUGHT HAS OCCURRED TO ME, CORPORAL. BUT THEIR SHIP IS WRECKED AND THEY'RE A BIT DISORGANIZED AT THE MOMENT. IF WE MOVE FAST-
MMMMMMMMKREEEEEK
NOT GOOD.

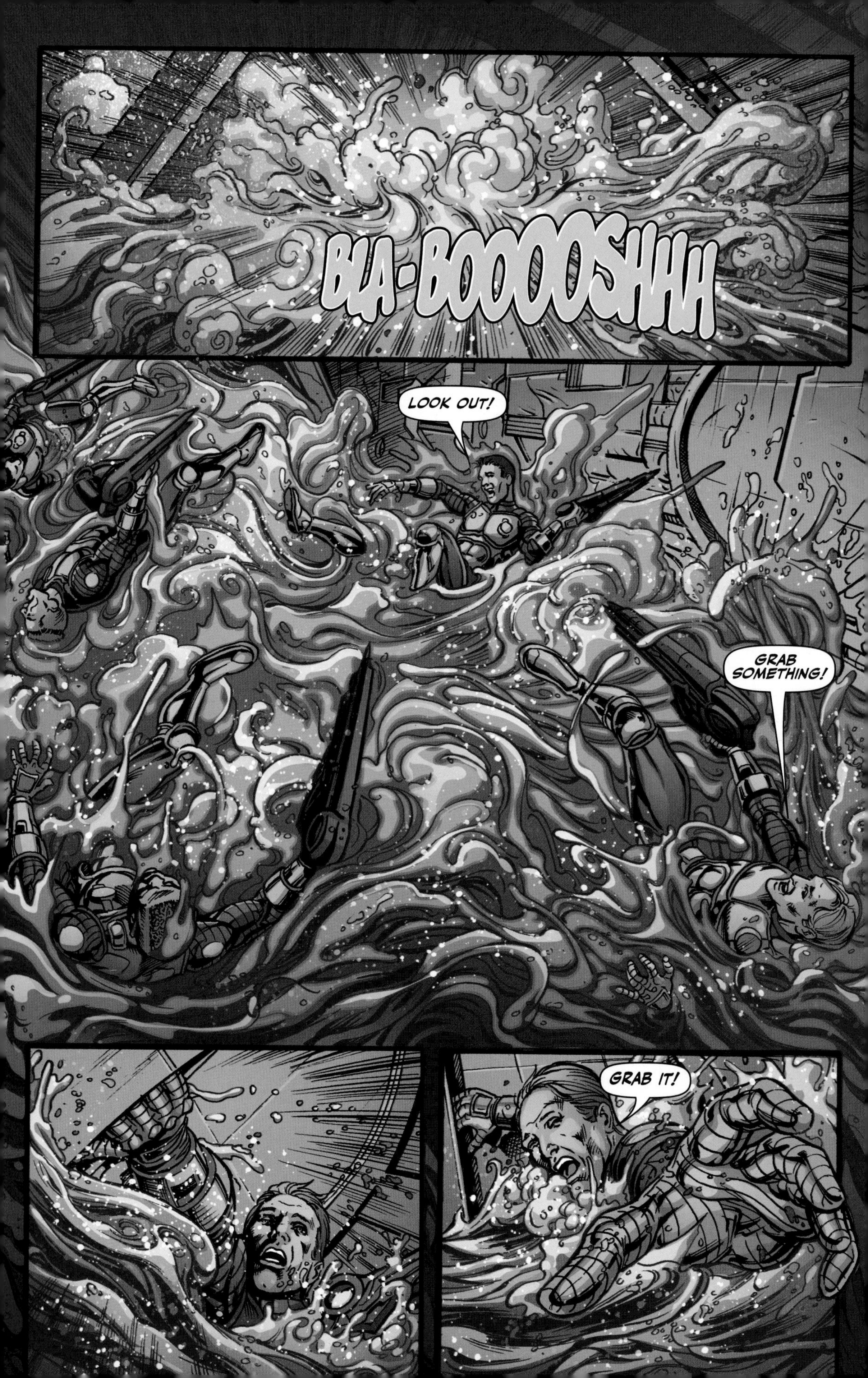
BLA-BOOOOSHHH
LOOK OUT!
GRAB SOMETHING!
GRAB IT!

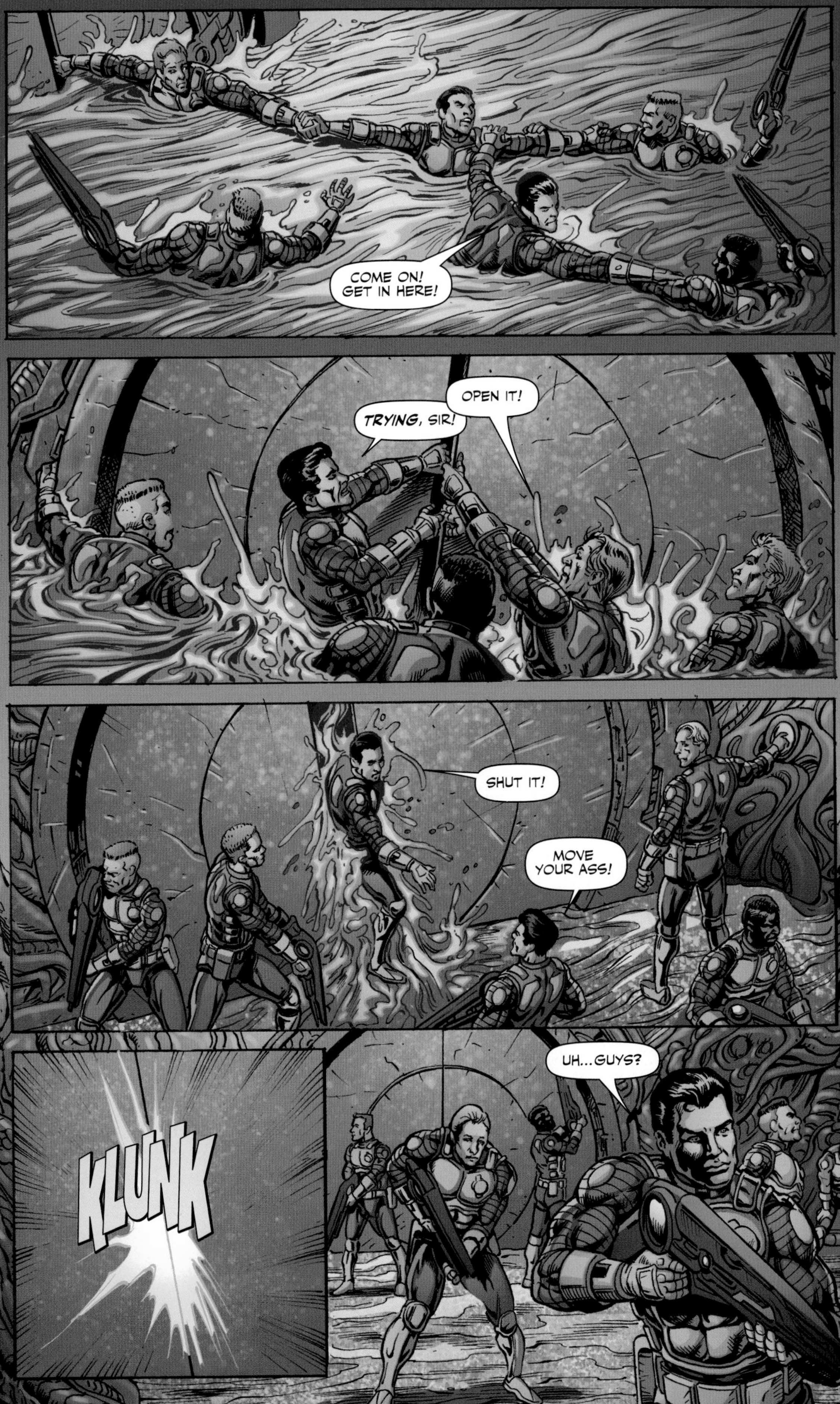
COME ON! GET IN HERE!
OPEN IT!
TRYING, SIR!
SHUT IT!
MOVE YOUR ASS!
KLUNK
UH...GUYS?

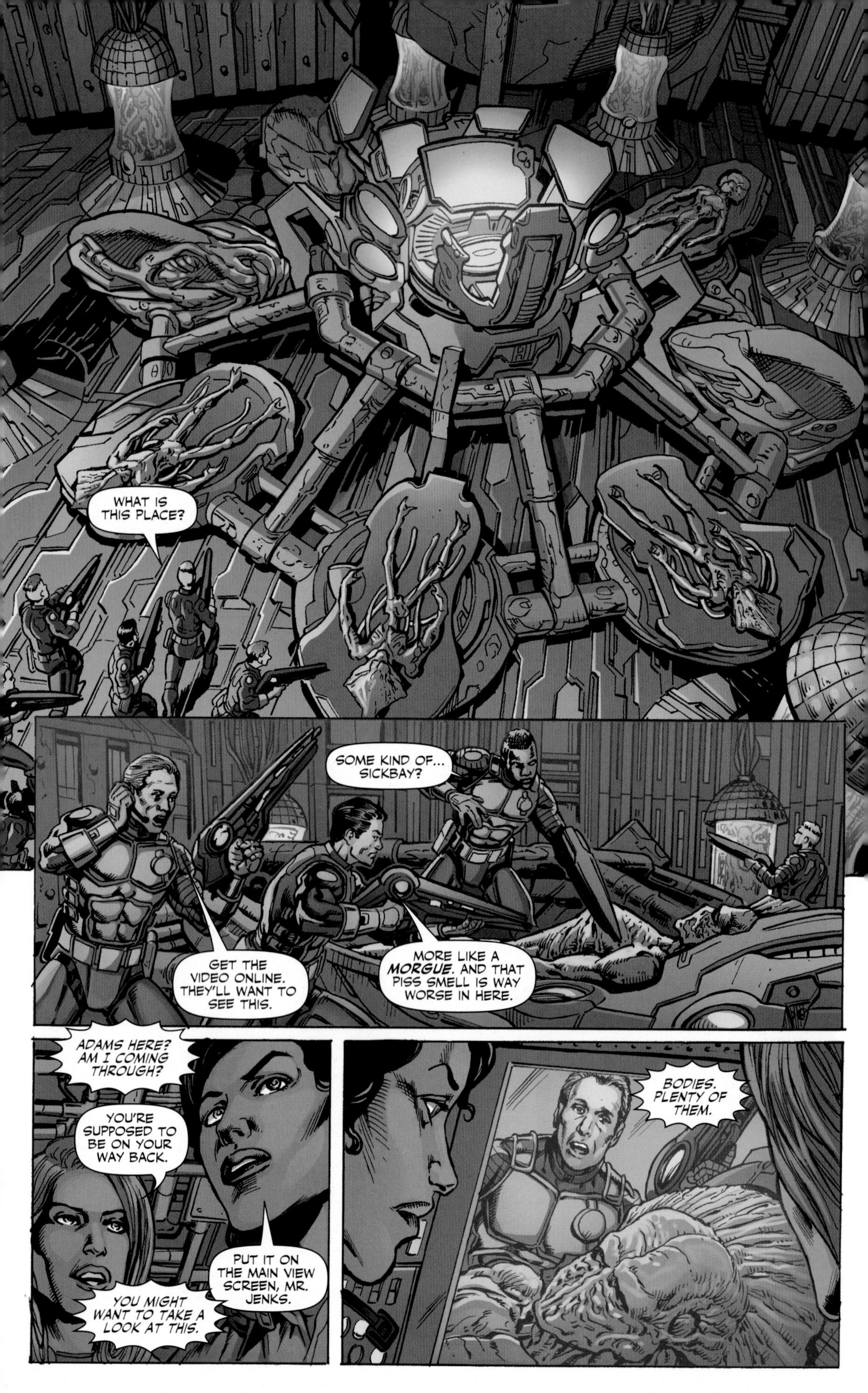
WHAT IS THIS PLACE?
SOME KIND OF... SICKBAY?
GET THE VIDEO ONLINE. THEY'LL WANT TO SEE THIS.
MORE LIKE A *MORGUE*. AND THAT PISS SMELL IS WAY WORSE IN HERE.
ADAMS HERE? AM I COMING THROUGH?
YOU'RE SUPPOSED TO BE ON YOUR WAY BACK.
YOU MIGHT WANT TO TAKE A LOOK AT THIS.
PUT IT ON THE MAIN VIEW SCREEN, MR. JENKS.
BODIES. PLENTY OF THEM.

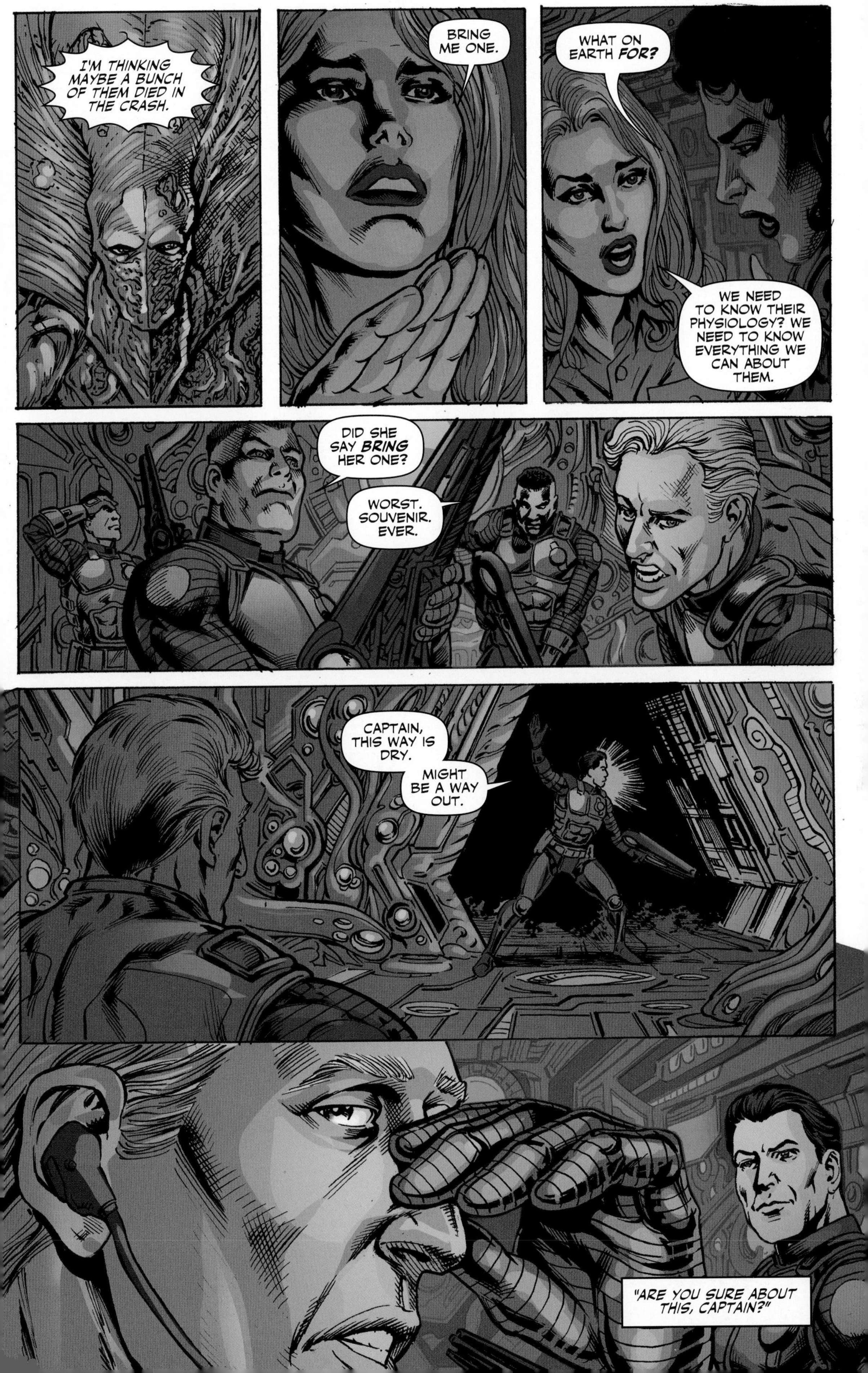
I'M THINKING MAYBE A BUNCH OF THEM DIED IN THE CRASH.
BRING ME ONE.
WHAT ON EARTH FOR?
WE NEED TO KNOW THEIR PHYSIOLOGY? WE NEED TO KNOW EVERYTHING WE CAN ABOUT THEM.
DID SHE SAY BRING HER ONE?
WORST. SOUVENIR. EVER.
CAPTAIN, THIS WAY IS DRY.
MIGHT BE A WAY OUT.
"ARE YOU SURE ABOUT THIS, CAPTAIN?"

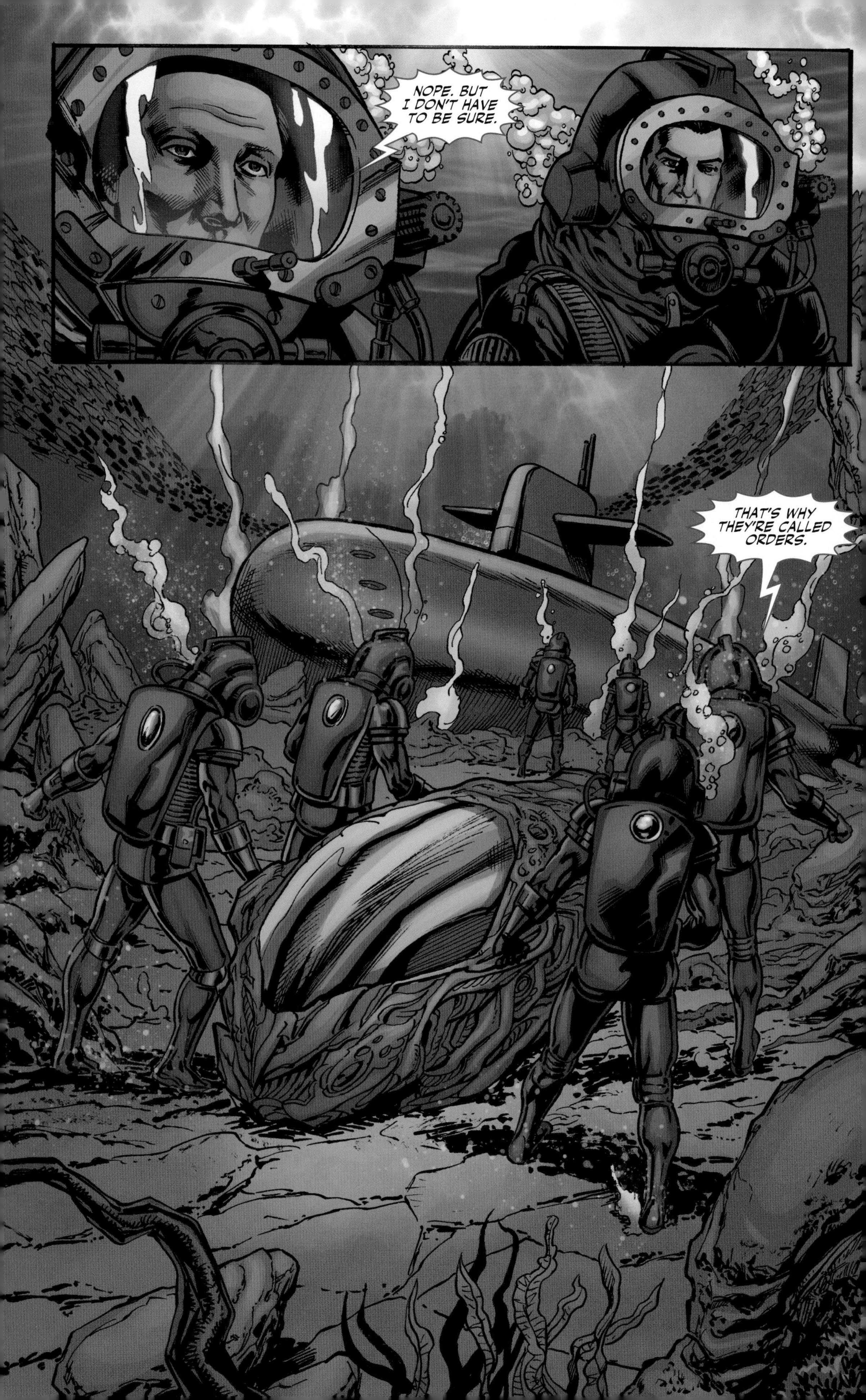
NOPE. BUT I DON'T HAVE TO BE SURE.
THAT'S WHY THEY'RE CALLED ORDERS.

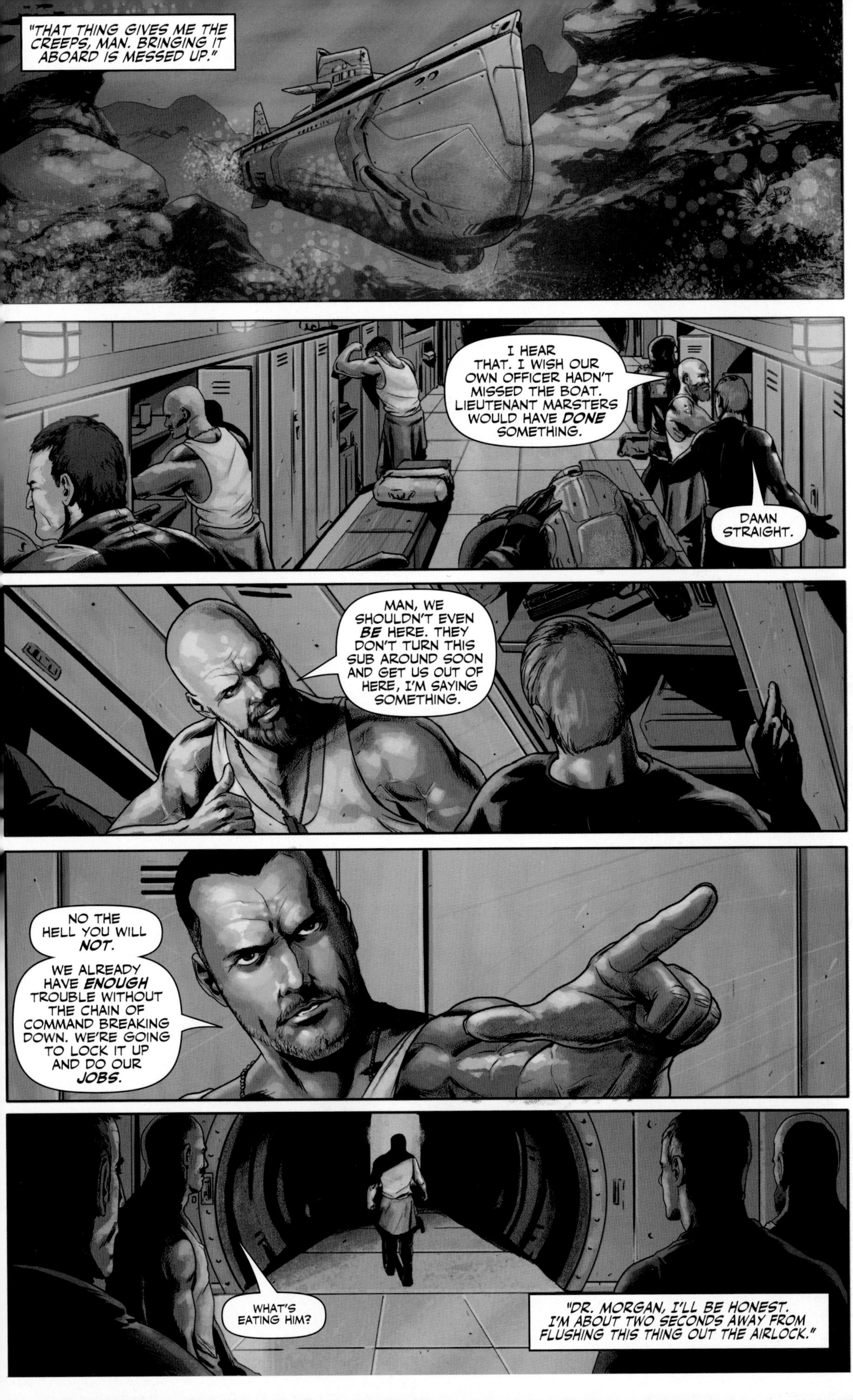
"THAT THING GIVES ME THE CREEPS, MAN. BRINGING IT ABOARD IS MESSED UP."
I HEAR THAT. I WISH OUR OWN OFFICER HADN'T MISSED THE BOAT. LIEUTENANT MARSTERS WOULD HAVE DONE SOMETHING.
DAMN STRAIGHT.
MAN, WE SHOULDN'T EVEN BE HERE. THEY DON'T TURN THIS SUB AROUND SOON AND GET US OUT OF HERE, I'M SAYING SOMETHING.
NO THE HELL YOU WILL NOT.
WE ALREADY HAVE ENOUGH TROUBLE WITHOUT THE CHAIN OF COMMAND BREAKING DOWN. WE'RE GOING TO LOCK IT UP AND DO OUR JOBS.
WHAT'S EATING HIM?
"DR. MORGAN, I'LL BE HONEST. I'M ABOUT TWO SECONDS AWAY FROM FLUSHING THIS THING OUT THE AIRLOCK."

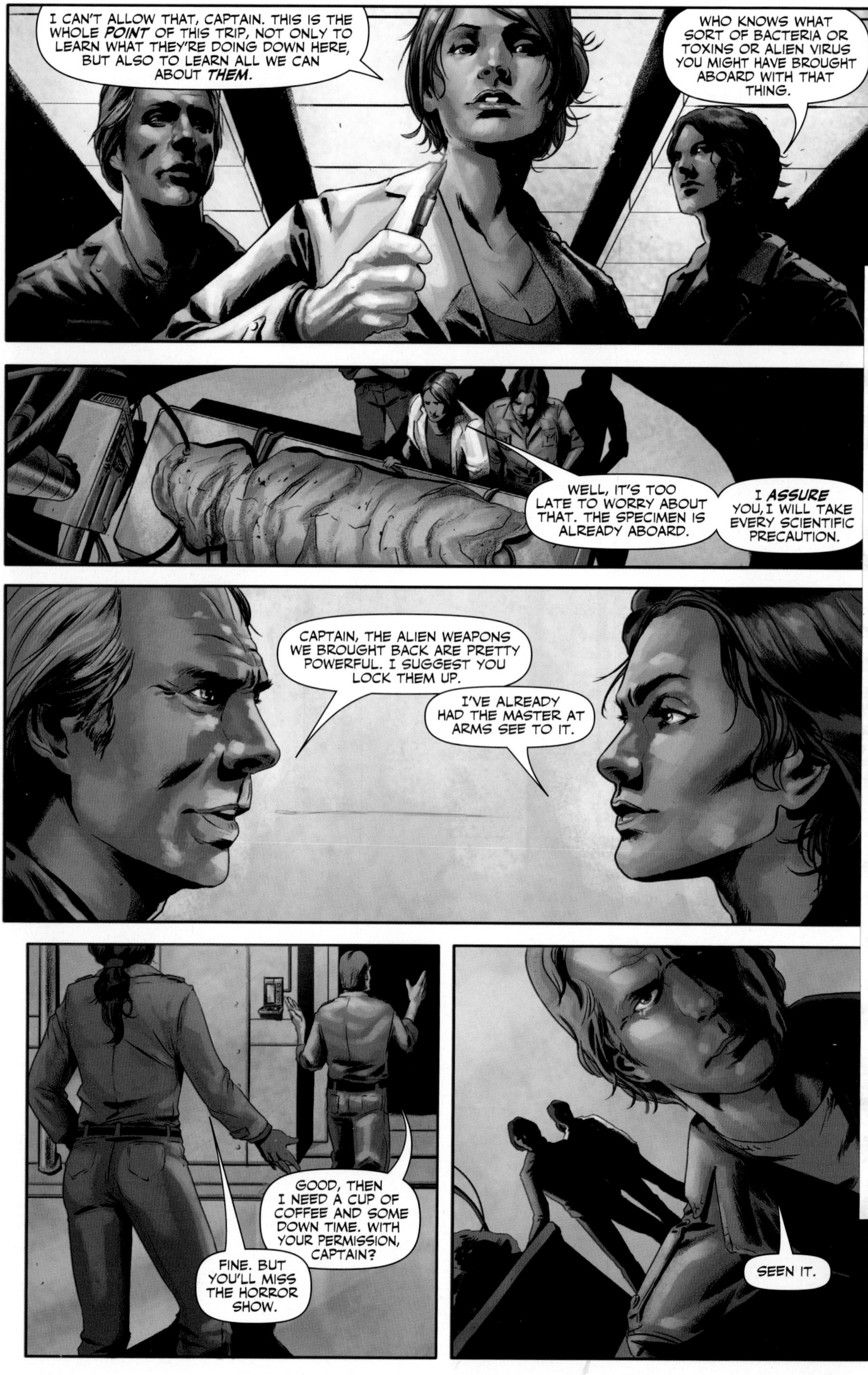
I CAN'T ALLOW THAT, CAPTAIN. THIS IS THE WHOLE POINT OF THIS TRIP, NOT ONLY TO LEARN WHAT THEY'RE DOING DOWN HERE, BUT ALSO TO LEARN ALL WE CAN ABOUT THEM.
WHO KNOWS WHAT SORT OF BACTERIA OR TOXINS OR ALIEN VIRUS YOU MIGHT HAVE BROUGHT ABOARD WITH THAT THING.
WELL, IT'S TOO LATE TO WORRY ABOUT THAT. THE SPECIMEN IS ALREADY ABOARD.
I ASSURE YOU, I WILL TAKE EVERY SCIENTIFIC PRECAUTION.
CAPTAIN, THE ALIEN WEAPONS WE BROUGHT BACK ARE PRETTY POWERFUL. I SUGGEST YOU LOCK THEM UP.
I'VE ALREADY HAD THE MASTER AT ARMS SEE TO IT.
GOOD, THEN I NEED A CUP OF COFFEE AND SOME DOWN TIME. WITH YOUR PERMISSION, CAPTAIN?
FINE. BUT YOU'LL MISS THE HORROR SHOW.
SEEN IT.

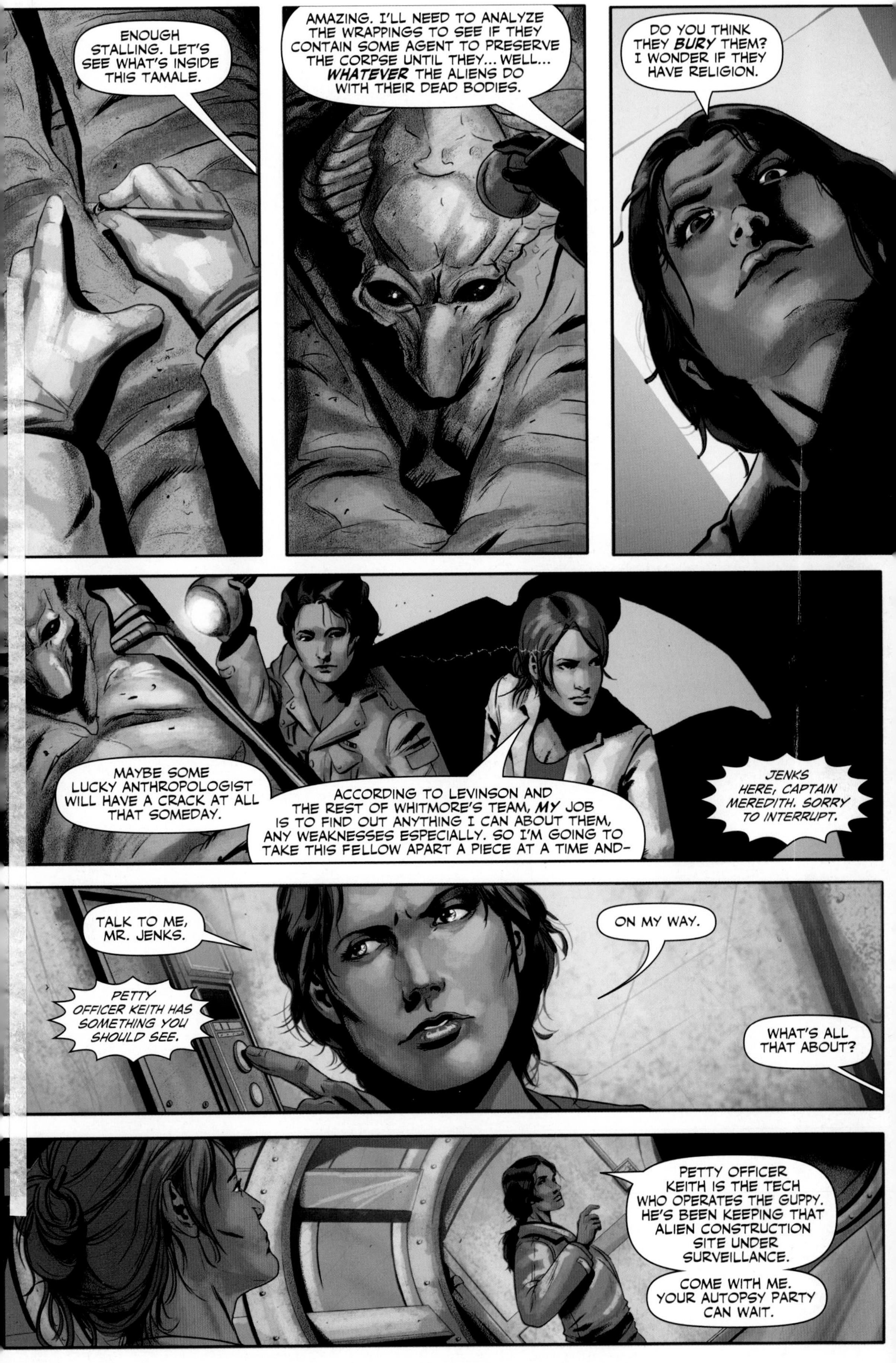
ENOUGH STALLING. LET'S SEE WHAT'S INSIDE THIS TAMALE.
AMAZING. I'LL NEED TO ANALYZE THE WRAPPINGS TO SEE IF THEY CONTAIN SOME AGENT TO PRESERVE THE CORPSE UNTIL THEY... WELL... WHATEVER THE ALIENS DO WITH THEIR DEAD BODIES.
DO YOU THINK THEY BURY THEM? I WONDER IF THEY HAVE RELIGION.
MAYBE SOME LUCKY ANTHROPOLOGIST WILL HAVE A CRACK AT ALL THAT SOMEDAY.
ACCORDING TO LEVINSON AND THE REST OF WHITMORE'S TEAM, MY JOB IS TO FIND OUT ANYTHING I CAN ABOUT THEM, ANY WEAKNESSES ESPECIALLY. SO I'M GOING TO TAKE THIS FELLOW APART A PIECE AT A TIME AND-
JENKS HERE, CAPTAIN MEREDITH. SORRY TO INTERRUPT.
TALK TO ME, MR. JENKS.
PETTY OFFICER KEITH HAS SOMETHING YOU SHOULD SEE.
ON MY WAY.
WHAT'S ALL THAT ABOUT?
PETTY OFFICER KEITH IS THE TECH WHO OPERATES THE GUPPY. HE'S BEEN KEEPING THAT ALIEN CONSTRUCTION SITE UNDER SURVEILLANCE.
COME WITH ME. YOUR AUTOPSY PARTY CAN WAIT.

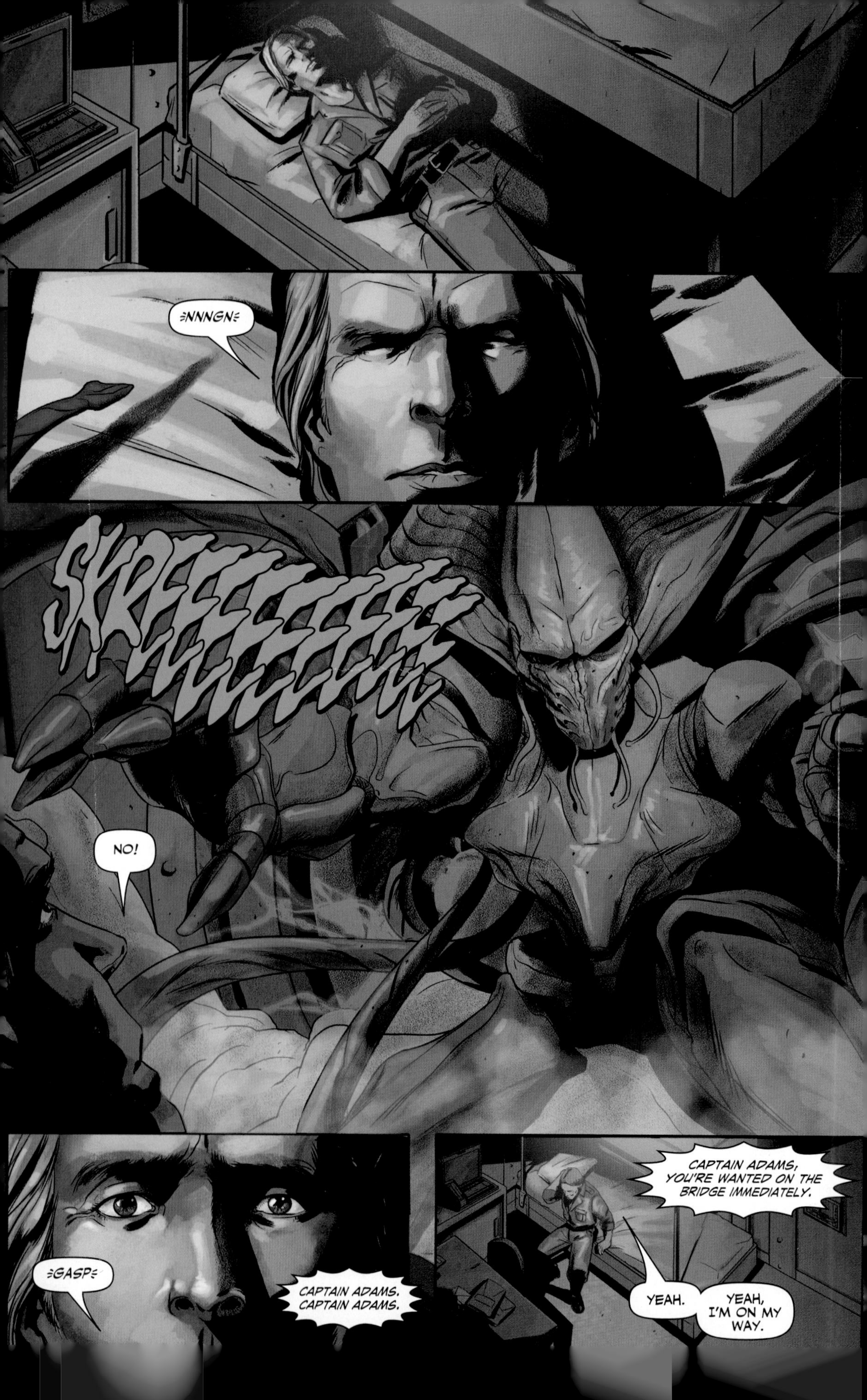
NNNGN
SKREEEEEEEEE
NO!
GASP
CAPTAIN ADAMS. CAPTAIN ADAMS.
CAPTAIN ADAMS, YOU'RE WANTED ON THE BRIDGE IMMEDIATELY.
YEAH.
YEAH, I'M ON MY WAY.

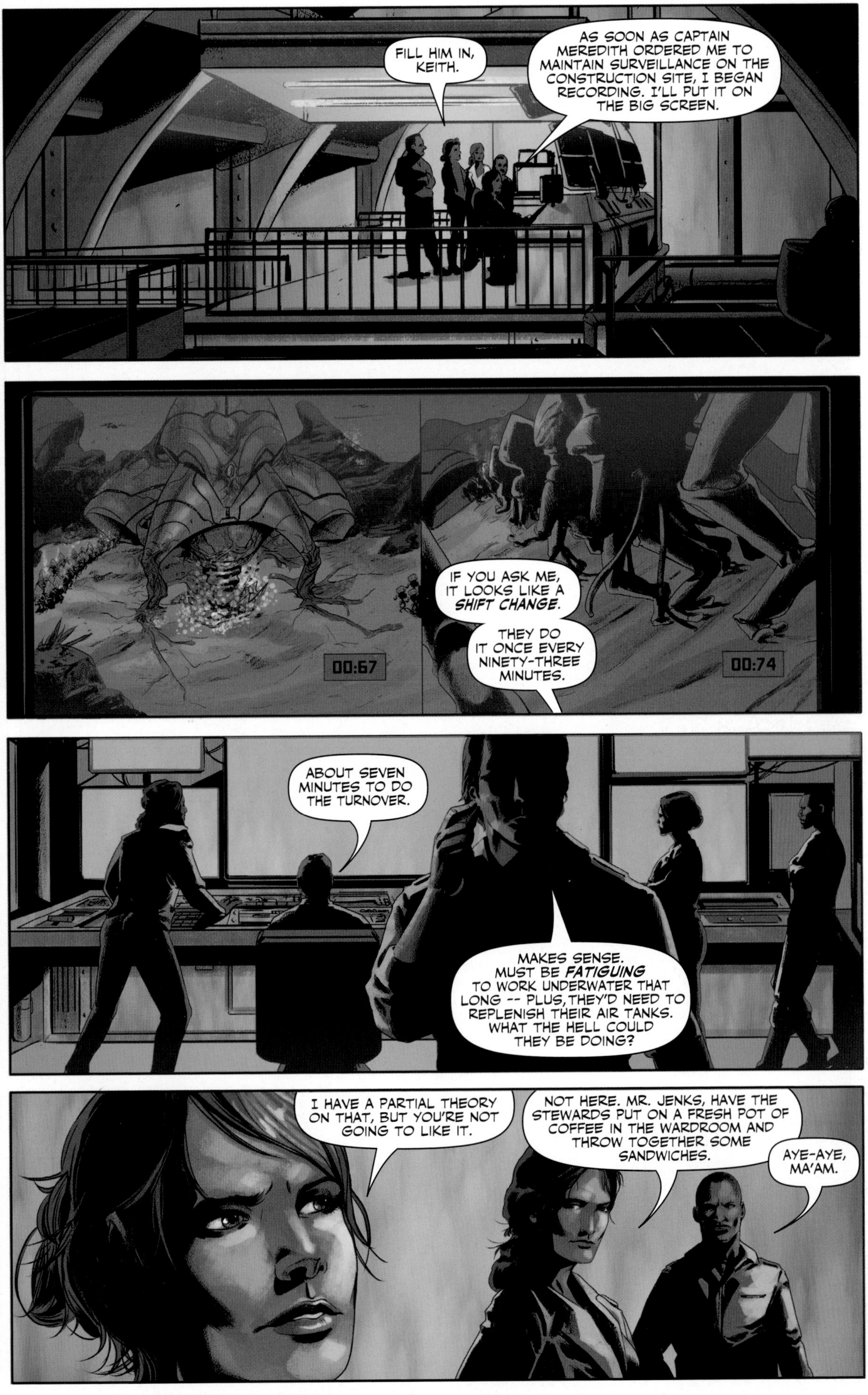
FILL HIM IN, KEITH.
AS SOON AS CAPTAIN MEREDITH ORDERED ME TO MAINTAIN SURVEILLANCE ON THE CONSTRUCTION SITE, I BEGAN RECORDING. I'LL PUT IT ON THE BIG SCREEN.
00:67
00:74
IF YOU ASK ME, IT LOOKS LIKE A *SHIFT CHANGE*.
THEY DO IT ONCE EVERY NINETY-THREE MINUTES.
ABOUT SEVEN MINUTES TO DO THE TURNOVER.
MAKES SENSE. MUST BE *FATIGUING* TO WORK UNDERWATER THAT LONG -- PLUS, THEY'D NEED TO REPLENISH THEIR AIR TANKS. WHAT THE HELL COULD THEY BE DOING?
I HAVE A PARTIAL THEORY ON THAT, BUT YOU'RE NOT GOING TO LIKE IT.
NOT HERE. MR. JENKS, HAVE THE STEWARDS PUT ON A FRESH POT OF COFFEE IN THE WARDROOM AND THROW TOGETHER SOME SANDWICHES.
AYE-AYE, MA'AM.

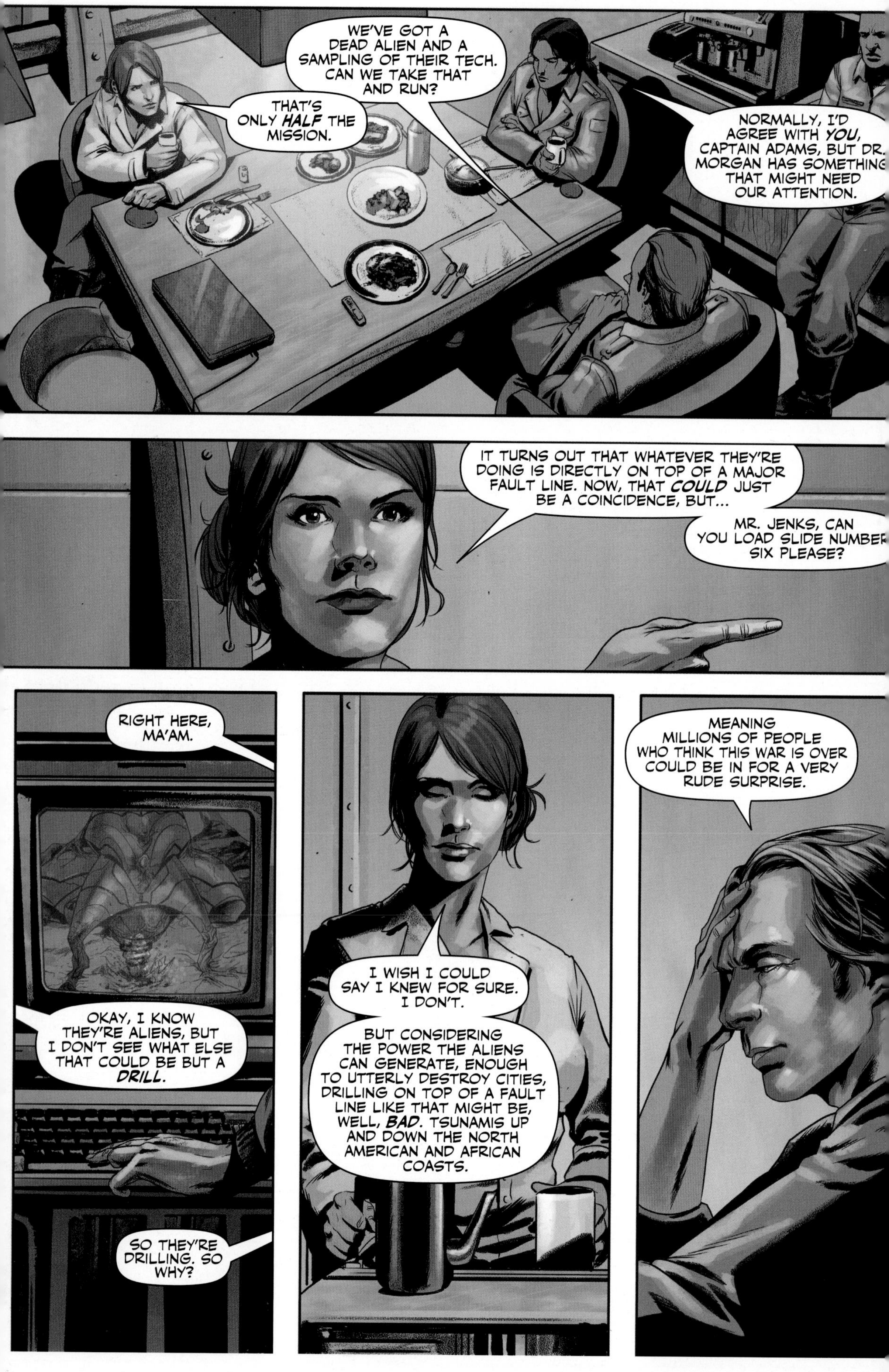

WE'VE GOT A DEAD ALIEN AND A SAMPLING OF THEIR TECH. CAN WE TAKE THAT AND RUN?
THAT'S ONLY *HALF* THE MISSION.
NORMALLY, I'D AGREE WITH *YOU*, CAPTAIN ADAMS, BUT DR. MORGAN HAS SOMETHING THAT MIGHT NEED OUR ATTENTION.
IT TURNS OUT THAT WHATEVER THEY'RE DOING IS DIRECTLY ON TOP OF A MAJOR FAULT LINE. NOW, THAT *COULD* JUST BE A COINCIDENCE, BUT...
MR. JENKS, CAN YOU LOAD SLIDE NUMBER SIX PLEASE?
RIGHT HERE, MA'AM.
OKAY, I KNOW THEY'RE ALIENS, BUT I DON'T SEE WHAT ELSE THAT COULD BE BUT A *DRILL*.
SO THEY'RE DRILLING. SO WHY?
I WISH I COULD SAY I KNEW FOR SURE. I DON'T.
BUT CONSIDERING THE POWER THE ALIENS CAN GENERATE, ENOUGH TO UTTERLY DESTROY CITIES, DRILLING ON TOP OF A FAULT LINE LIKE THAT MIGHT BE, WELL, *BAD*. TSUNAMIS UP AND DOWN THE NORTH AMERICAN AND AFRICAN COASTS.
MEANING MILLIONS OF PEOPLE WHO THINK THIS WAR IS OVER COULD BE IN FOR A VERY RUDE SURPRISE.

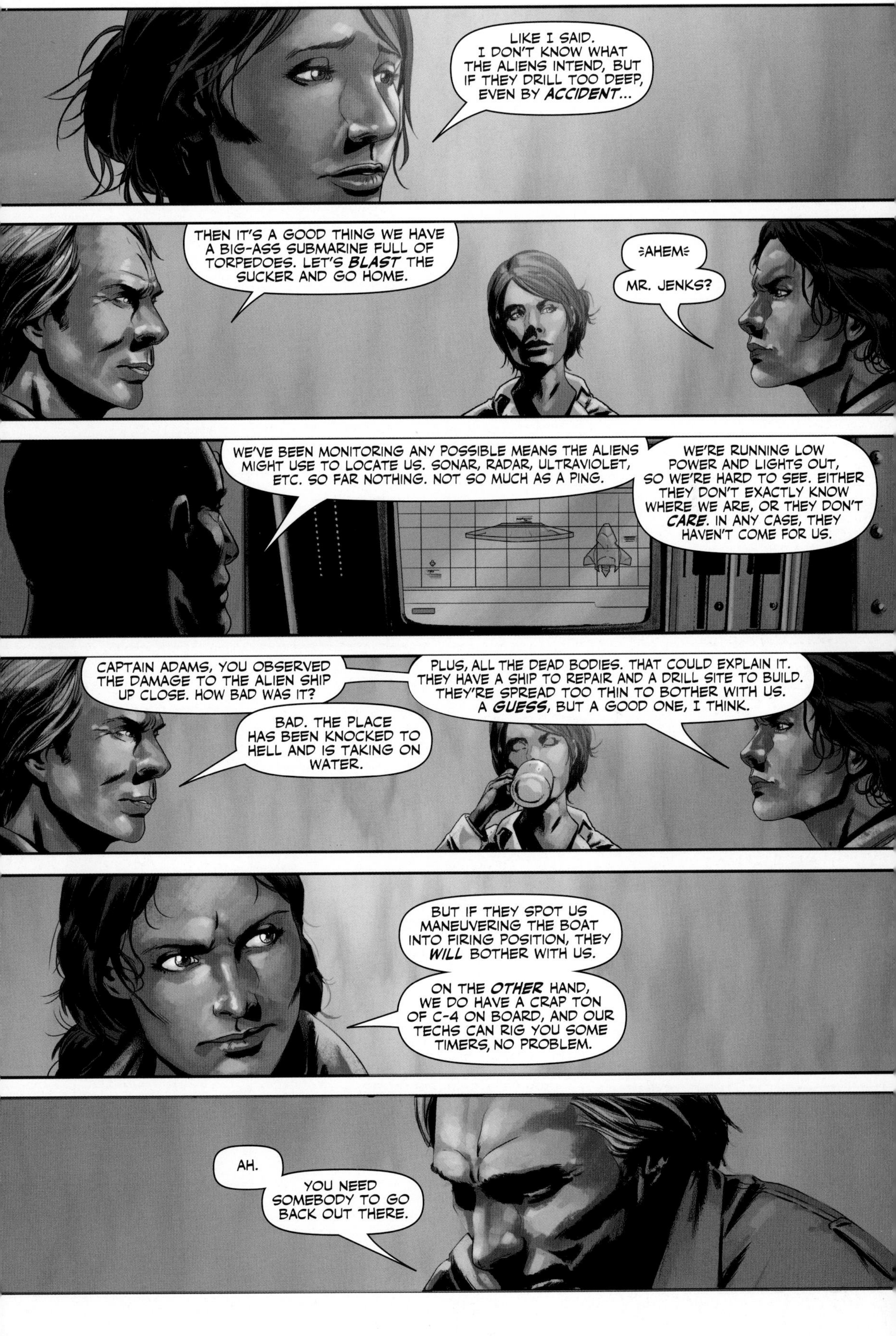
LIKE I SAID. I DON'T KNOW WHAT THE ALIENS INTEND, BUT IF THEY DRILL TOO DEEP, EVEN BY ACCIDENT...
THEN IT'S A GOOD THING WE HAVE A BIG-ASS SUBMARINE FULL OF TORPEDOES. LET'S BLAST THE SUCKER AND GO HOME.
AHEM
MR. JENKS?
WE'VE BEEN MONITORING ANY POSSIBLE MEANS THE ALIENS MIGHT USE TO LOCATE US. SONAR, RADAR, ULTRAVIOLET, ETC. SO FAR NOTHING. NOT SO MUCH AS A PING.
WE'RE RUNNING LOW POWER AND LIGHTS OUT, SO WE'RE HARD TO SEE. EITHER THEY DON'T EXACTLY KNOW WHERE WE ARE, OR THEY DON'T CARE. IN ANY CASE, THEY HAVEN'T COME FOR US.
CAPTAIN ADAMS, YOU OBSERVED THE DAMAGE TO THE ALIEN SHIP UP CLOSE. HOW BAD WAS IT?
BAD. THE PLACE HAS BEEN KNOCKED TO HELL AND IS TAKING ON WATER.
PLUS, ALL THE DEAD BODIES. THAT COULD EXPLAIN IT. THEY HAVE A SHIP TO REPAIR AND A DRILL SITE TO BUILD. THEY'RE SPREAD TOO THIN TO BOTHER WITH US. A GUESS, BUT A GOOD ONE, I THINK.
BUT IF THEY SPOT US MANEUVERING THE BOAT INTO FIRING POSITION, THEY WILL BOTHER WITH US.
ON THE OTHER HAND, WE DO HAVE A CRAP TON OF C-4 ON BOARD, AND OUR TECHS CAN RIG YOU SOME TIMERS, NO PROBLEM.
AH.
YOU NEED SOMEBODY TO GO BACK OUT THERE.

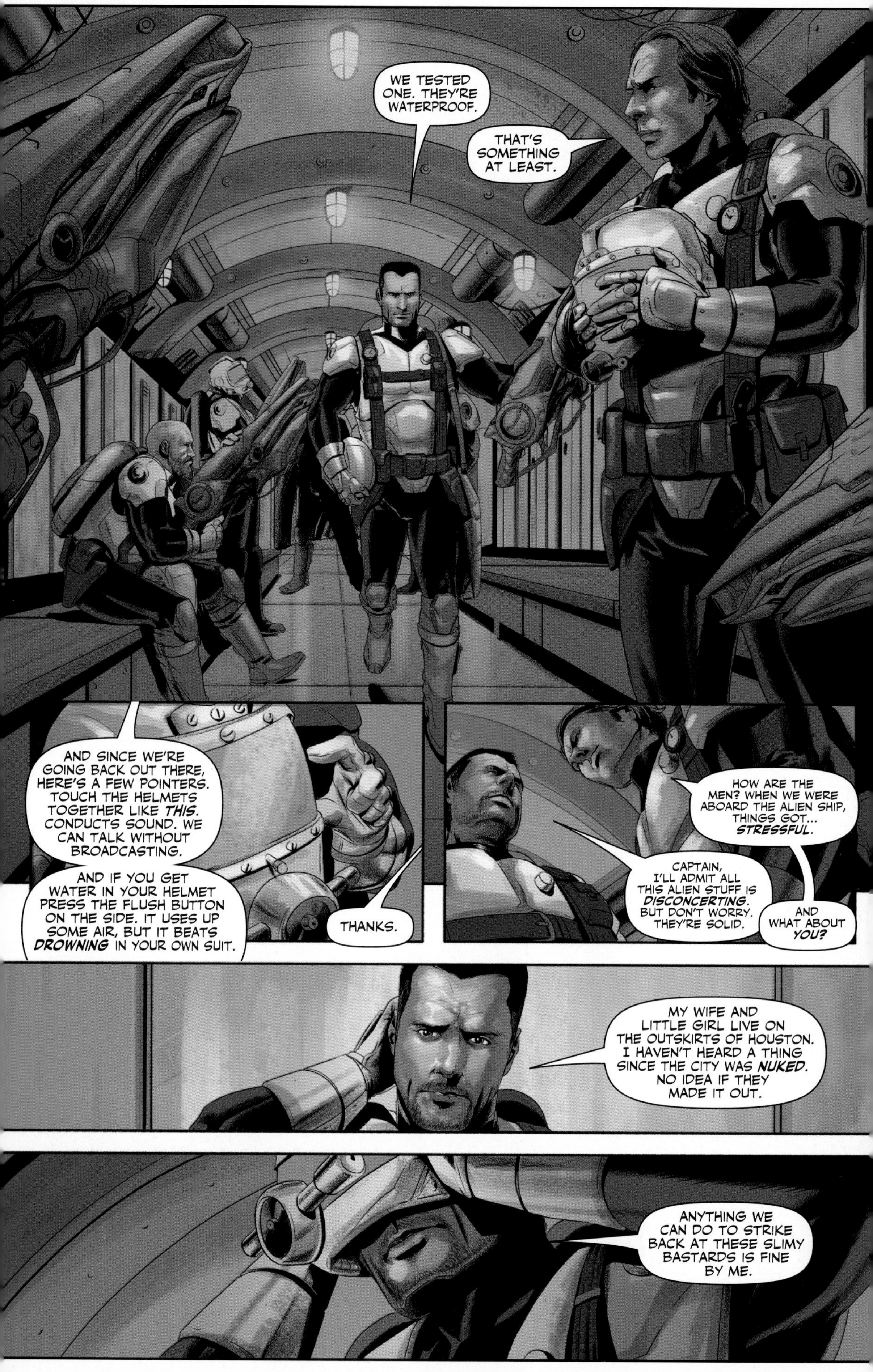
WE TESTED ONE. THEY'RE WATERPROOF.
THAT'S SOMETHING AT LEAST.
AND SINCE WE'RE GOING BACK OUT THERE, HERE'S A FEW POINTERS. TOUCH THE HELMETS TOGETHER LIKE *THIS*. CONDUCTS SOUND. WE CAN TALK WITHOUT BROADCASTING.
AND IF YOU GET WATER IN YOUR HELMET PRESS THE FLUSH BUTTON ON THE SIDE. IT USES UP SOME AIR, BUT IT BEATS *DROWNING* IN YOUR OWN SUIT.
THANKS.
HOW ARE THE MEN? WHEN WE WERE ABOARD THE ALIEN SHIP, THINGS GOT... *STRESSFUL*.
CAPTAIN, I'LL ADMIT ALL THIS ALIEN STUFF IS *DISCONCERTING*. BUT DON'T WORRY. THEY'RE SOLID.
AND WHAT ABOUT *YOU?*
MY WIFE AND LITTLE GIRL LIVE ON THE OUTSKIRTS OF HOUSTON. I HAVEN'T HEARD A THING SINCE THE CITY WAS *NUKED*. NO IDEA IF THEY MADE IT OUT.
ANYTHING WE CAN DO TO STRIKE BACK AT THESE SLIMY BASTARDS IS FINE BY ME.

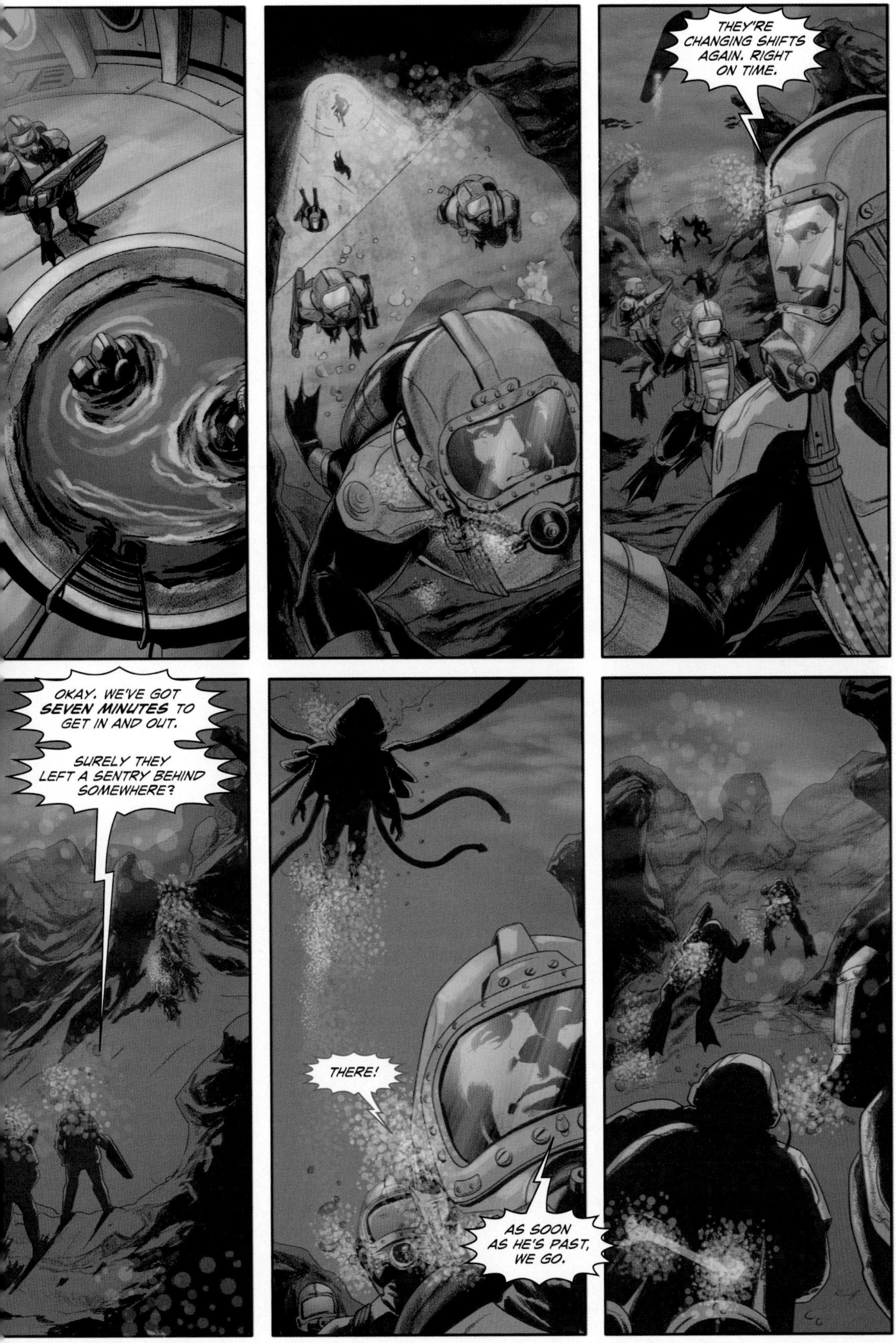
THEY'RE CHANGING SHIFTS AGAIN. RIGHT ON TIME.
OKAY. WE'VE GOT SEVEN MINUTES TO GET IN AND OUT.
SURELY THEY LEFT A SENTRY BEHIND SOMEWHERE?
THERE!
AS SOON AS HE'S PAST, WE GO.

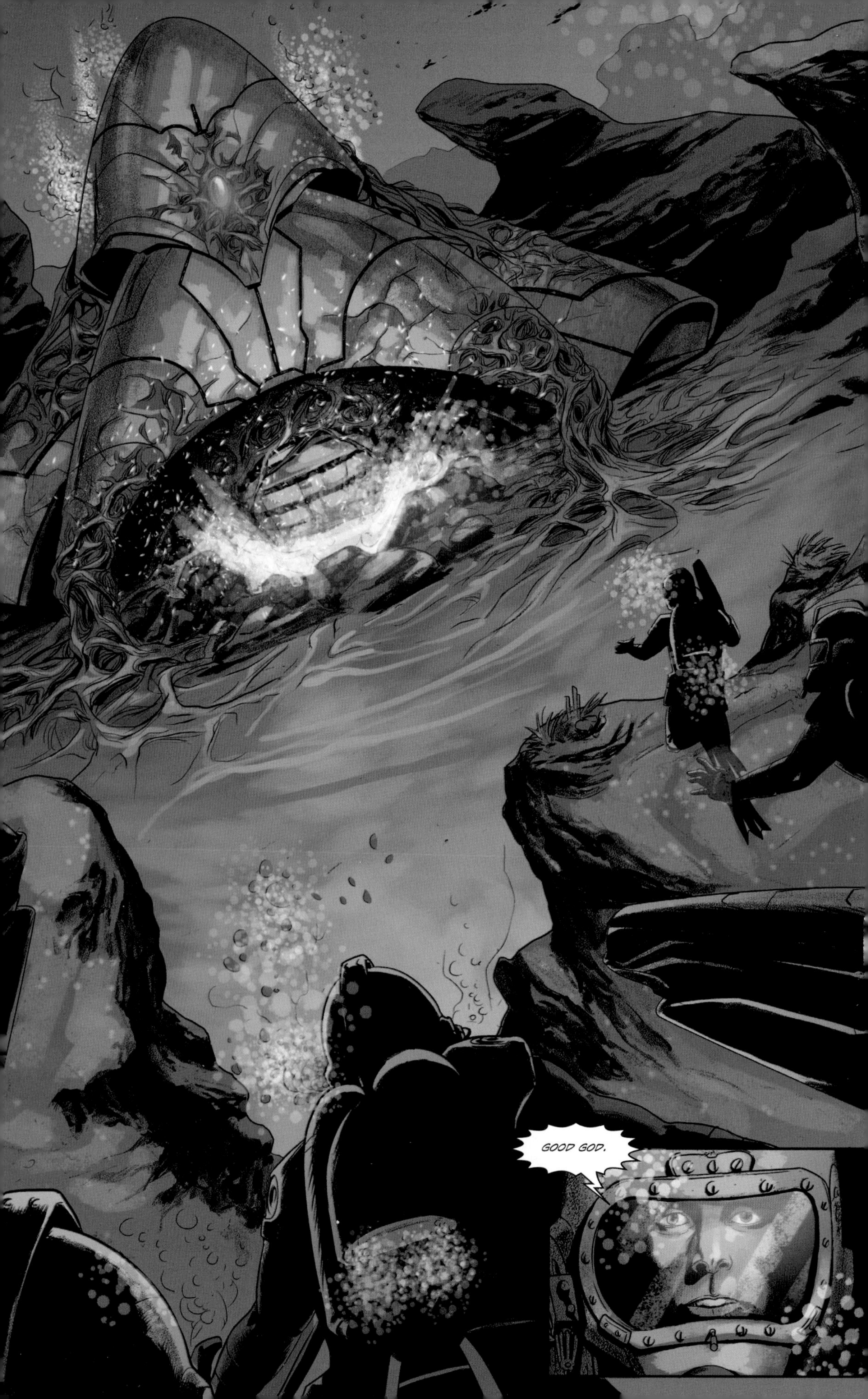
GOOD GOD.

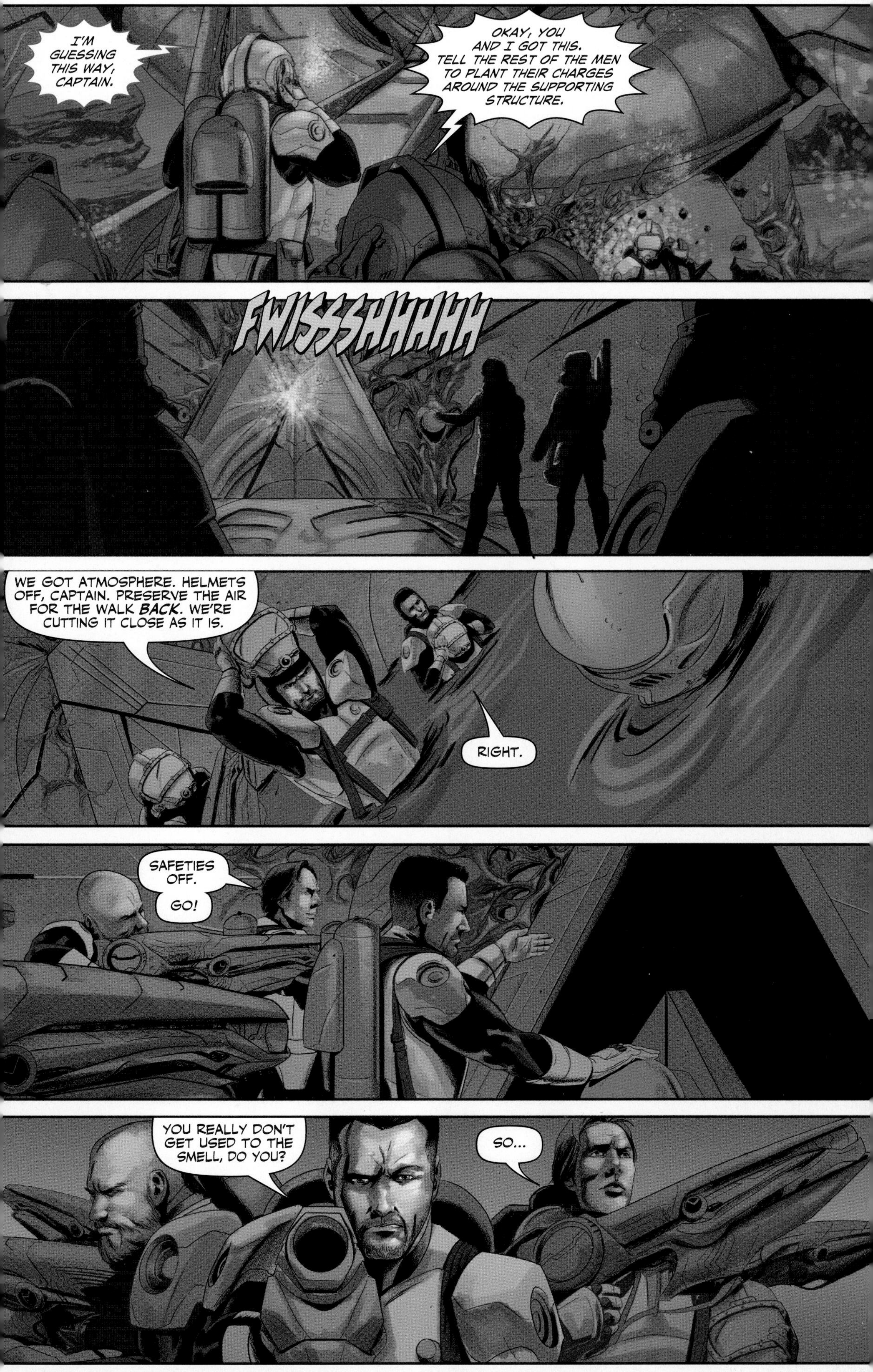
I'M GUESSING THIS WAY, CAPTAIN.
OKAY, YOU AND I GOT THIS. TELL THE REST OF THE MEN TO PLANT THEIR CHARGES AROUND THE SUPPORTING STRUCTURE.
FWISSSHHHHH
WE GOT ATMOSPHERE. HELMETS OFF, CAPTAIN. PRESERVE THE AIR FOR THE WALK BACK. WE'RE CUTTING IT CLOSE AS IT IS.
RIGHT.
SAFETIES OFF.
GO!
YOU REALLY DON'T GET USED TO THE SMELL, DO YOU?
SO...

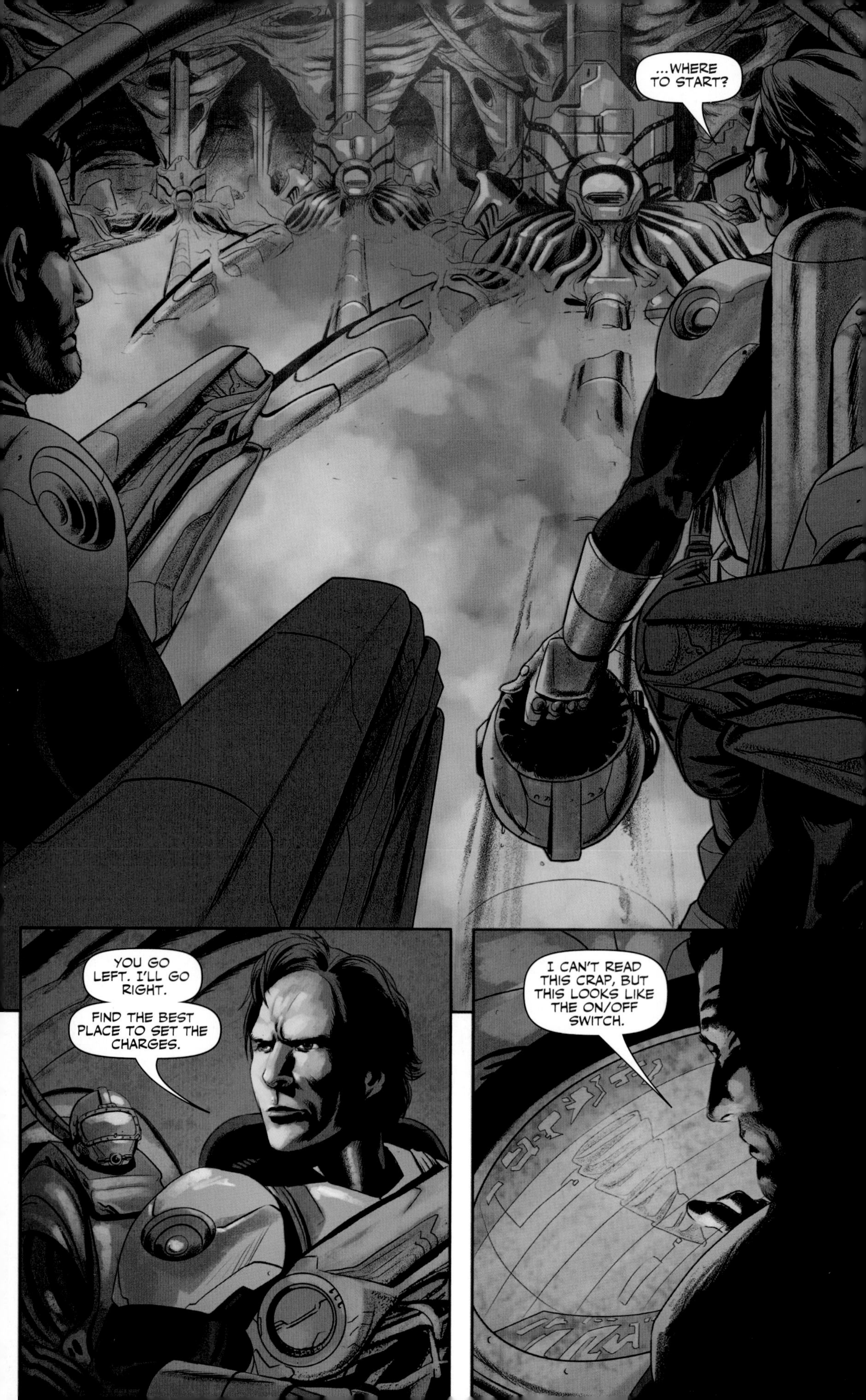
...WHERE TO START?
YOU GO LEFT. I'LL GO RIGHT.
FIND THE BEST PLACE TO SET THE CHARGES.
I CAN'T READ THIS CRAP, BUT THIS LOOKS LIKE THE ON/OFF SWITCH.

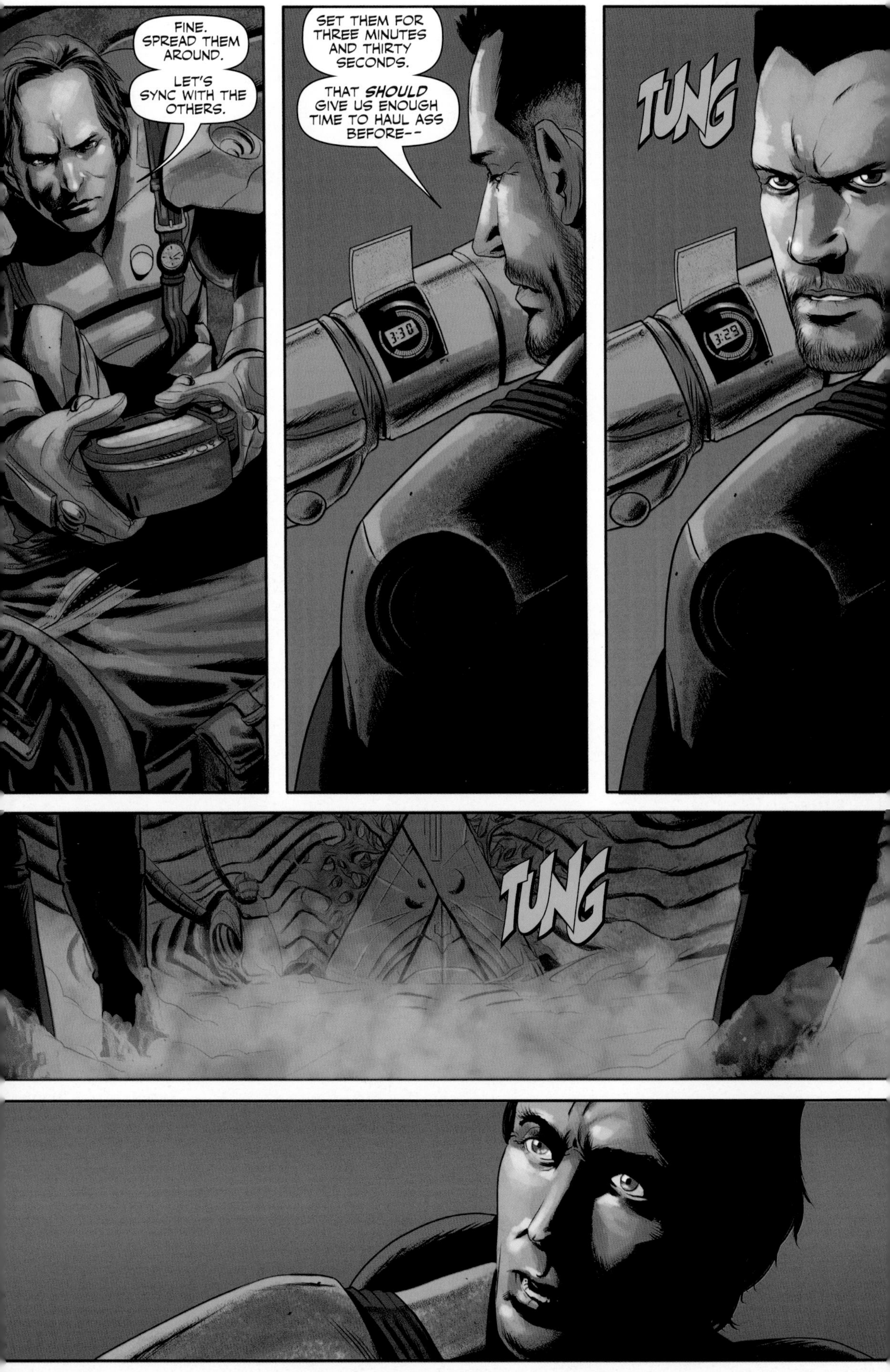
FINE. SPREAD THEM AROUND.
LET'S SYNC WITH THE OTHERS.
SET THEM FOR THREE MINUTES AND THIRTY SECONDS.
THAT SHOULD GIVE US ENOUGH TIME TO HAUL ASS BEFORE--
3:30
TUNG
3:29
TUNG

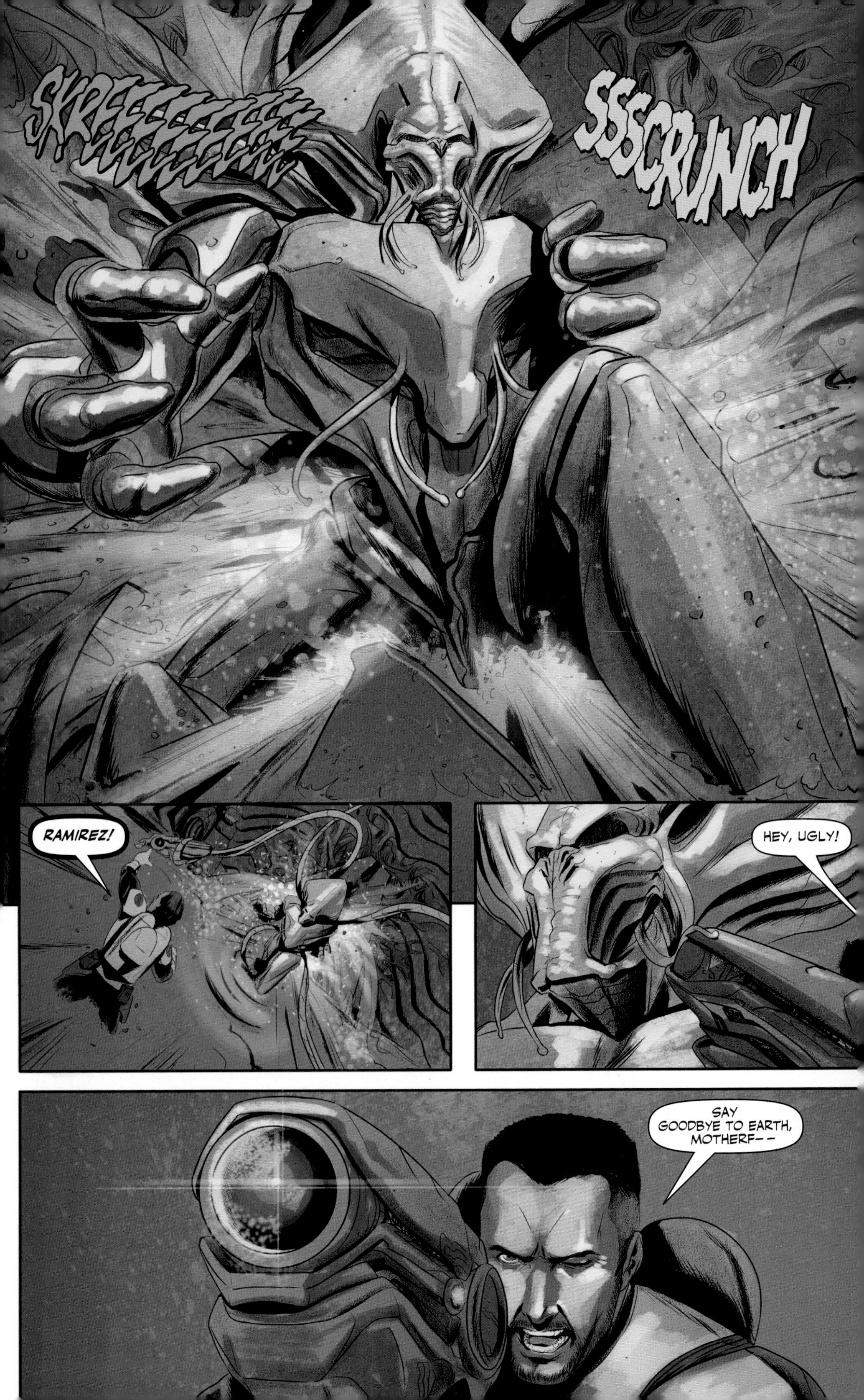
SKREEEEEEEEEE
SSSCRUNCH
RAMIREZ!
HEY, UGLY!
SAY GOODBYE TO EARTH, MOTHERF--

VZZZAP

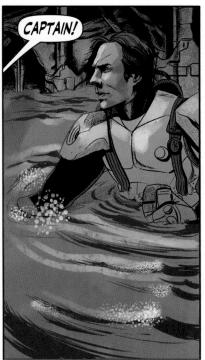

CAPTAIN!

HURRY, CAPTAIN! THE DOOR'S TRYING TO CLOSE.

SET THE CHARGES AND LET'S GET THE *HELL* OUT OF HERE!

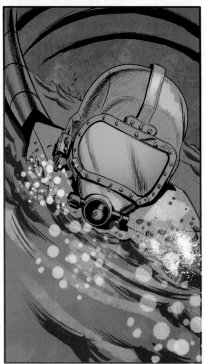

CAPTAIN!

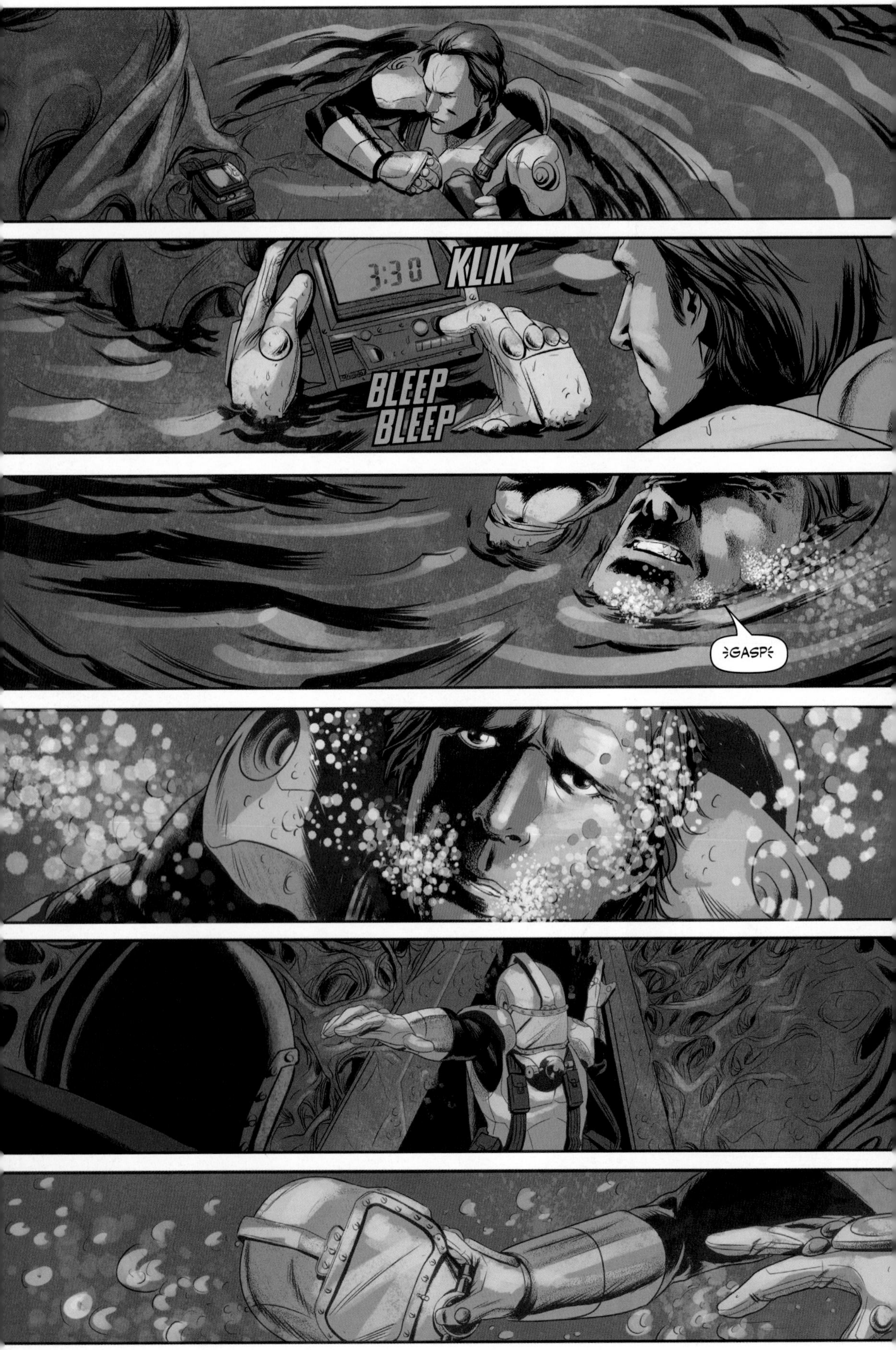
3:30
KLIK
BLEEP
BLEEP
GASP

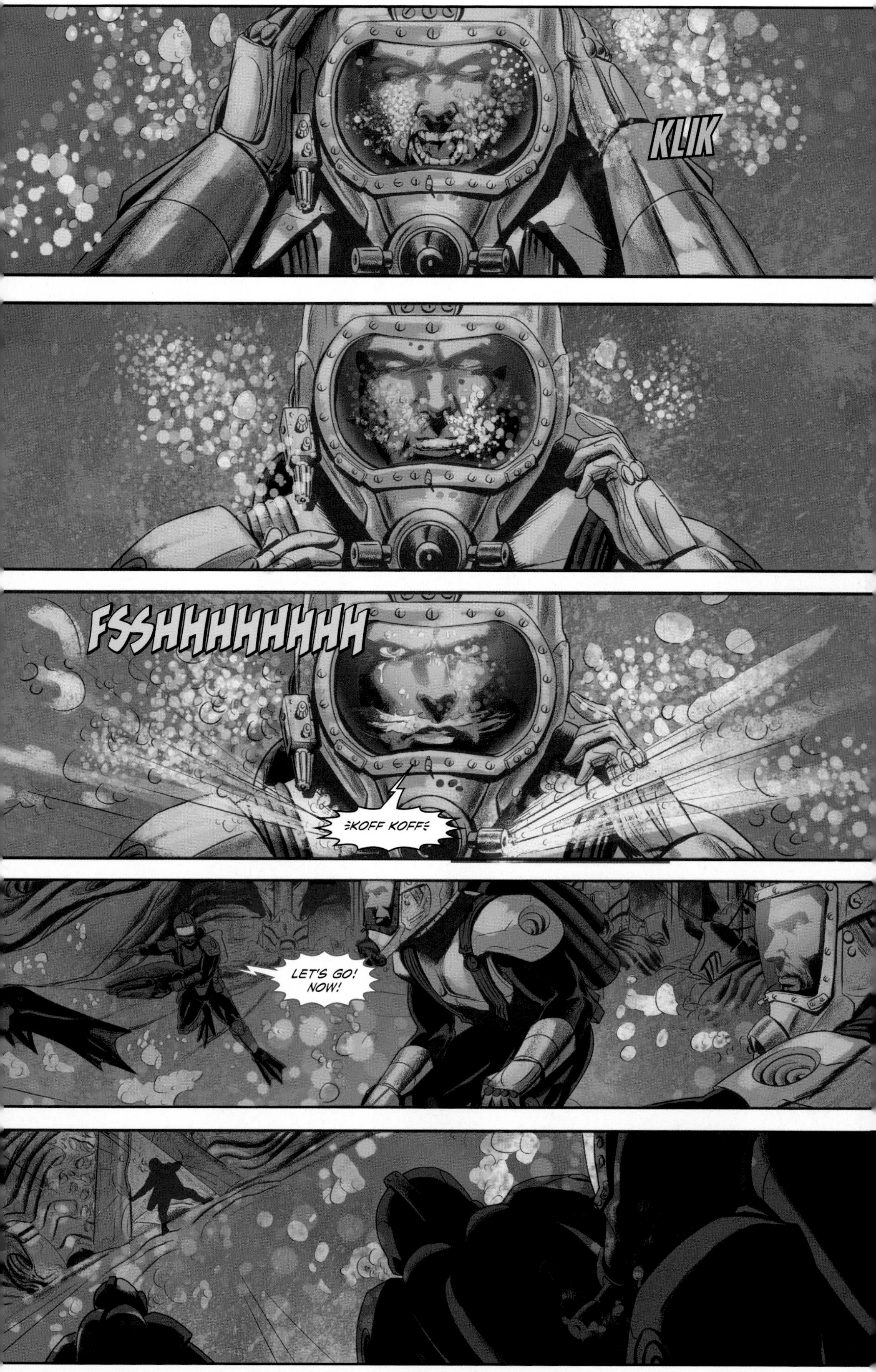
KLIK
FSSHHHHHHHHH
KOFF KOFF
LET'S GO! NOW!

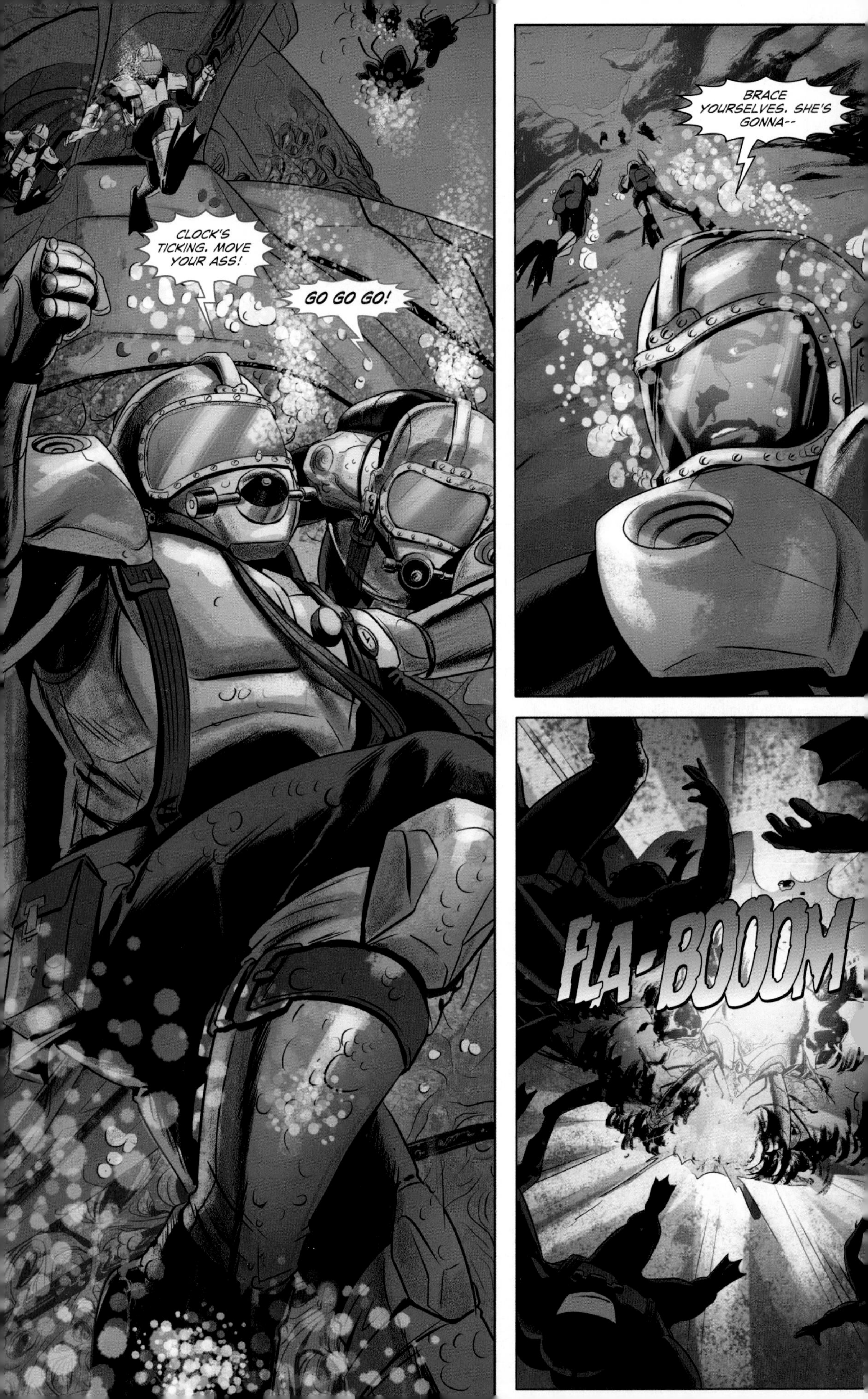
CLOCK'S TICKING. MOVE YOUR ASS!
GO GO GO!
BRACE YOURSELVES. SHE'S GONNA--
FLA-BOOOM

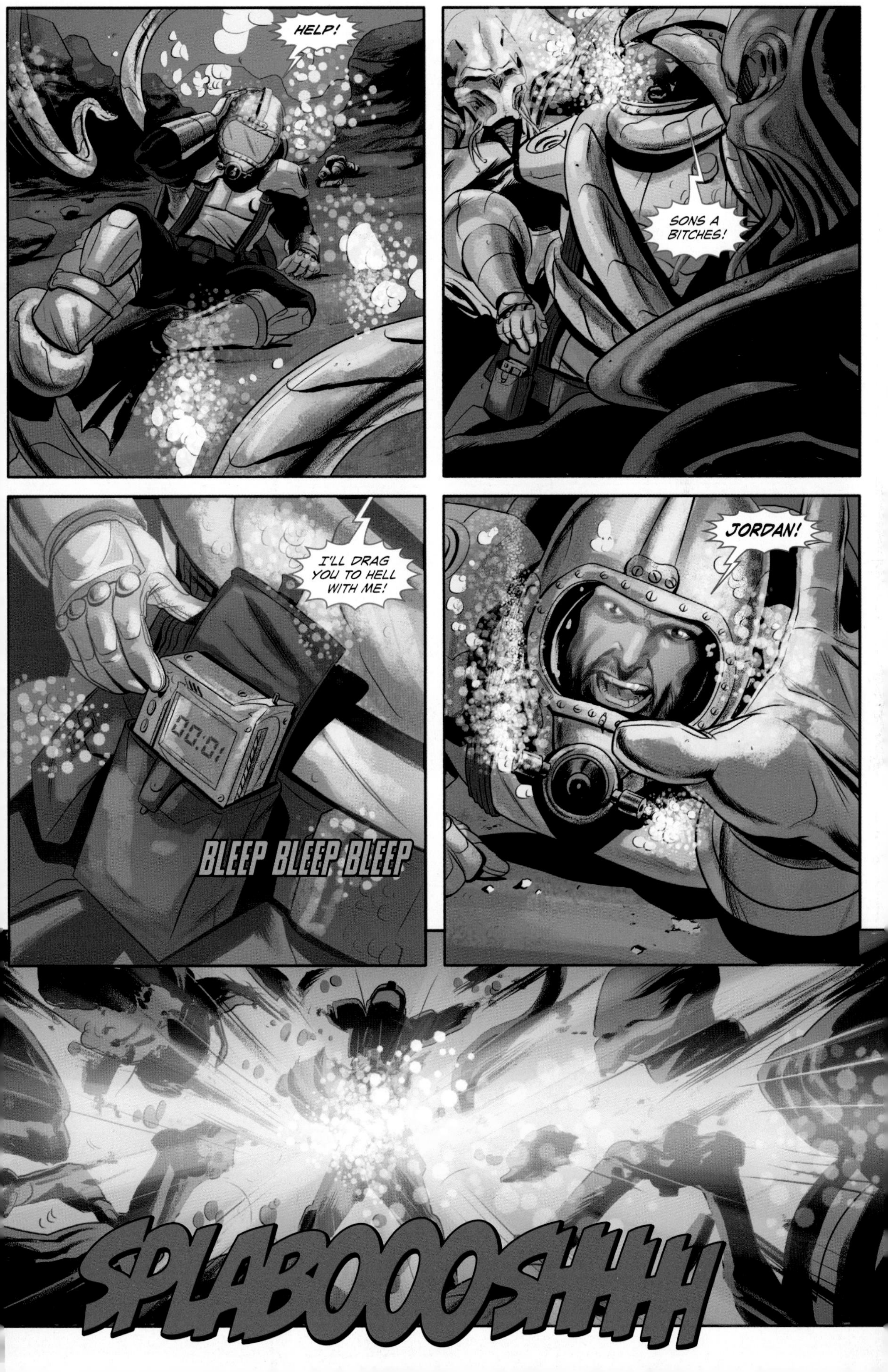
HELP!
SONS A BITCHES!
I'LL DRAG YOU TO HELL WITH ME!
00:01
BLEEP BLEEP BLEEP
JORDAN!
SPLABOOOSHHH

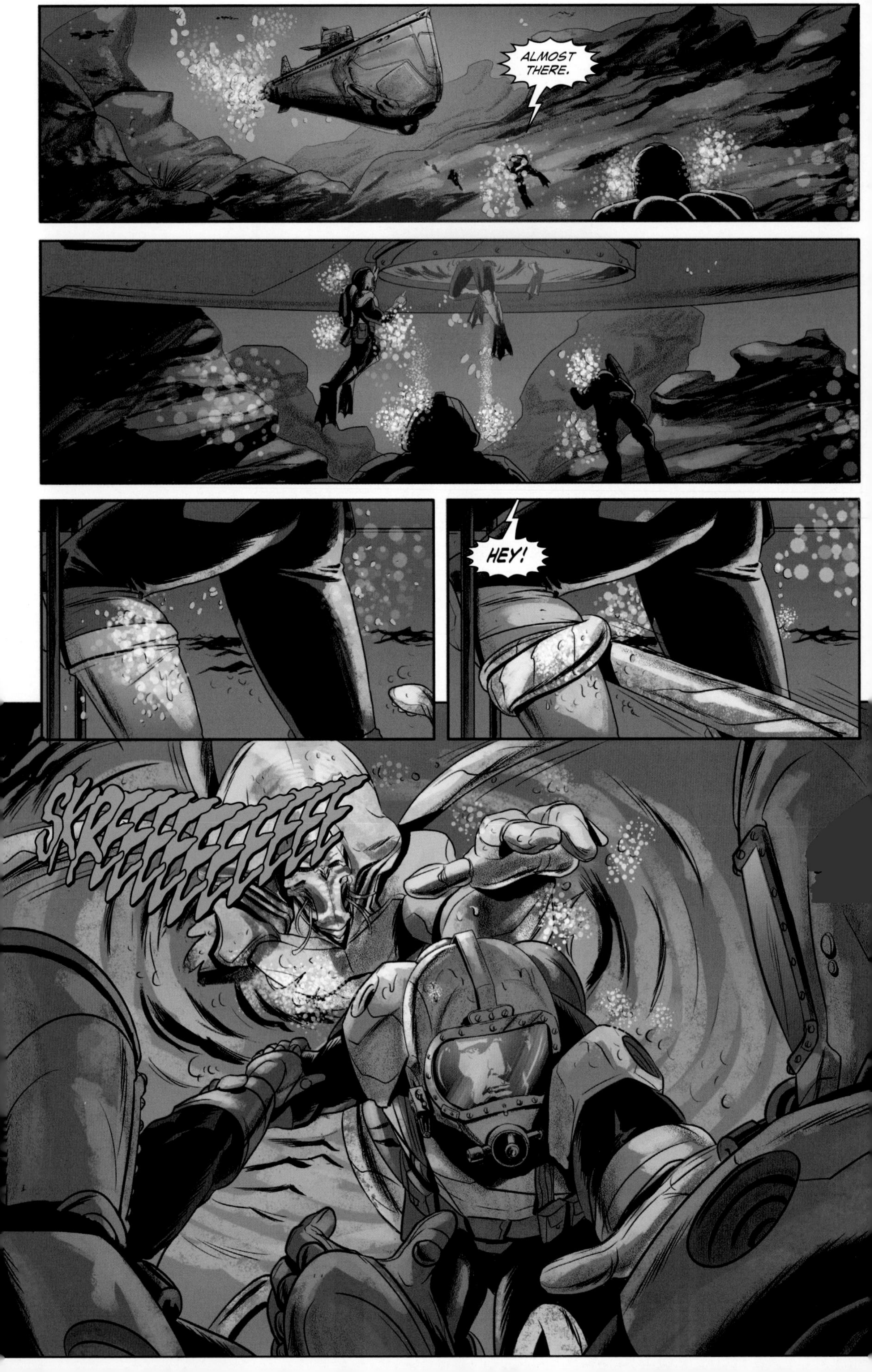
ALMOST THERE.
HEY!
SKREEEEEEEEEEEE

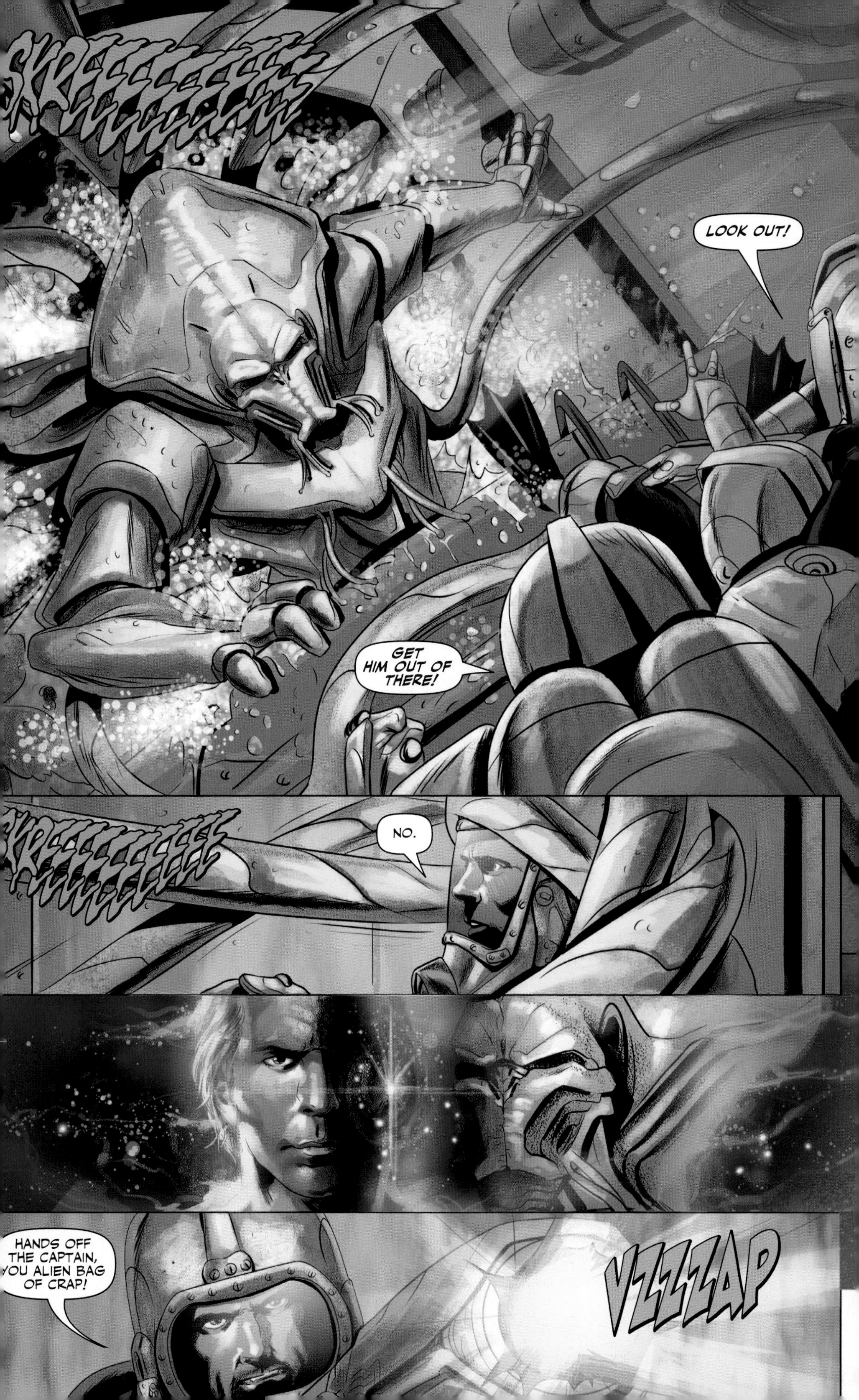
SKREEEEEEEEE
LOOK OUT!
GET HIM OUT OF THERE!
SKREEEEEEEEEE
NO.
HANDS OFF THE CAPTAIN, YOU ALIEN BAG OF CRAP!
VZZZAP

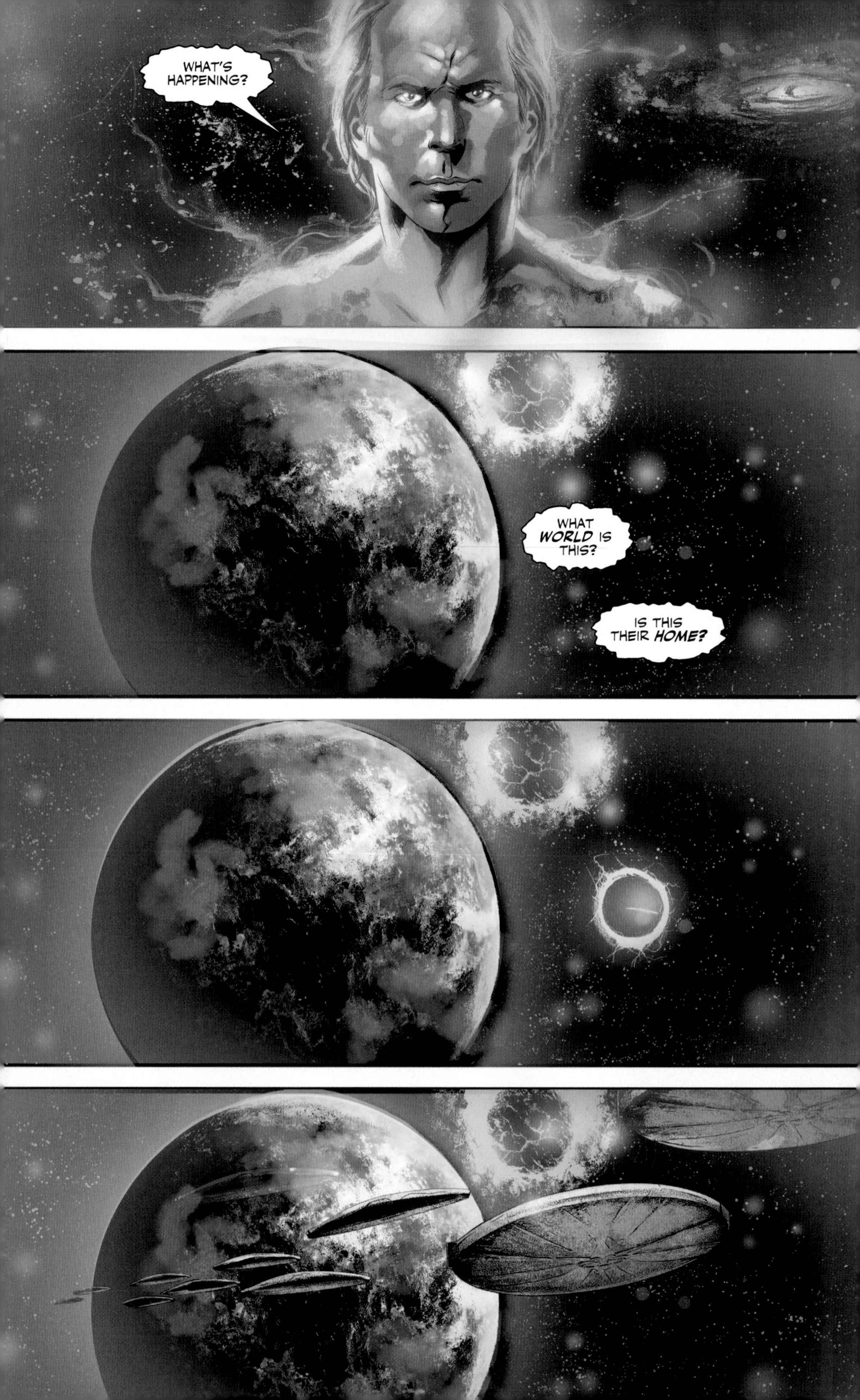
WHAT'S HAPPENING?
WHAT *WORLD* IS THIS?
IS THIS THEIR *HOME?*

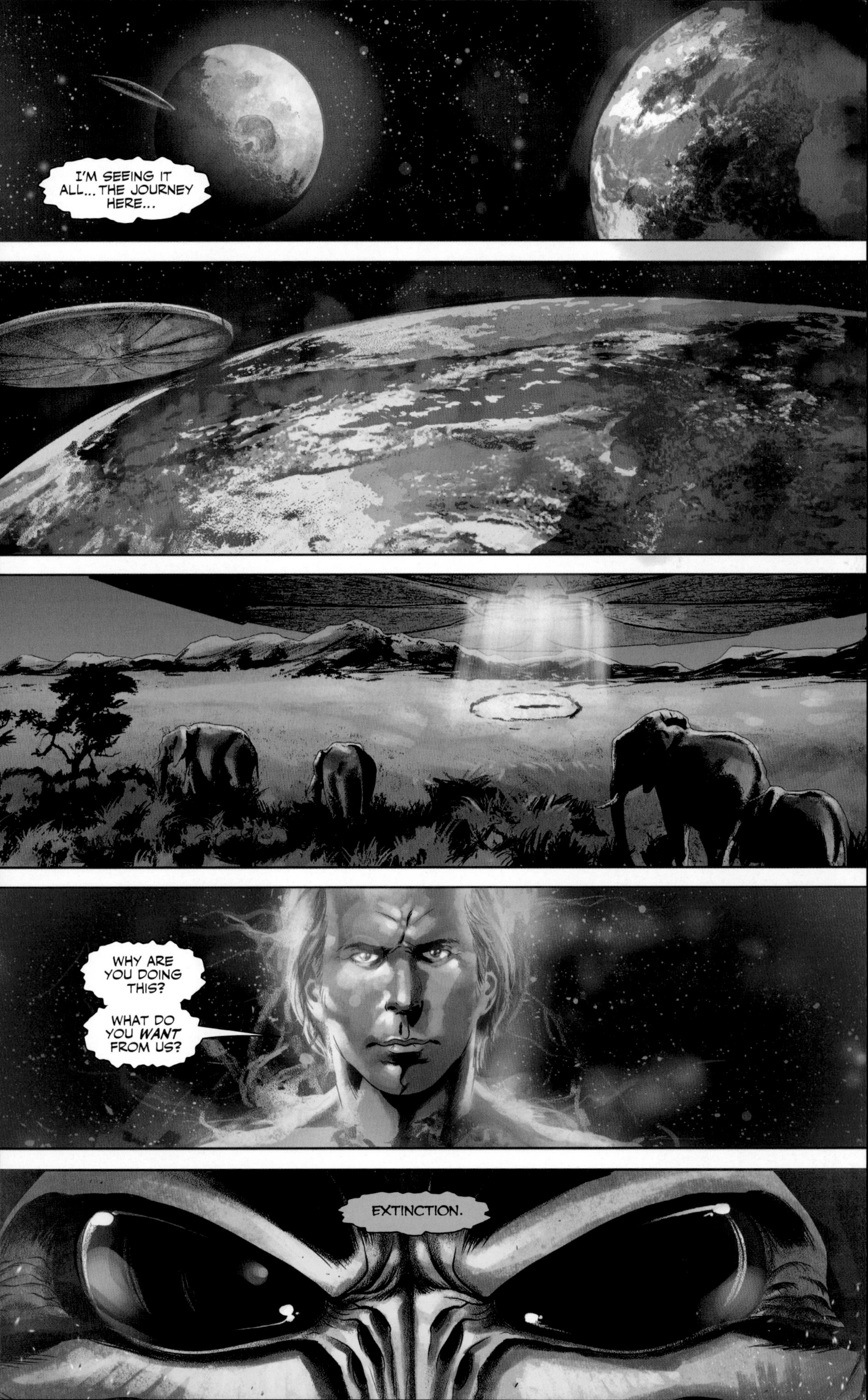
I'M SEEING IT ALL... THE JOURNEY HERE...
WHY ARE YOU DOING THIS?
WHAT DO YOU *WANT* FROM US?
EXTINCTION.

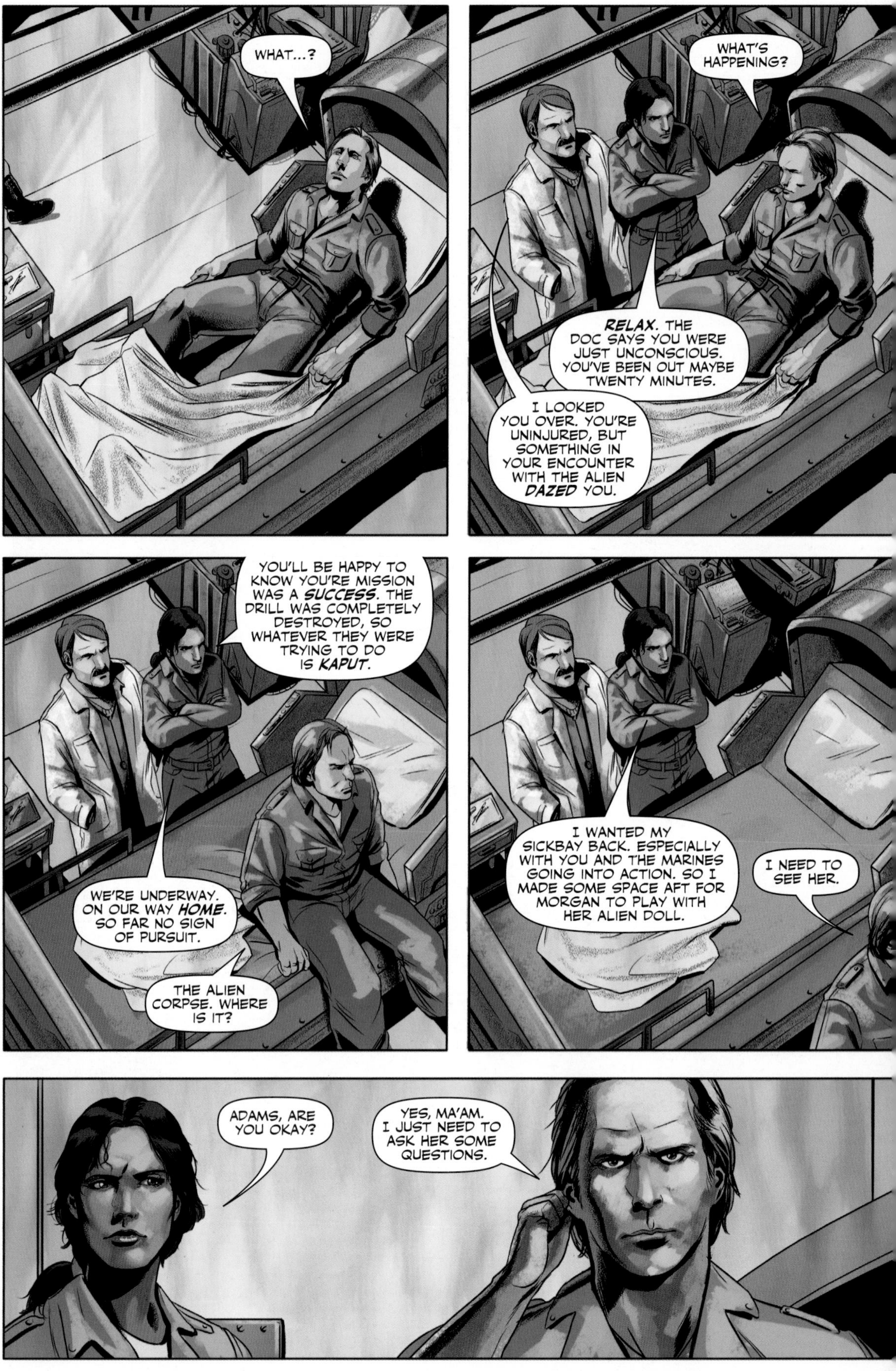
WHAT...?
WHAT'S HAPPENING?
RELAX. THE DOC SAYS YOU WERE JUST UNCONSCIOUS. YOU'VE BEEN OUT MAYBE TWENTY MINUTES.
I LOOKED YOU OVER. YOU'RE UNINJURED, BUT SOMETHING IN YOUR ENCOUNTER WITH THE ALIEN DAZED YOU.
YOU'LL BE HAPPY TO KNOW YOU'RE MISSION WAS A SUCCESS. THE DRILL WAS COMPLETELY DESTROYED, SO WHATEVER THEY WERE TRYING TO DO IS KAPUT.
WE'RE UNDERWAY. ON OUR WAY HOME. SO FAR NO SIGN OF PURSUIT.
THE ALIEN CORPSE. WHERE IS IT?
I WANTED MY SICKBAY BACK. ESPECIALLY WITH YOU AND THE MARINES GOING INTO ACTION. SO I MADE SOME SPACE AFT FOR MORGAN TO PLAY WITH HER ALIEN DOLL.
I NEED TO SEE HER.
ADAMS, ARE YOU OKAY?
YES, MA'AM. I JUST NEED TO ASK HER SOME QUESTIONS.

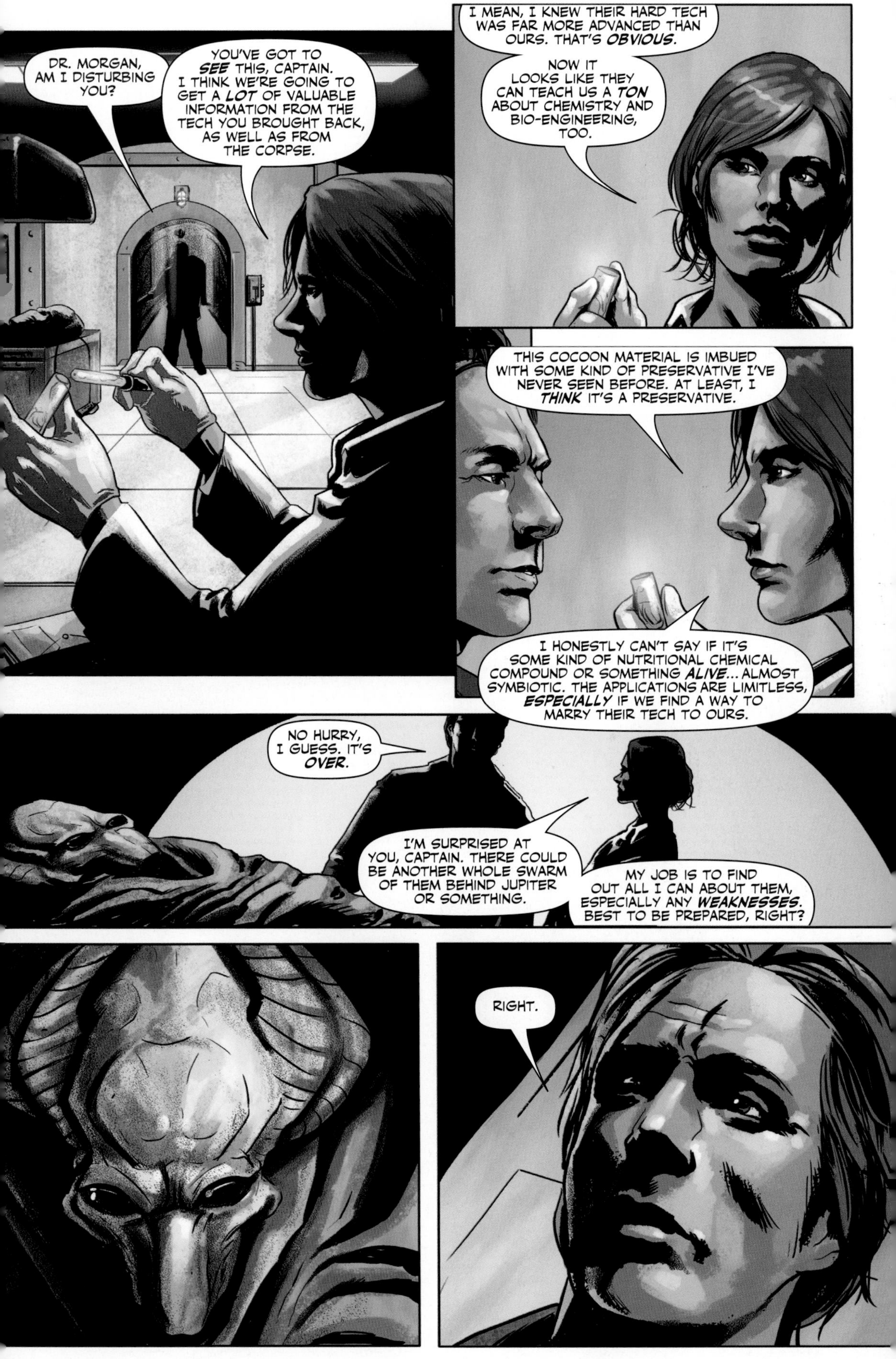
DR. MORGAN, AM I DISTURBING YOU?
YOU'VE GOT TO SEE THIS, CAPTAIN. I THINK WE'RE GOING TO GET A LOT OF VALUABLE INFORMATION FROM THE TECH YOU BROUGHT BACK, AS WELL AS FROM THE CORPSE.
I MEAN, I KNEW THEIR HARD TECH WAS FAR MORE ADVANCED THAN OURS. THAT'S OBVIOUS.
NOW IT LOOKS LIKE THEY CAN TEACH US A TON ABOUT CHEMISTRY AND BIO-ENGINEERING, TOO.
THIS COCOON MATERIAL IS IMBUED WITH SOME KIND OF PRESERVATIVE I'VE NEVER SEEN BEFORE. AT LEAST, I THINK IT'S A PRESERVATIVE.
I HONESTLY CAN'T SAY IF IT'S SOME KIND OF NUTRITIONAL CHEMICAL COMPOUND OR SOMETHING ALIVE... ALMOST SYMBIOTIC. THE APPLICATIONS ARE LIMITLESS, ESPECIALLY IF WE FIND A WAY TO MARRY THEIR TECH TO OURS.
NO HURRY, I GUESS. IT'S OVER.
I'M SURPRISED AT YOU, CAPTAIN. THERE COULD BE ANOTHER WHOLE SWARM OF THEM BEHIND JUPITER OR SOMETHING.
MY JOB IS TO FIND OUT ALL I CAN ABOUT THEM, ESPECIALLY ANY WEAKNESSES. BEST TO BE PREPARED, RIGHT?
RIGHT.

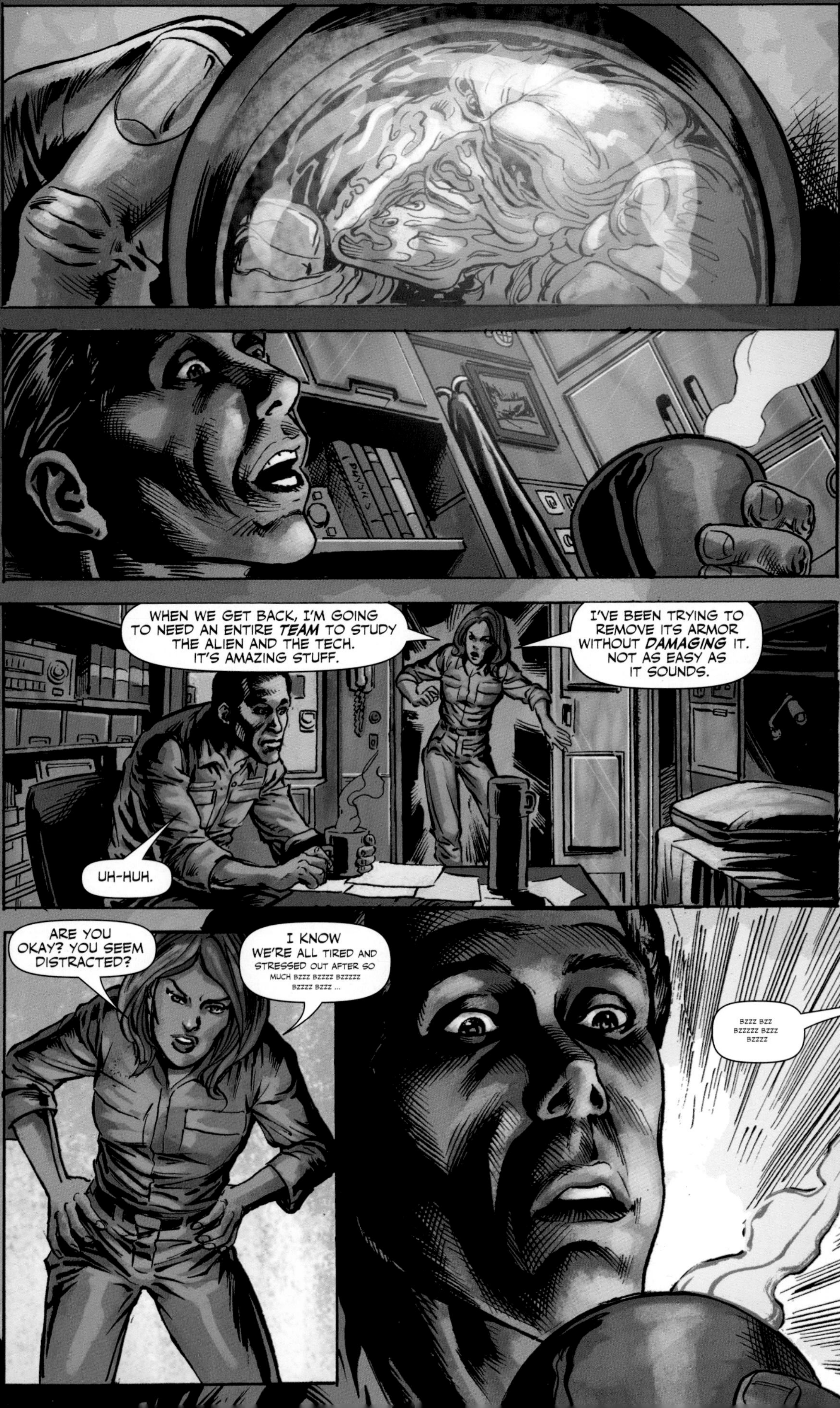
WHEN WE GET BACK, I'M GOING TO NEED AN ENTIRE *TEAM* TO STUDY THE ALIEN AND THE TECH. IT'S AMAZING STUFF.
I'VE BEEN TRYING TO REMOVE ITS ARMOR WITHOUT *DAMAGING* IT. NOT AS EASY AS IT SOUNDS.
UH-HUH.
ARE YOU OKAY? YOU SEEM DISTRACTED?
I KNOW WE'RE ALL TIRED AND STRESSED OUT AFTER SO MUCH BZZZ BZZZZ BZZZZZ BZZZZ BZZZ ...
BZZZ BZZ BZZZZZ BZZZ BZZZZ

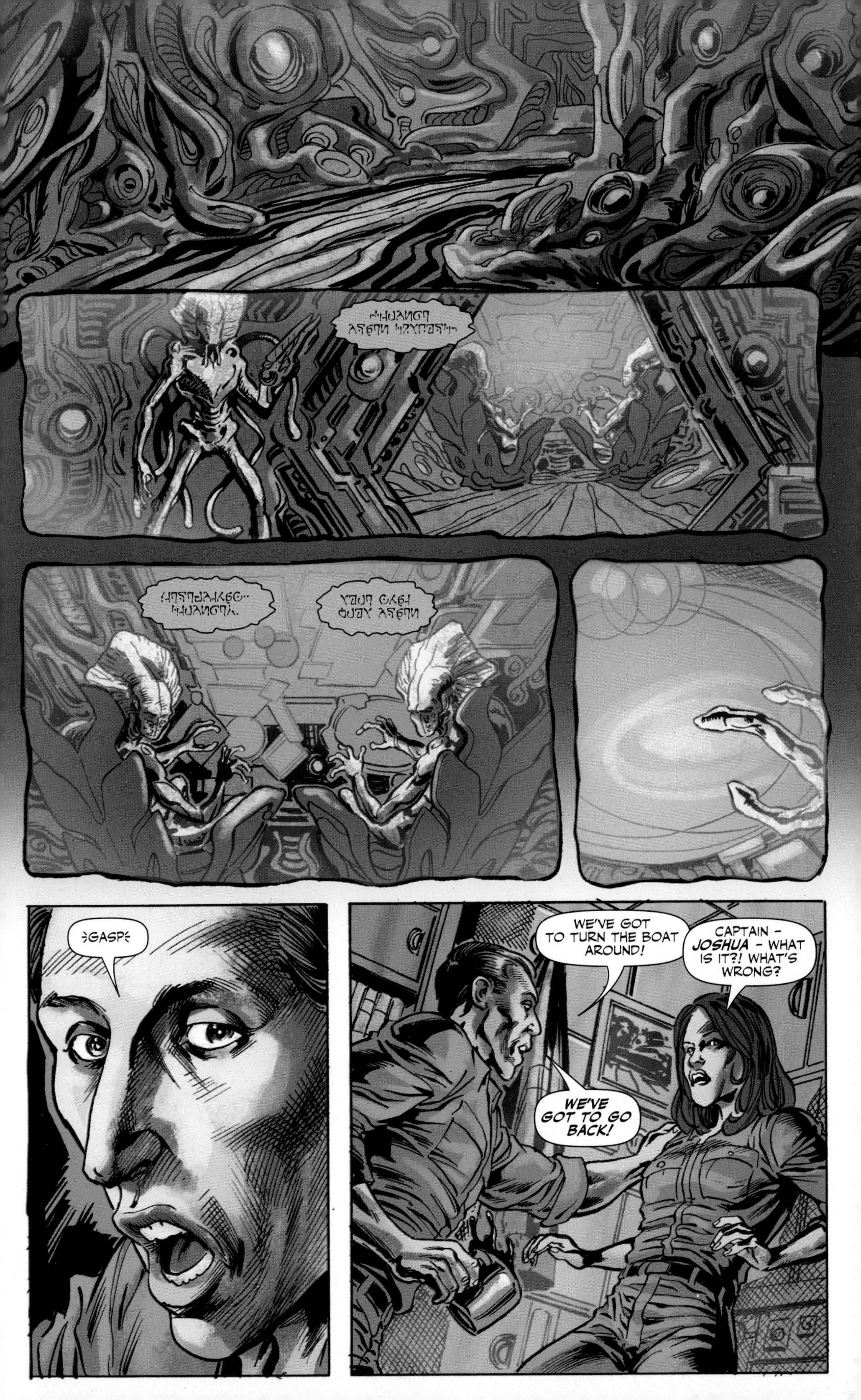
GASP
WE'VE GOT TO TURN THE BOAT AROUND!
CAPTAIN - JOSHUA - WHAT IS IT?! WHAT'S WRONG?
WE'VE GOT TO GO BACK!

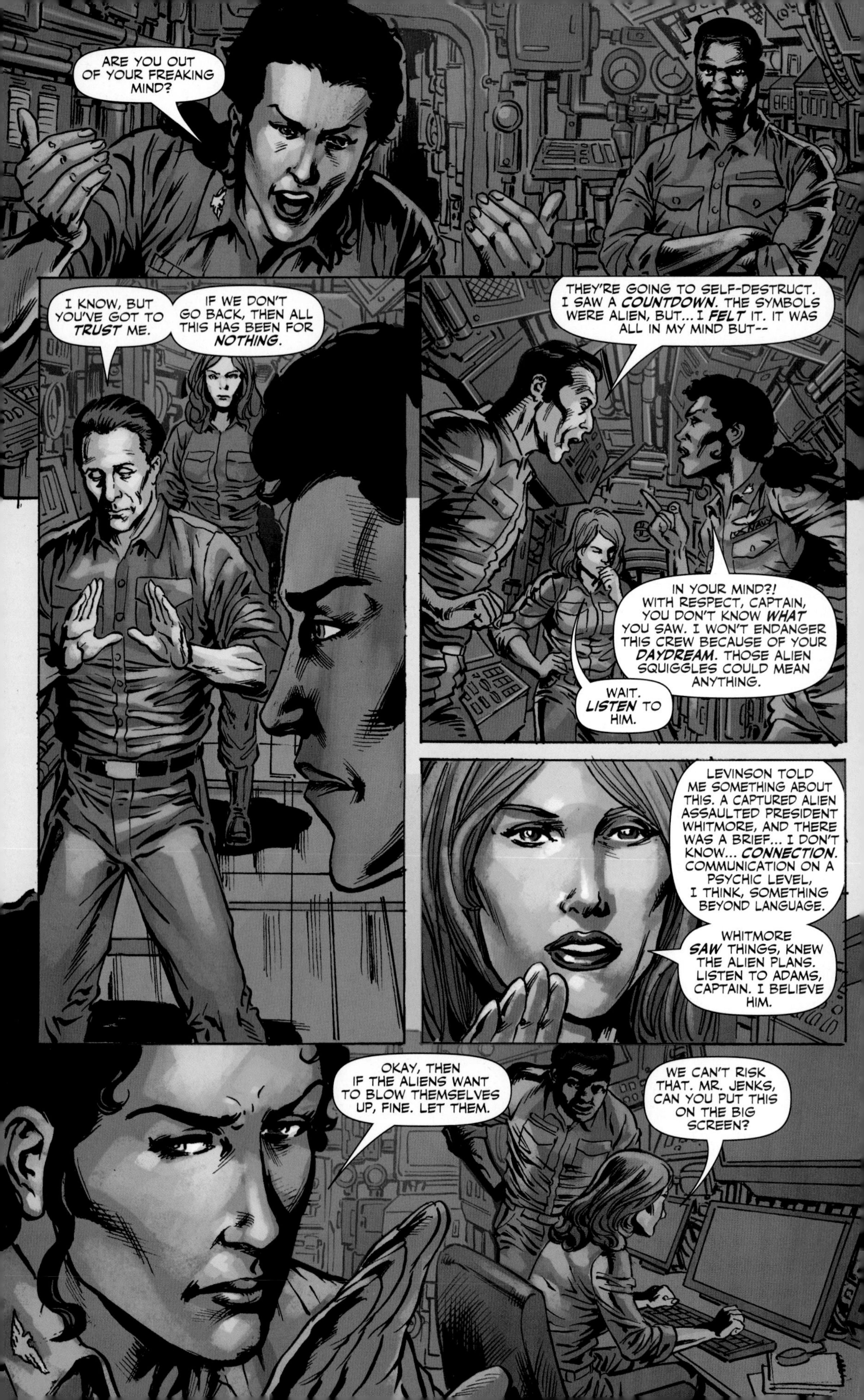
ARE YOU OUT OF YOUR FREAKING MIND?
I KNOW, BUT YOU'VE GOT TO TRUST ME.
IF WE DON'T GO BACK, THEN ALL THIS HAS BEEN FOR NOTHING.
THEY'RE GOING TO SELF-DESTRUCT. I SAW A COUNTDOWN. THE SYMBOLS WERE ALIEN, BUT... I FELT IT. IT WAS ALL IN MY MIND BUT--
IN YOUR MIND?! WITH RESPECT, CAPTAIN, YOU DON'T KNOW WHAT YOU SAW. I WON'T ENDANGER THIS CREW BECAUSE OF YOUR DAYDREAM. THOSE ALIEN SQUIGGLES COULD MEAN ANYTHING.
WAIT. LISTEN TO HIM.
LEVINSON TOLD ME SOMETHING ABOUT THIS. A CAPTURED ALIEN ASSAULTED PRESIDENT WHITMORE, AND THERE WAS A BRIEF... I DON'T KNOW... CONNECTION. COMMUNICATION ON A PSYCHIC LEVEL, I THINK, SOMETHING BEYOND LANGUAGE.
WHITMORE SAW THINGS, KNEW THE ALIEN PLANS. LISTEN TO ADAMS, CAPTAIN. I BELIEVE HIM.
OKAY, THEN IF THE ALIENS WANT TO BLOW THEMSELVES UP, FINE. LET THEM.
WE CAN'T RISK THAT. MR. JENKS, CAN YOU PUT THIS ON THE BIG SCREEN?

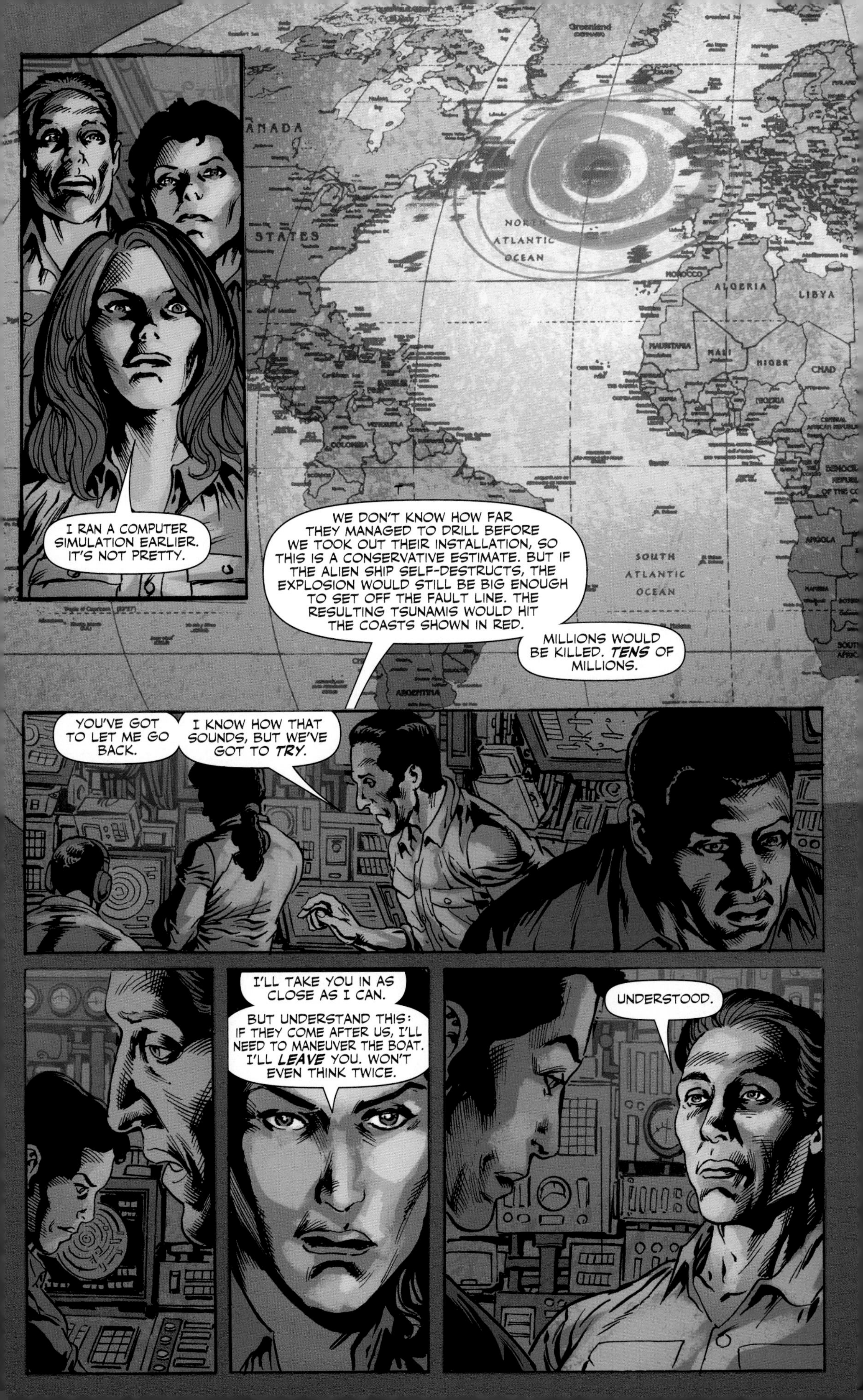
I RAN A COMPUTER SIMULATION EARLIER. IT'S NOT PRETTY.
WE DON'T KNOW HOW FAR THEY MANAGED TO DRILL BEFORE WE TOOK OUT THEIR INSTALLATION, SO THIS IS A CONSERVATIVE ESTIMATE. BUT IF THE ALIEN SHIP SELF-DESTRUCTS, THE EXPLOSION WOULD STILL BE BIG ENOUGH TO SET OFF THE FAULT LINE. THE RESULTING TSUNAMIS WOULD HIT THE COASTS SHOWN IN RED.
MILLIONS WOULD BE KILLED. TENS OF MILLIONS.
CANADA
STATES
NORTH ATLANTIC OCEAN
SOUTH ATLANTIC OCEAN
ALGERIA
LIBYA
CHAD
ANGOLA
YOU'VE GOT TO LET ME GO BACK.
I KNOW HOW THAT SOUNDS, BUT WE'VE GOT TO TRY.
I'LL TAKE YOU IN AS CLOSE AS I CAN.
BUT UNDERSTAND THIS: IF THEY COME AFTER US, I'LL NEED TO MANEUVER THE BOAT. I'LL LEAVE YOU. WON'T EVEN THINK TWICE.
UNDERSTOOD.

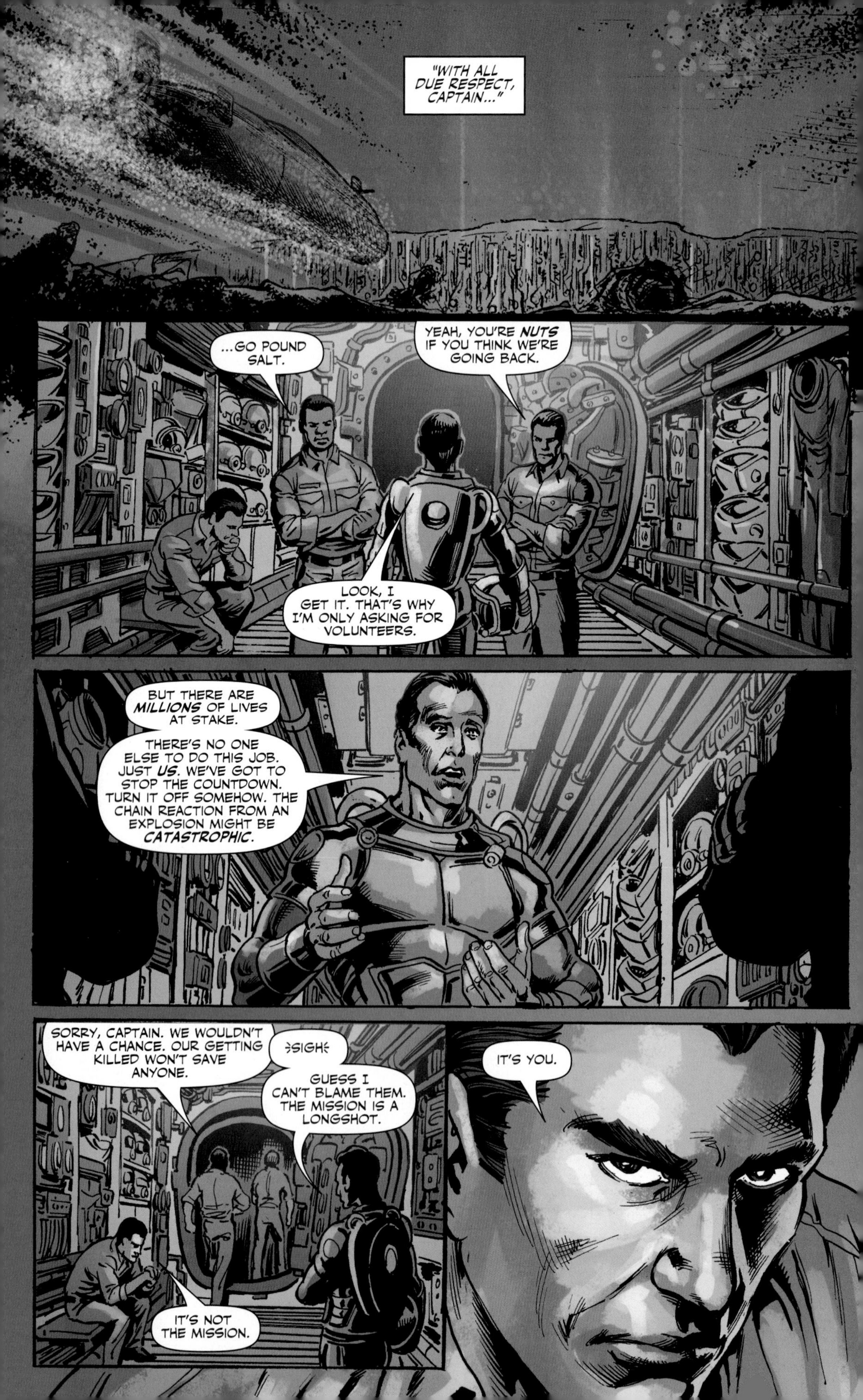
"WITH ALL DUE RESPECT, CAPTAIN..."
...GO POUND SALT.
YEAH, YOU'RE NUTS IF YOU THINK WE'RE GOING BACK.
LOOK, I GET IT. THAT'S WHY I'M ONLY ASKING FOR VOLUNTEERS.
BUT THERE ARE MILLIONS OF LIVES AT STAKE.
THERE'S NO ONE ELSE TO DO THIS JOB. JUST US. WE'VE GOT TO STOP THE COUNTDOWN. TURN IT OFF SOMEHOW. THE CHAIN REACTION FROM AN EXPLOSION MIGHT BE CATASTROPHIC.
SORRY, CAPTAIN. WE WOULDN'T HAVE A CHANCE. OUR GETTING KILLED WON'T SAVE ANYONE.
SIGH
GUESS I CAN'T BLAME THEM. THE MISSION IS A LONGSHOT.
IT'S NOT THE MISSION.
IT'S YOU.

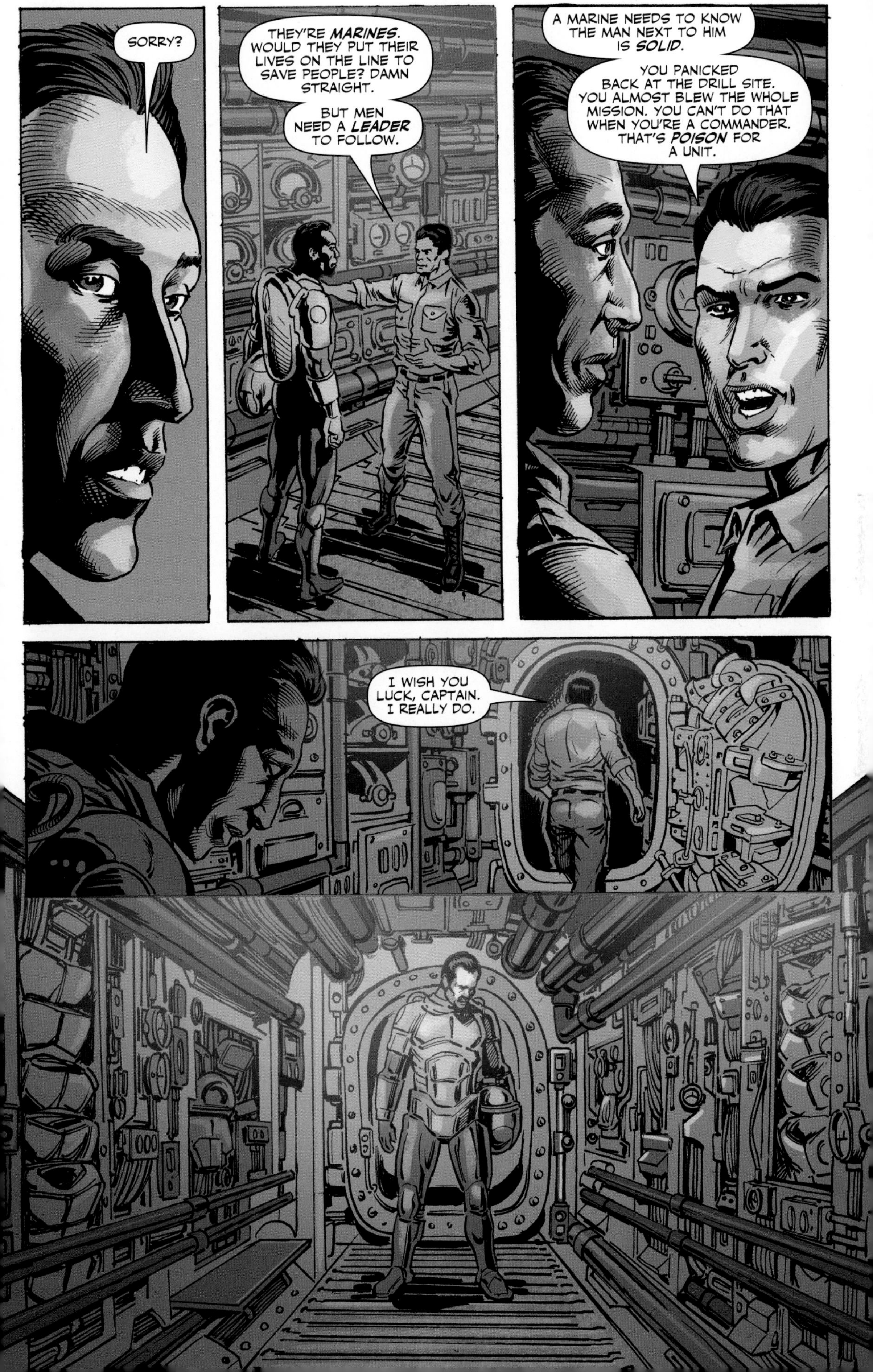
SORRY?
THEY'RE MARINES. WOULD THEY PUT THEIR LIVES ON THE LINE TO SAVE PEOPLE? DAMN STRAIGHT.
BUT MEN NEED A LEADER TO FOLLOW.
A MARINE NEEDS TO KNOW THE MAN NEXT TO HIM IS SOLID.
YOU PANICKED BACK AT THE DRILL SITE. YOU ALMOST BLEW THE WHOLE MISSION. YOU CAN'T DO THAT WHEN YOU'RE A COMMANDER. THAT'S POISON FOR A UNIT.
I WISH YOU LUCK, CAPTAIN. I REALLY DO.

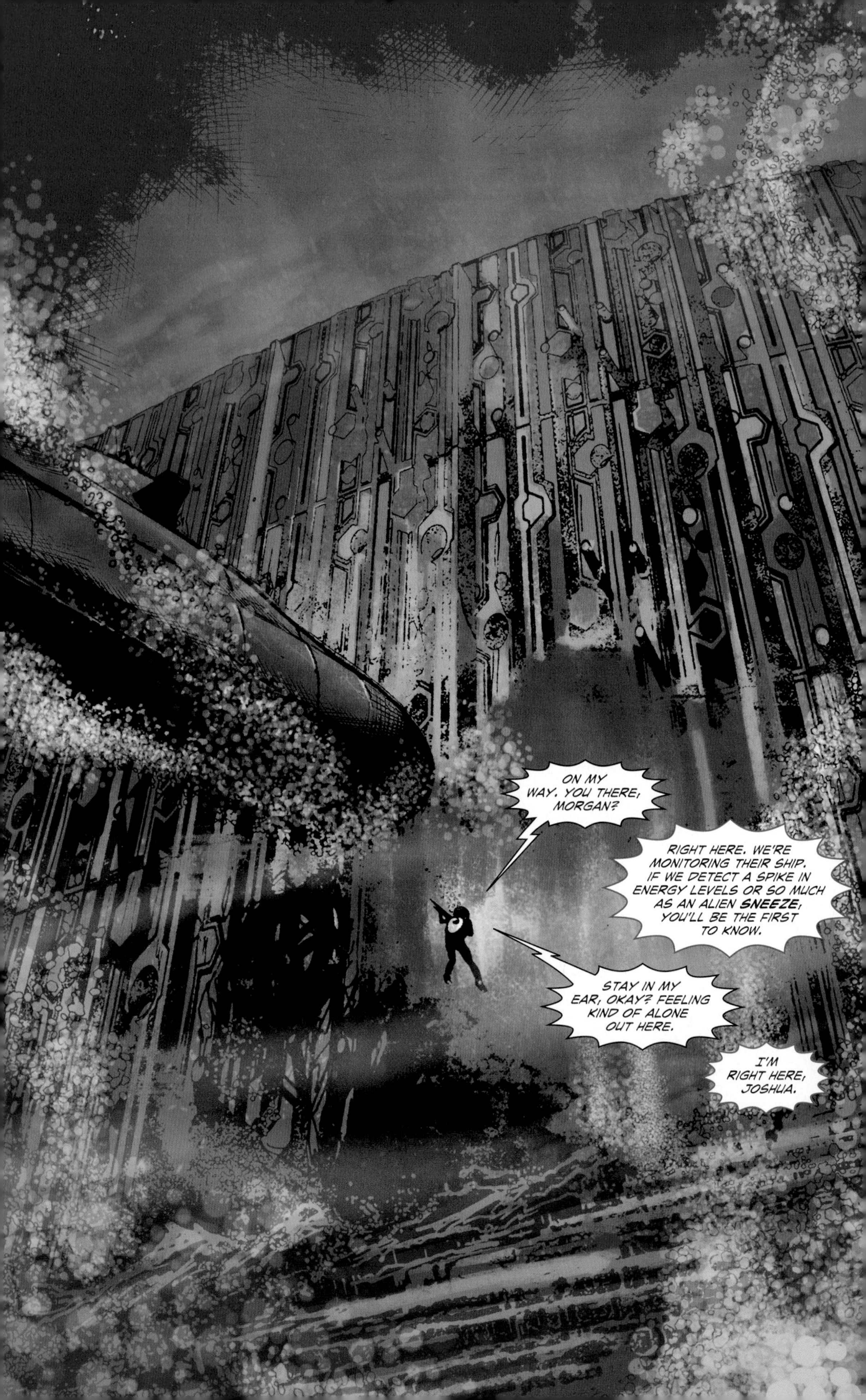
ON MY WAY. YOU THERE, MORGAN?
RIGHT HERE. WE'RE MONITORING THEIR SHIP. IF WE DETECT A SPIKE IN ENERGY LEVELS OR SO MUCH AS AN ALIEN SNEEZE, YOU'LL BE THE FIRST TO KNOW.
STAY IN MY EAR, OKAY? FEELING KIND OF ALONE OUT HERE.
I'M RIGHT HERE, JOSHUA.

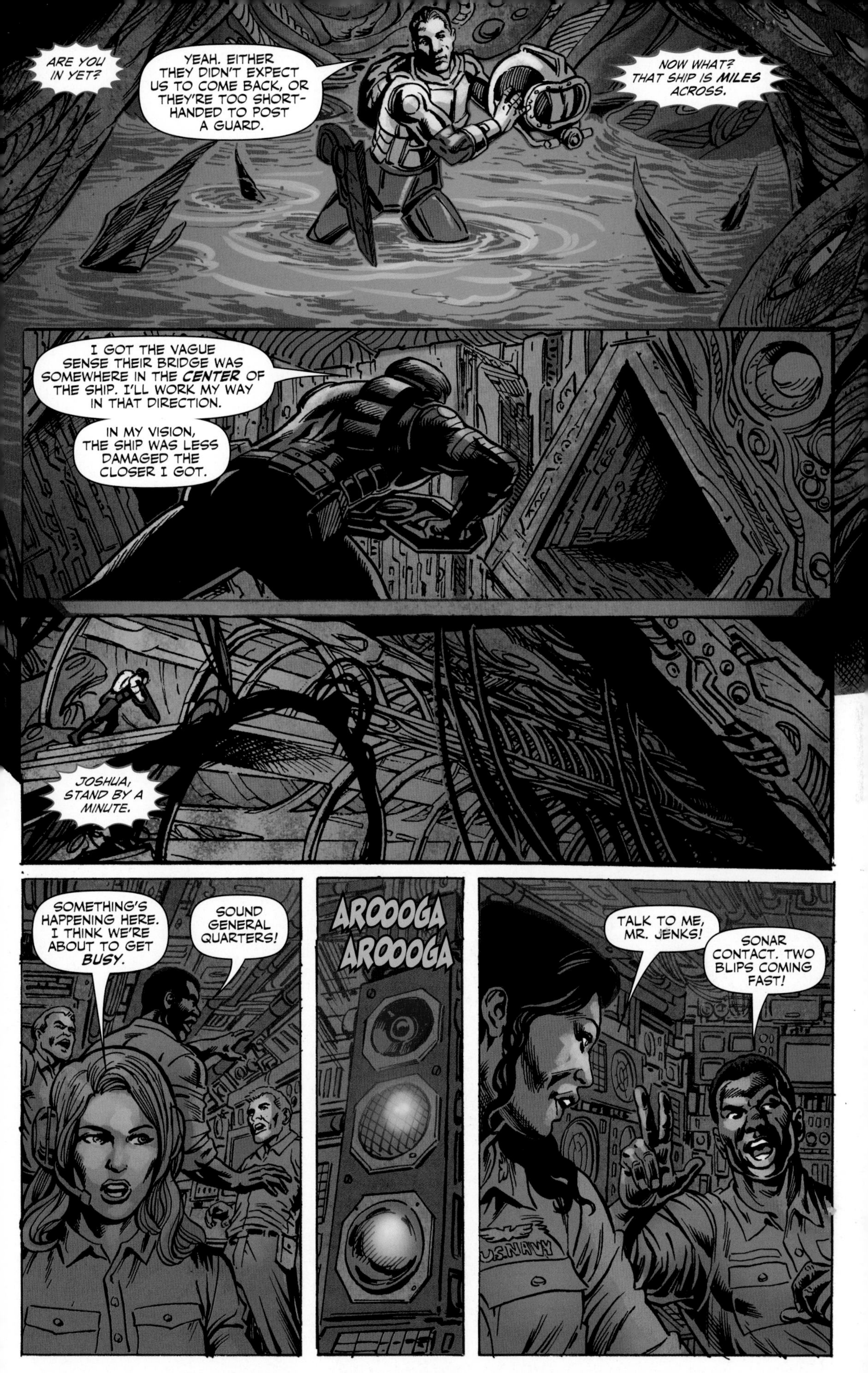

ARE YOU IN YET?
YEAH. EITHER THEY DIDN'T EXPECT US TO COME BACK, OR THEY'RE TOO SHORT-HANDED TO POST A GUARD.
NOW WHAT? THAT SHIP IS MILES ACROSS.
I GOT THE VAGUE SENSE THEIR BRIDGE WAS SOMEWHERE IN THE CENTER OF THE SHIP. I'LL WORK MY WAY IN THAT DIRECTION.
IN MY VISION, THE SHIP WAS LESS DAMAGED THE CLOSER I GOT.
JOSHUA, STAND BY A MINUTE.
SOMETHING'S HAPPENING HERE. I THINK WE'RE ABOUT TO GET BUSY.
SOUND GENERAL QUARTERS!
AROOOGA AROOOGA
TALK TO ME, MR. JENKS!
SONAR CONTACT. TWO BLIPS COMING FAST!

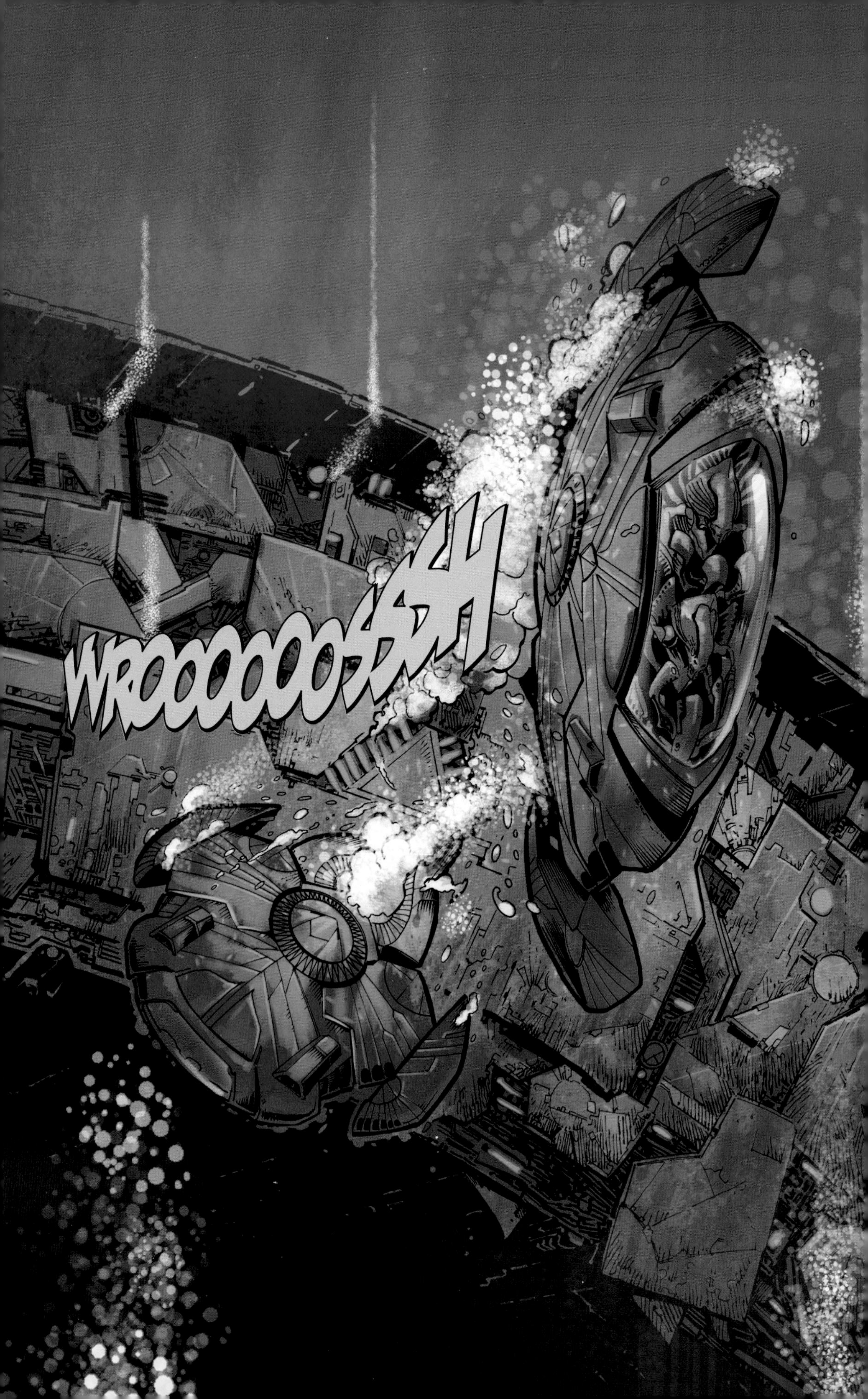
WROOOOOOSH

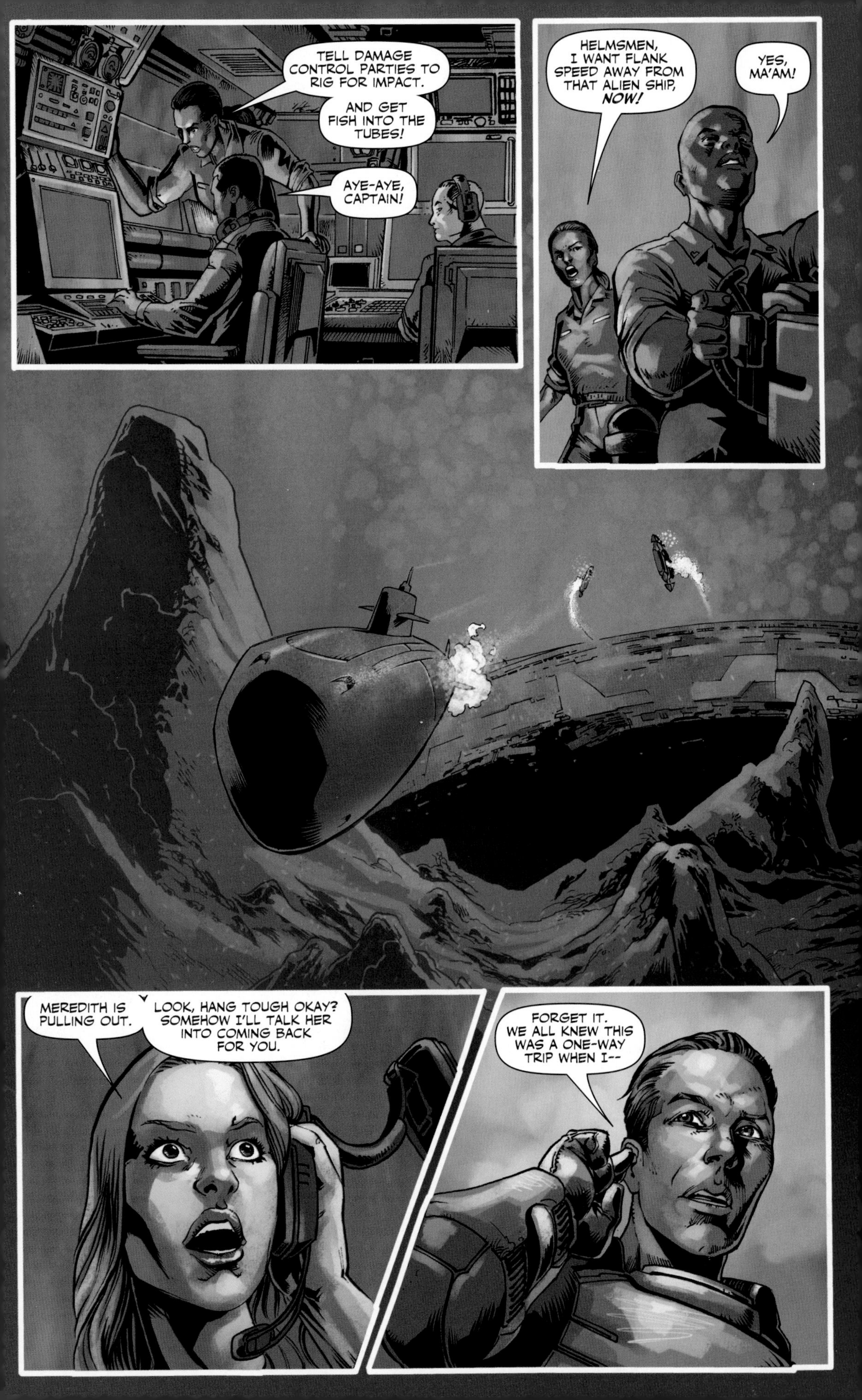
TELL DAMAGE CONTROL PARTIES TO RIG FOR IMPACT.
AND GET FISH INTO THE TUBES!
AYE-AYE, CAPTAIN!
HELMSMEN, I WANT FLANK SPEED AWAY FROM THAT ALIEN SHIP, NOW!
YES, MA'AM!
MEREDITH IS PULLING OUT.
LOOK, HANG TOUGH OKAY? SOMEHOW I'LL TALK HER INTO COMING BACK FOR YOU.
FORGET IT. WE ALL KNEW THIS WAS A ONE-WAY TRIP WHEN I--

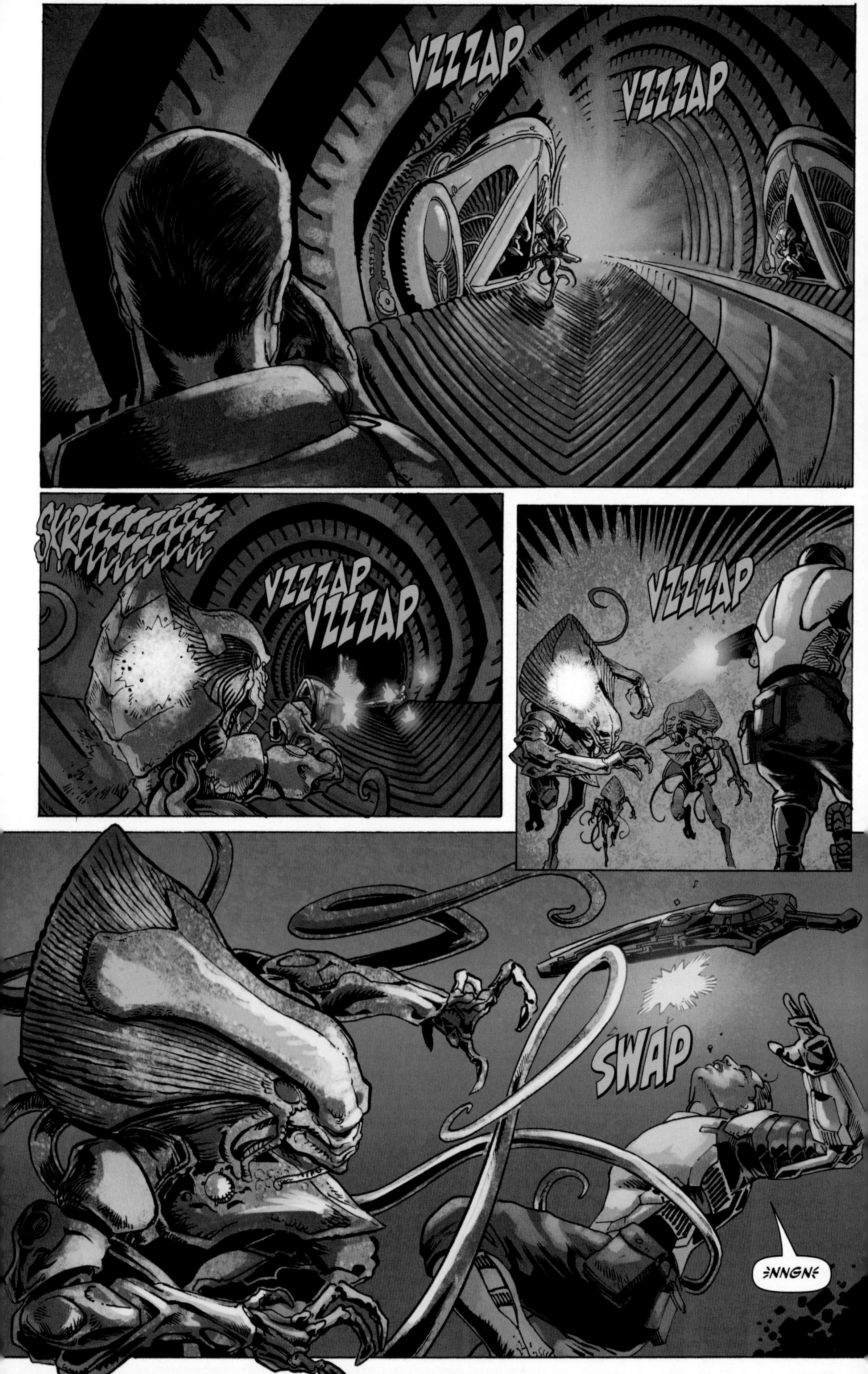
VZZZAP
VZZZAP
SKREEEEEEEEE
VZZZAP
VZZZAP
VZZZAP
SWAP
NNGN

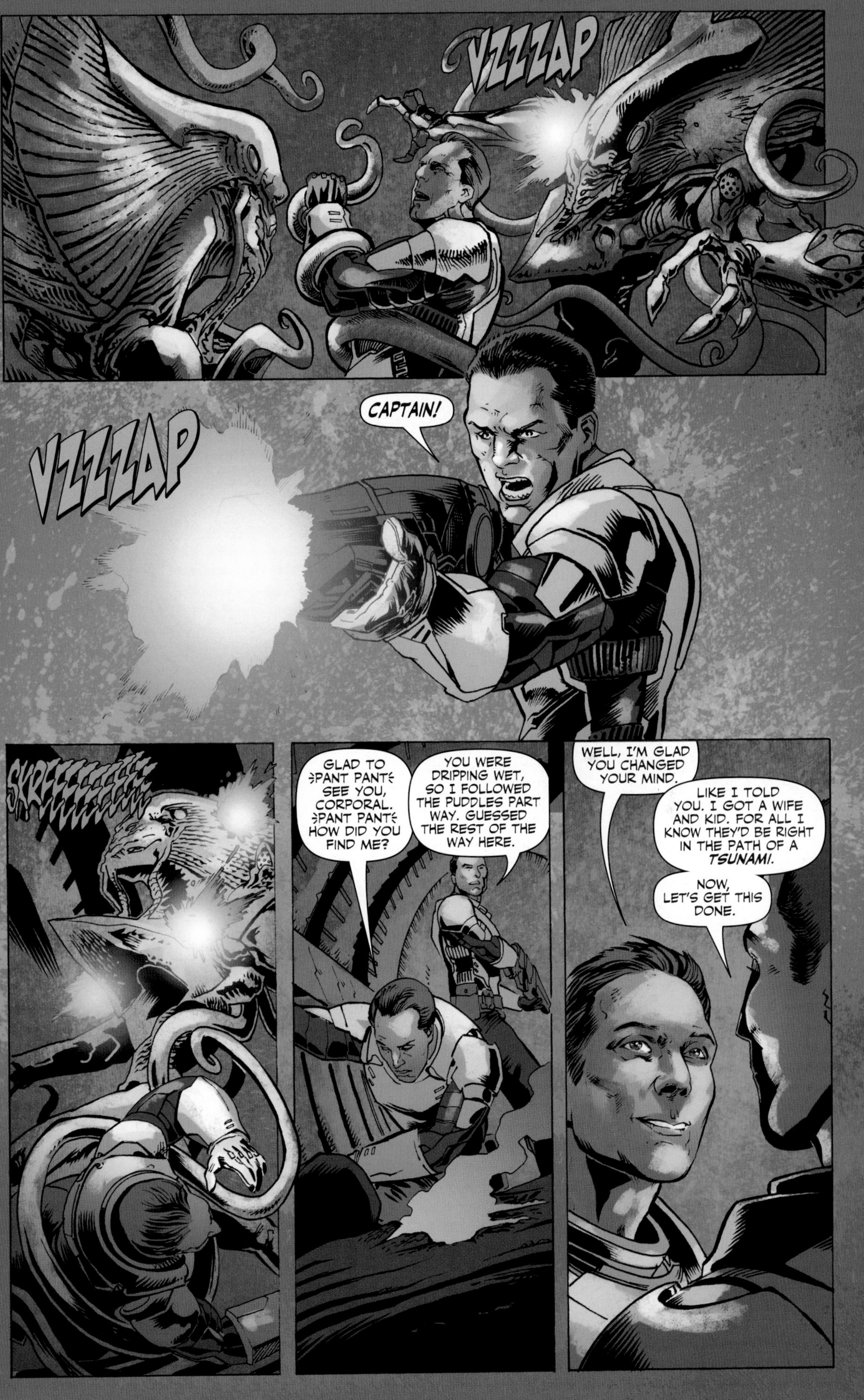
VZZZAP
CAPTAIN!
VZZZAP
SKREEEEEEEEEEE
GLAD TO ≥PANT PANT≤ SEE YOU, CORPORAL. ≥PANT PANT≤ HOW DID YOU FIND ME?
YOU WERE DRIPPING WET, SO I FOLLOWED THE PUDDLES PART WAY. GUESSED THE REST OF THE WAY HERE.
WELL, I'M GLAD YOU CHANGED YOUR MIND.
LIKE I TOLD YOU. I GOT A WIFE AND KID. FOR ALL I KNOW THEY'D BE RIGHT IN THE PATH OF A *TSUNAMI*.
NOW, LET'S GET THIS DONE.

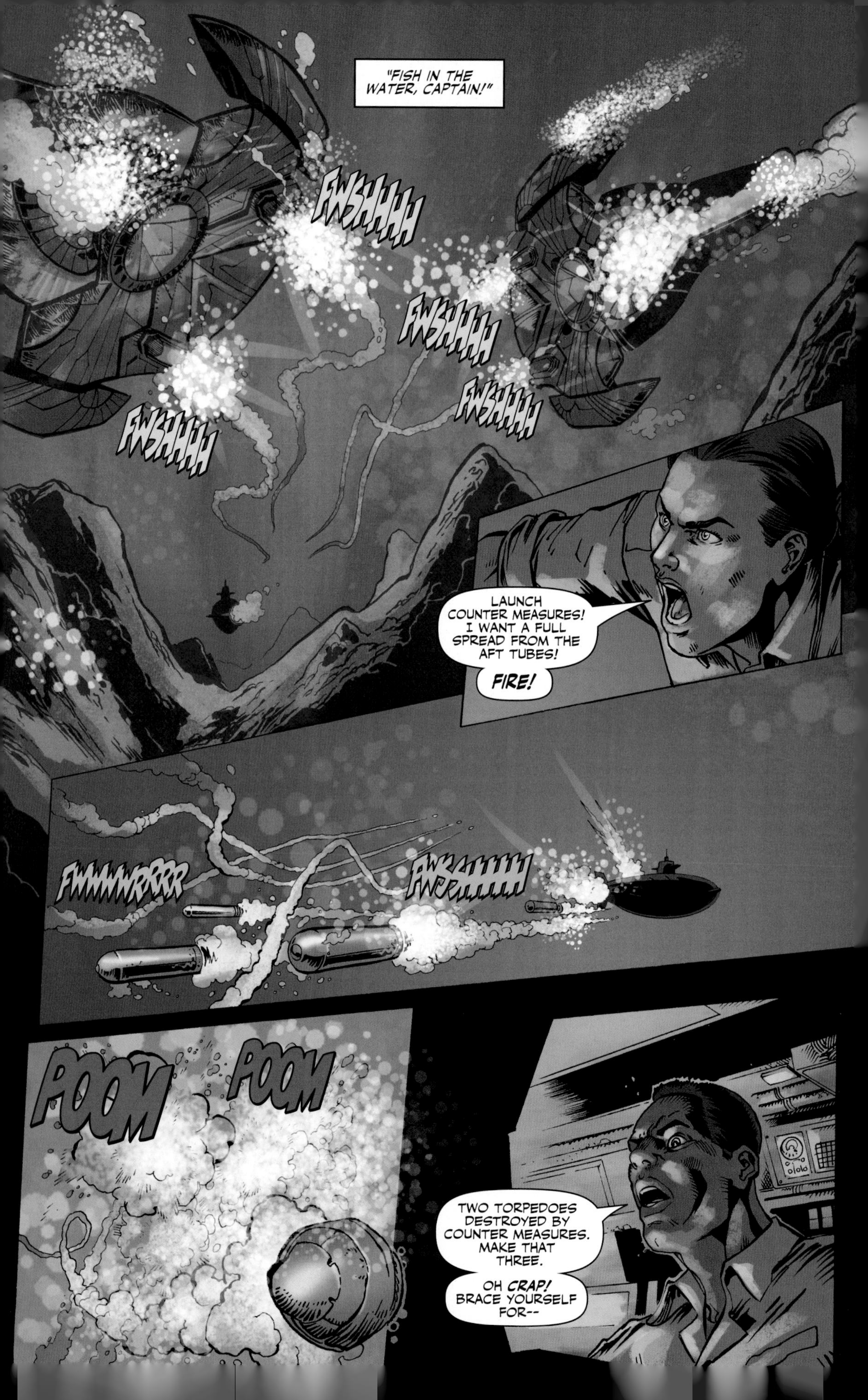
"FISH IN THE WATER, CAPTAIN!"
FWSHHHH
FWSHHHH
FWSHHHH
FWSHHHH
LAUNCH COUNTER MEASURES! I WANT A FULL SPREAD FROM THE AFT TUBES!
FIRE!
FWWWWRRRR
FWSHHHHH
POOM
POOM
TWO TORPEDOES DESTROYED BY COUNTER MEASURES. MAKE THAT THREE.
OH CRAP! BRACE YOURSELF FOR--

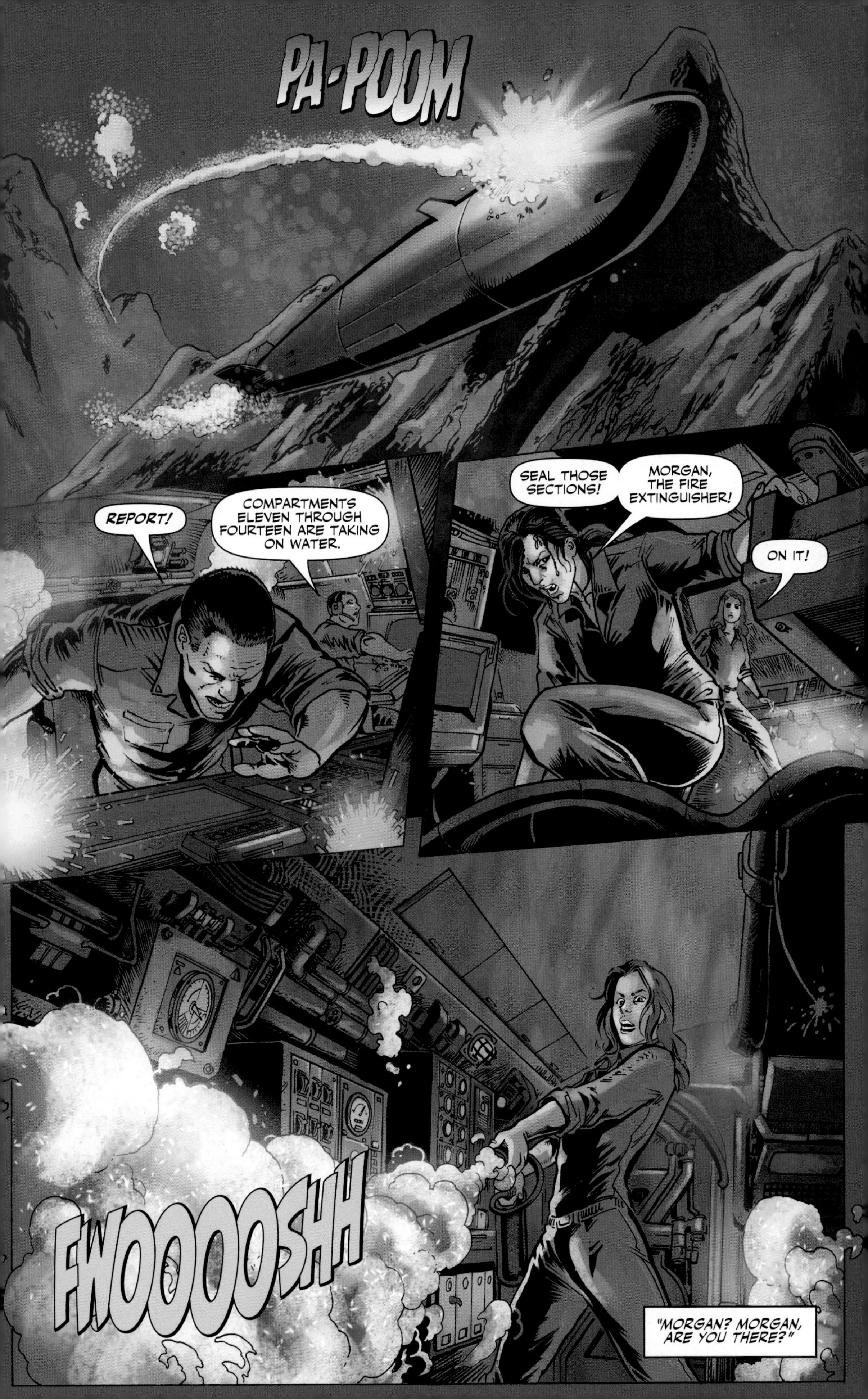
PA-POOM
REPORT!
COMPARTMENTS ELEVEN THROUGH FOURTEEN ARE TAKING ON WATER.
SEAL THOSE SECTIONS!
MORGAN, THE FIRE EXTINGUISHER!
ON IT!
FWOOOOSHH
"MORGAN? MORGAN, ARE YOU THERE?"

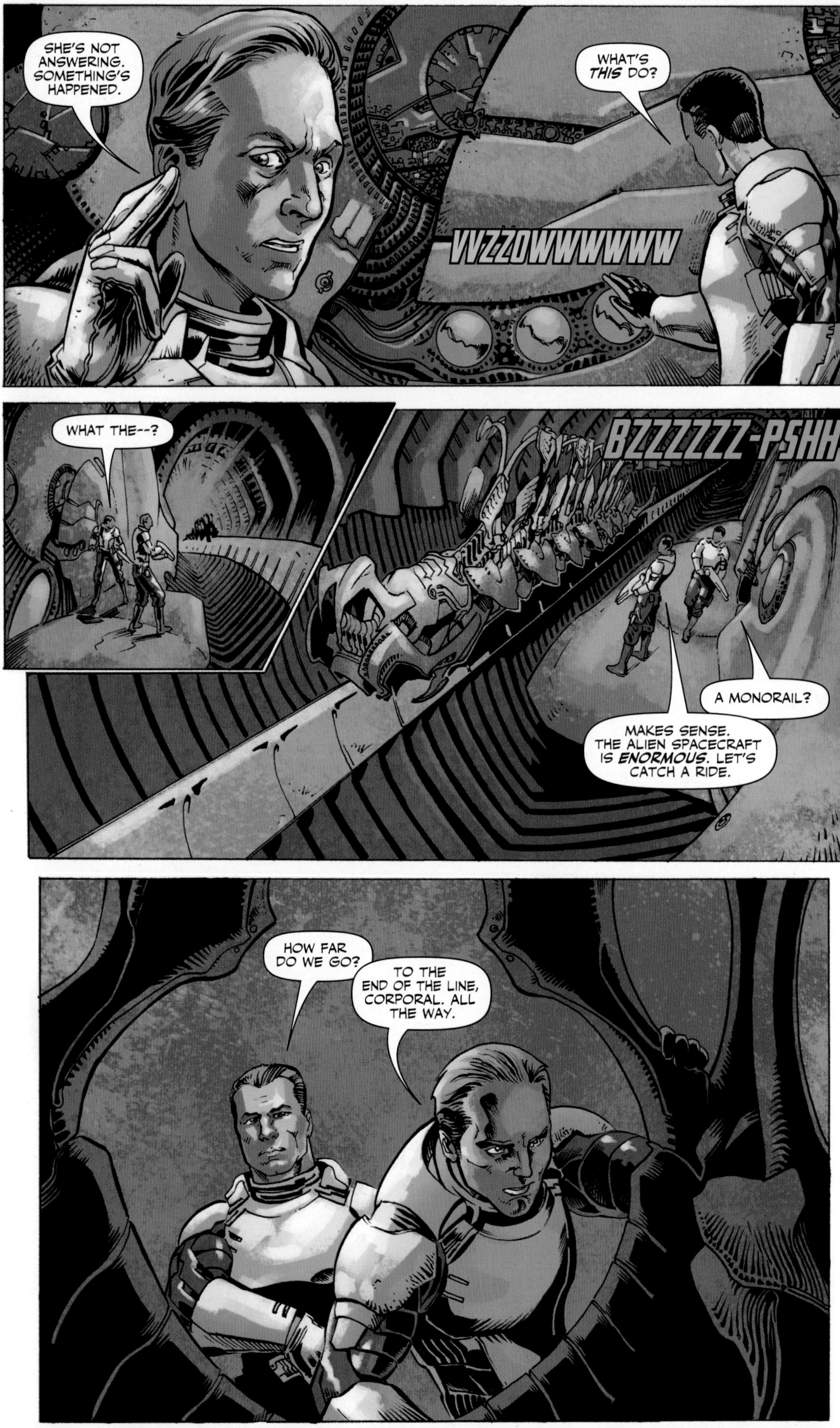
SHE'S NOT ANSWERING. SOMETHING'S HAPPENED.
WHAT'S *THIS* DO?
VVZZOWWWWWW
WHAT THE--?
BZZZZZZ-PSHH
A MONORAIL?
MAKES SENSE. THE ALIEN SPACECRAFT IS *ENORMOUS*. LET'S CATCH A RIDE.
HOW FAR DO WE GO?
TO THE END OF THE LINE, CORPORAL. ALL THE WAY.

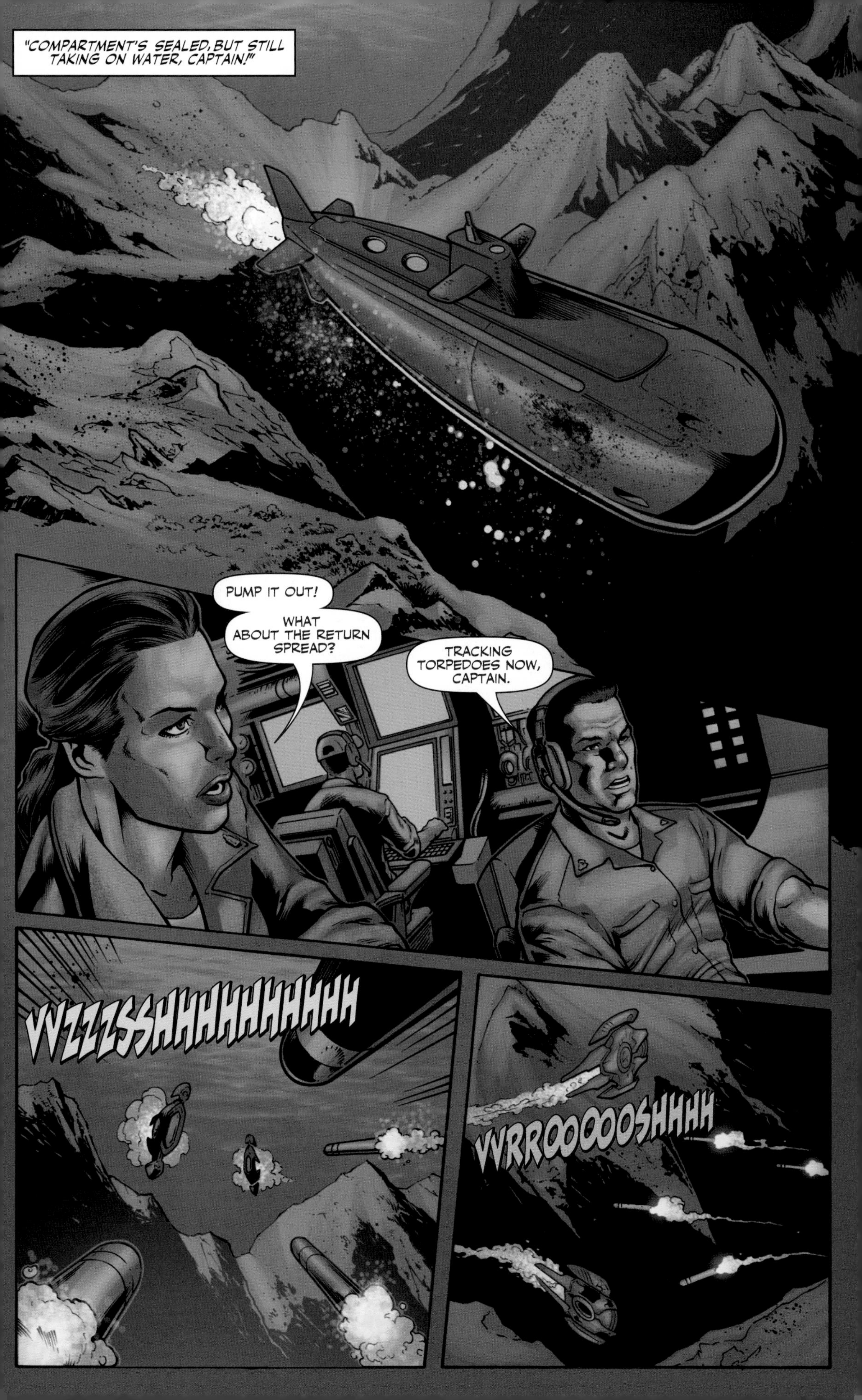
"COMPARTMENT'S SEALED, BUT STILL TAKING ON WATER, CAPTAIN!"
PUMP IT OUT!
WHAT ABOUT THE RETURN SPREAD?
TRACKING TORPEDOES NOW, CAPTAIN.
VVZZZZSSHHHHHHHHHHH
VVRROOOOOSHHHH

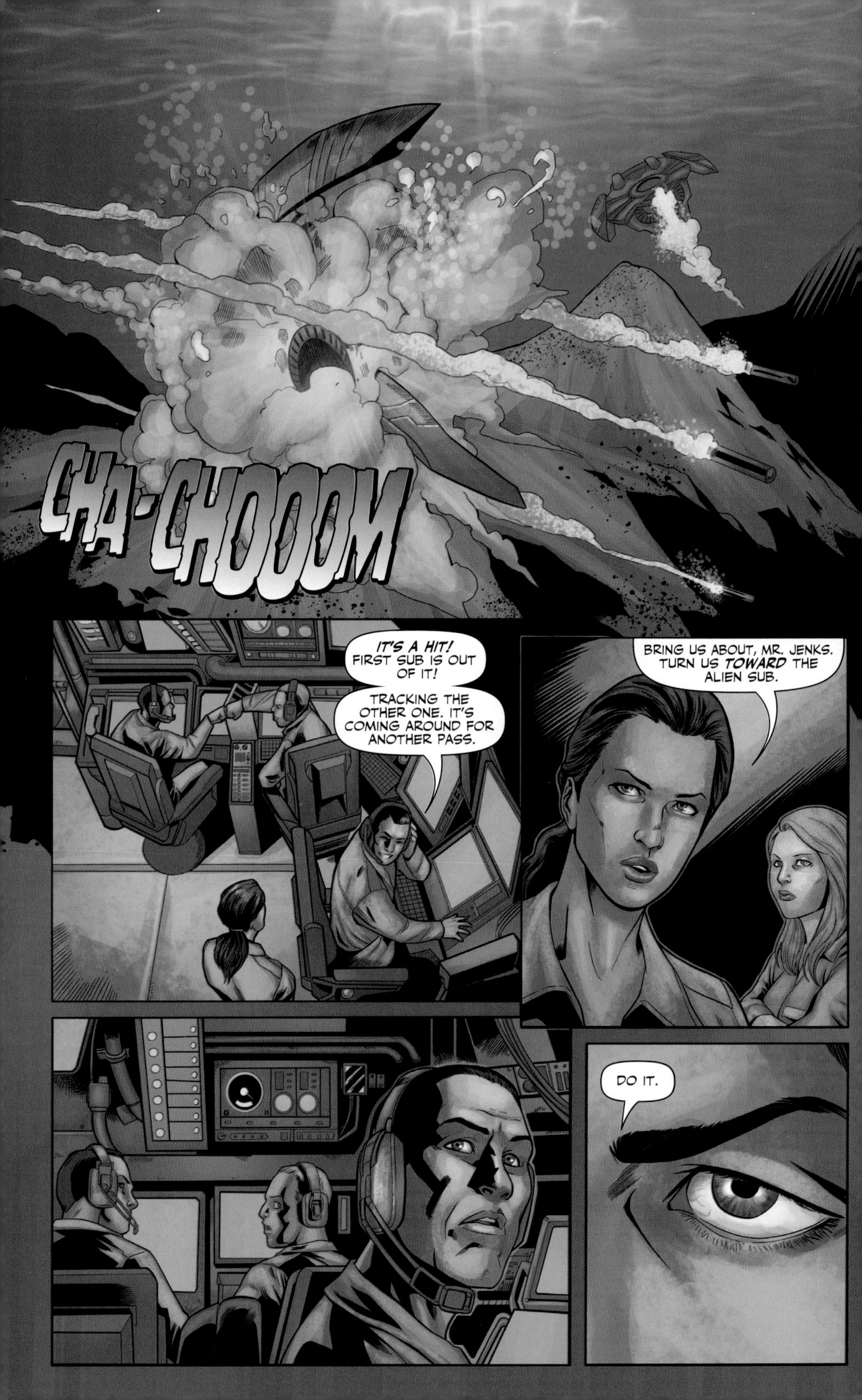
CHA-CHOOOM
IT'S A HIT! FIRST SUB IS OUT OF IT!
TRACKING THE OTHER ONE. IT'S COMING AROUND FOR ANOTHER PASS.
BRING US ABOUT, MR. JENKS. TURN US TOWARD THE ALIEN SUB.
DO IT.

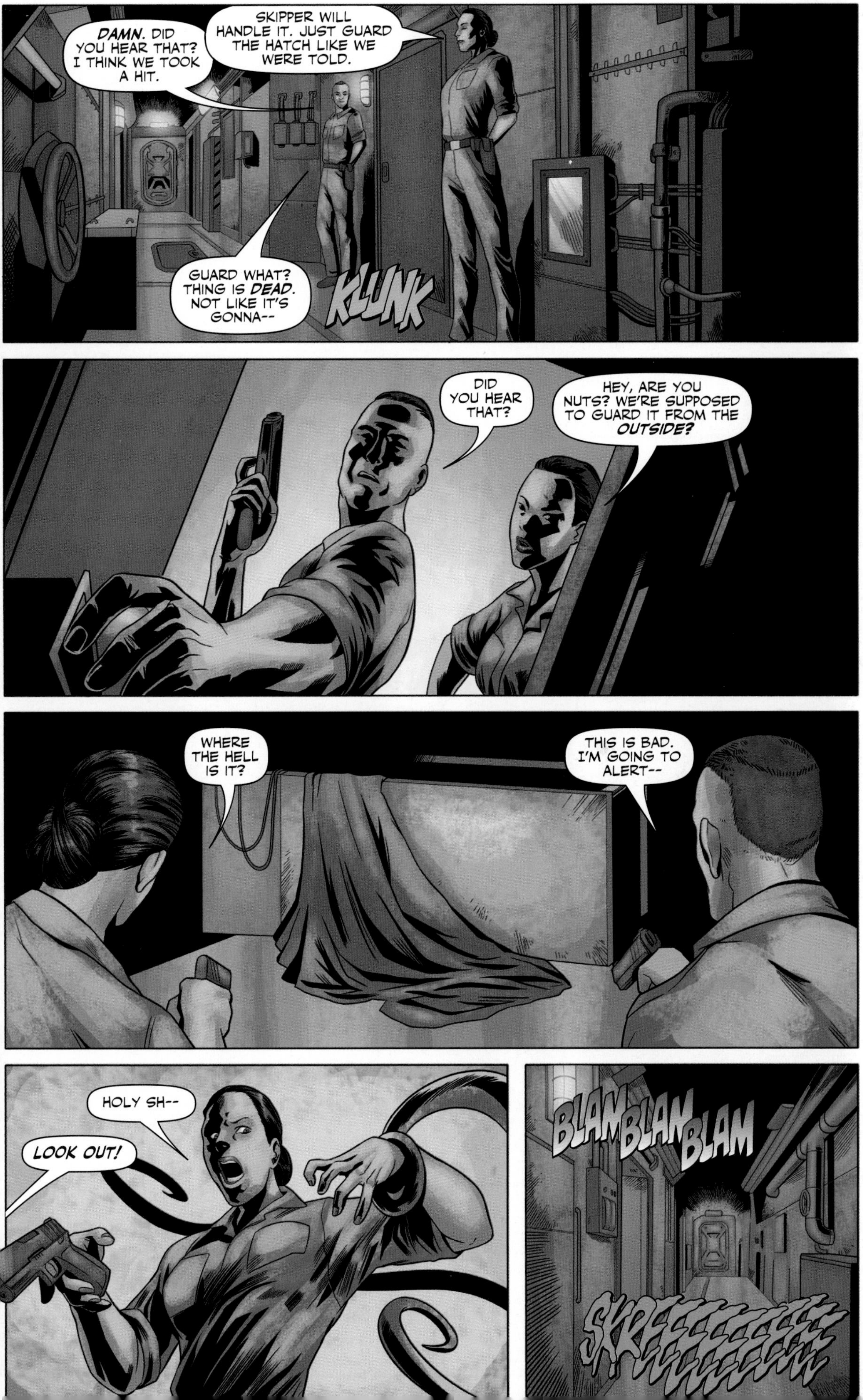

DAMN. DID YOU HEAR THAT? I THINK WE TOOK A HIT.
SKIPPER WILL HANDLE IT. JUST GUARD THE HATCH LIKE WE WERE TOLD.
GUARD WHAT? THING IS DEAD. NOT LIKE IT'S GONNA--
KLUNK
DID YOU HEAR THAT?
HEY, ARE YOU NUTS? WE'RE SUPPOSED TO GUARD IT FROM THE OUTSIDE?
WHERE THE HELL IS IT?
THIS IS BAD. I'M GOING TO ALERT--
HOLY SH--
LOOK OUT!
BLAM BLAM BLAM
SKREEEEEEEEE

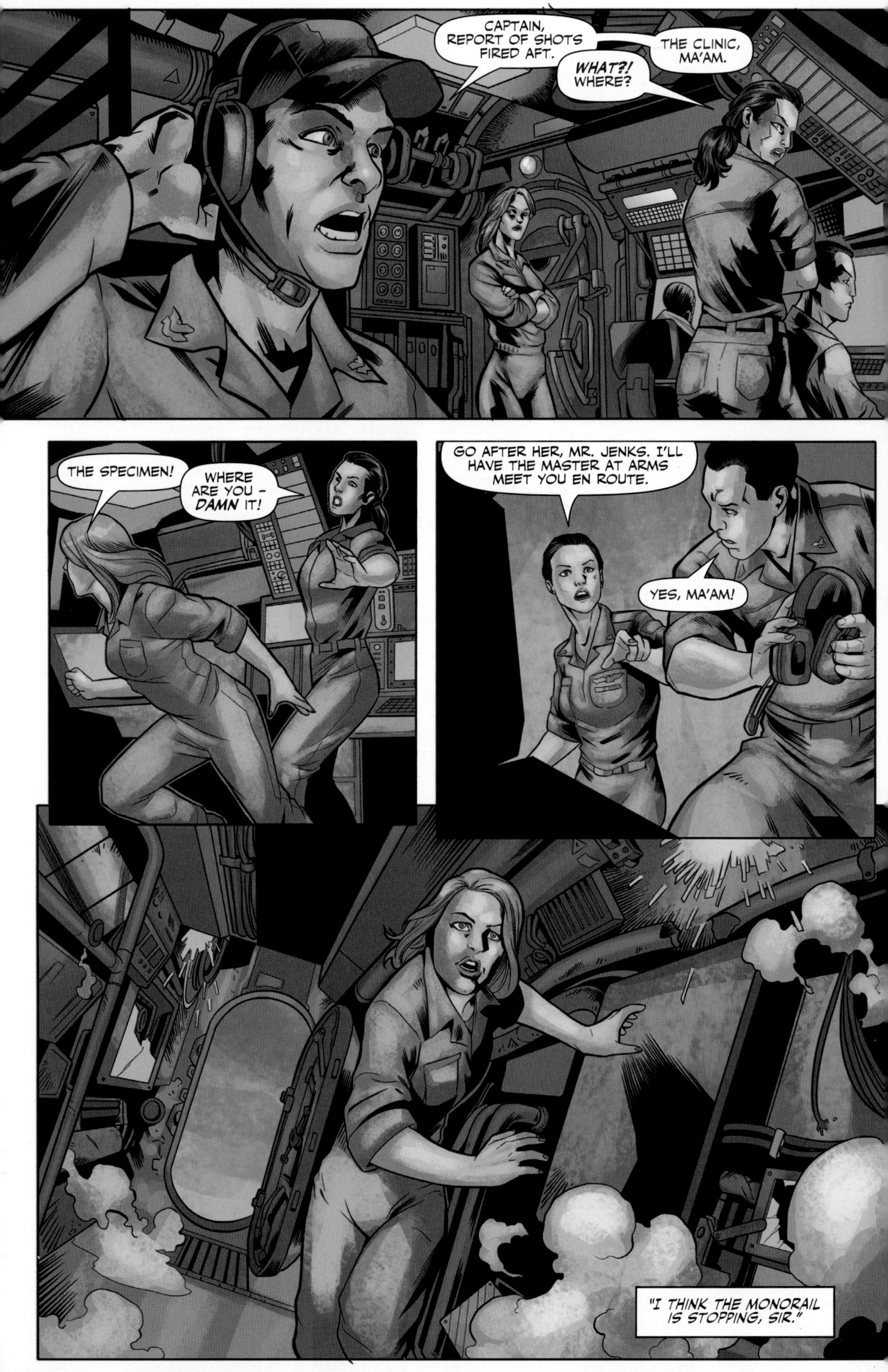
CAPTAIN, REPORT OF SHOTS FIRED AFT.
WHAT?! WHERE?
THE CLINIC, MA'AM.
THE SPECIMEN!
WHERE ARE YOU - DAMN IT!
GO AFTER HER, MR. JENKS. I'LL HAVE THE MASTER AT ARMS MEET YOU EN ROUTE.
YES, MA'AM!
"I THINK THE MONORAIL IS STOPPING, SIR."

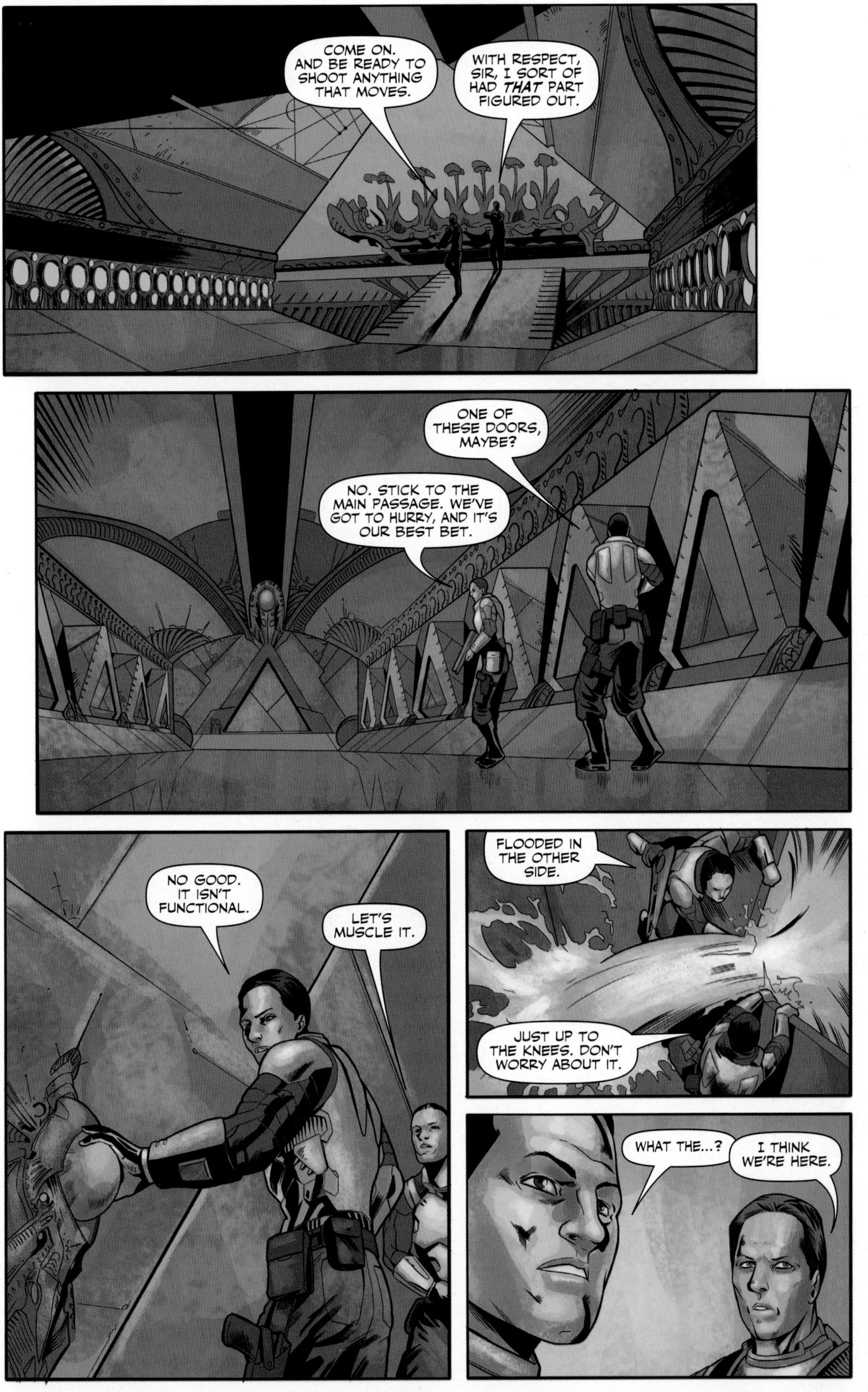
COME ON. AND BE READY TO SHOOT ANYTHING THAT MOVES.
WITH RESPECT, SIR, I SORT OF HAD *THAT* PART FIGURED OUT.
ONE OF THESE DOORS, MAYBE?
NO. STICK TO THE MAIN PASSAGE. WE'VE GOT TO HURRY, AND IT'S OUR BEST BET.
NO GOOD. IT ISN'T FUNCTIONAL.
LET'S MUSCLE IT.
FLOODED IN THE OTHER SIDE.
JUST UP TO THE KNEES. DON'T WORRY ABOUT IT.
WHAT THE...?
I THINK WE'RE HERE.

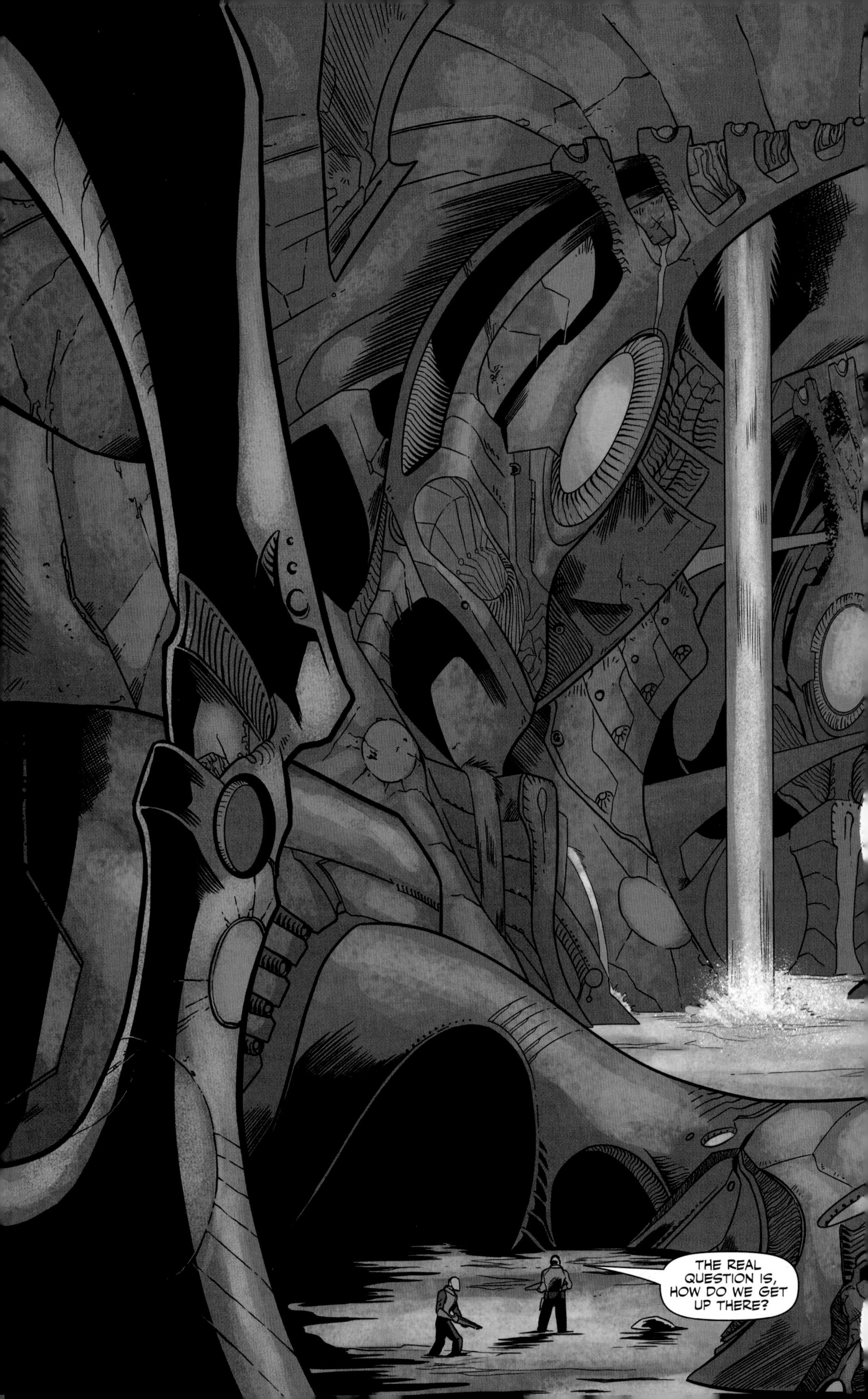
THE REAL QUESTION IS, HOW DO WE GET UP THERE?

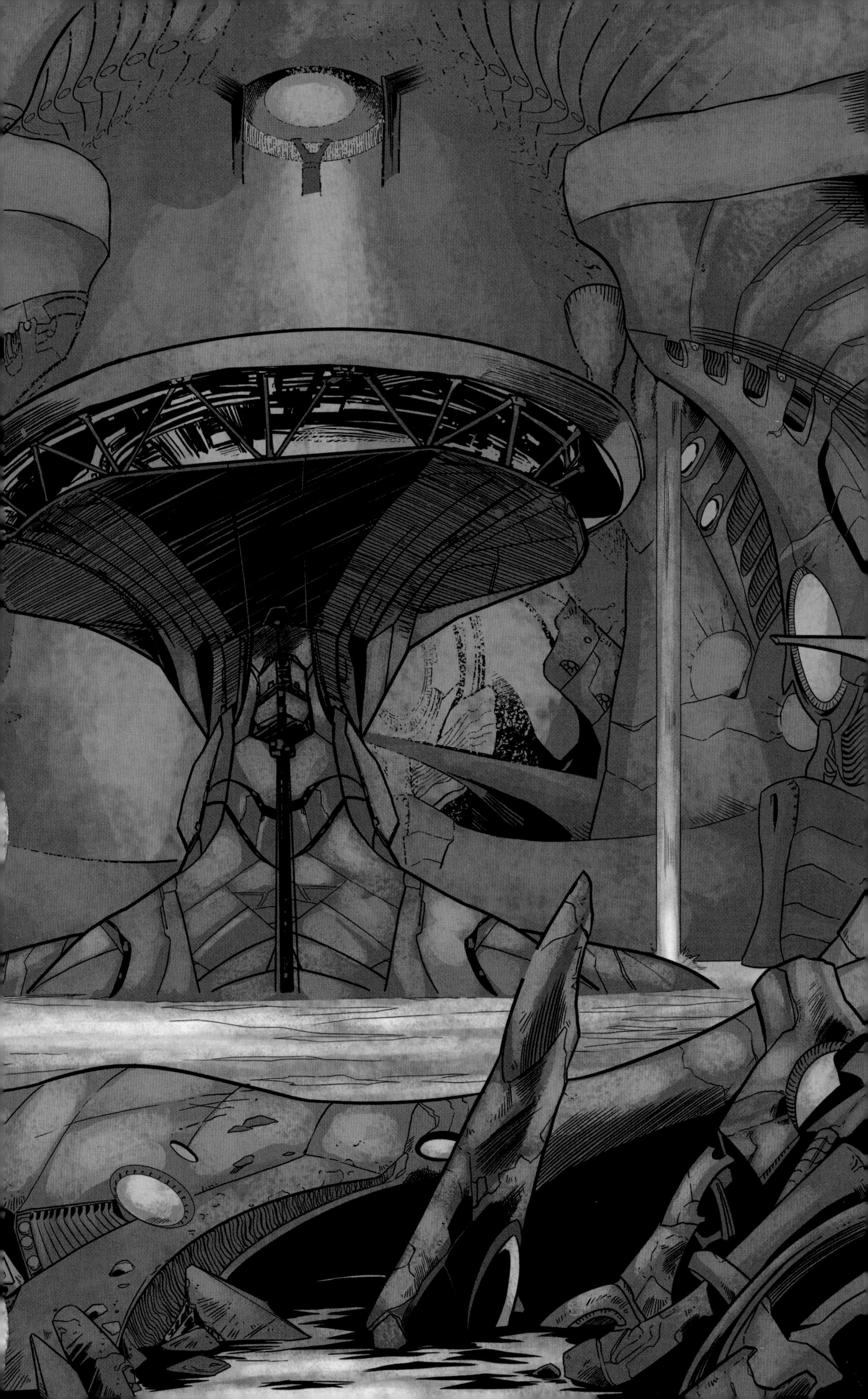

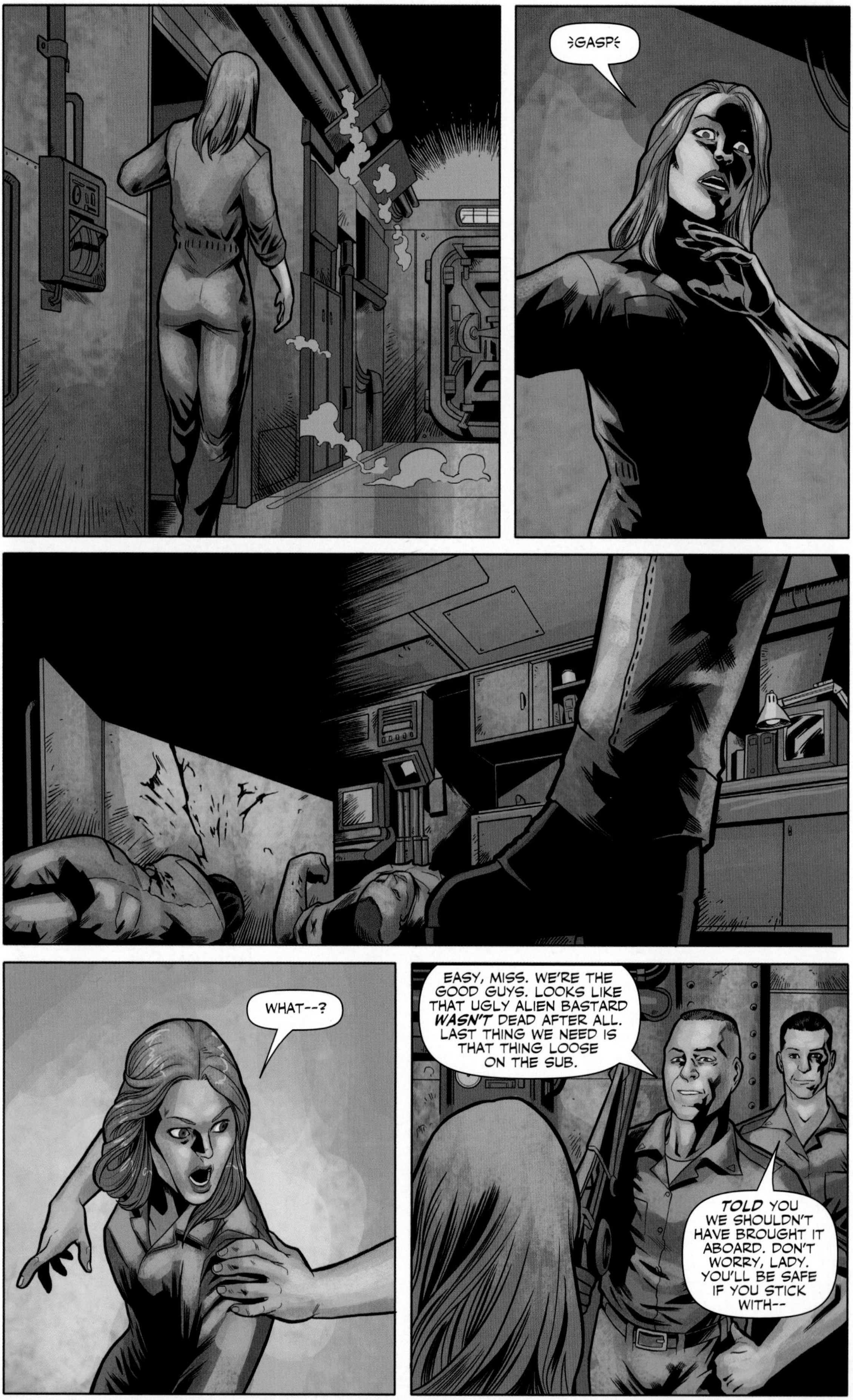
GASP
WHAT--?
EASY, MISS. WE'RE THE GOOD GUYS. LOOKS LIKE THAT UGLY ALIEN BASTARD WASN'T DEAD AFTER ALL. LAST THING WE NEED IS THAT THING LOOSE ON THE SUB.
TOLD YOU WE SHOULDN'T HAVE BROUGHT IT ABOARD. DON'T WORRY, LADY. YOU'LL BE SAFE IF YOU STICK WITH--

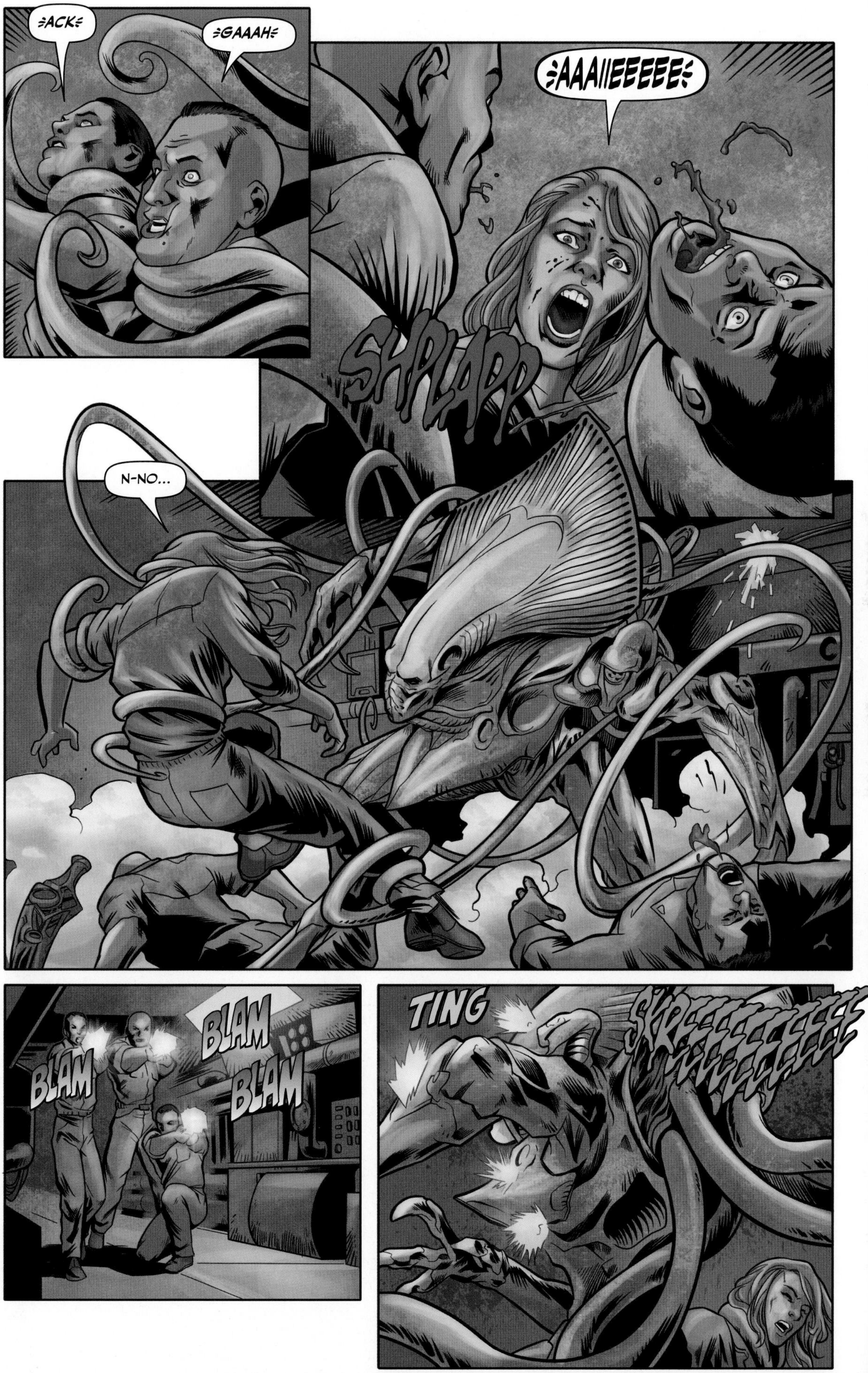
ACK
GAAAH
AAAIIEEEEE
SHPLAPP
N-NO...
BLAM
BLAM
BLAM
TING

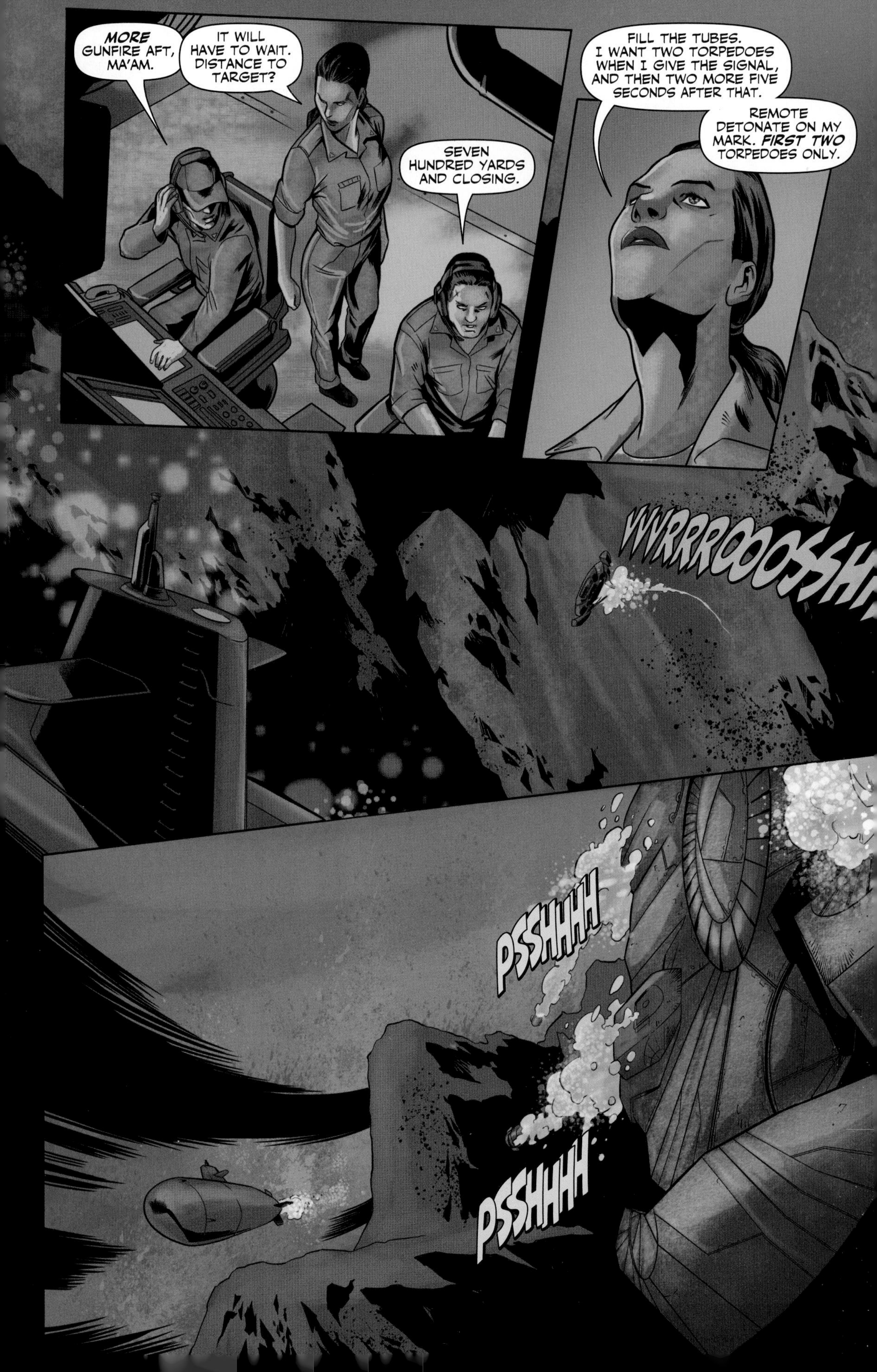
MORE GUNFIRE AFT, MA'AM.
IT WILL HAVE TO WAIT. DISTANCE TO TARGET?
SEVEN HUNDRED YARDS AND CLOSING.
FILL THE TUBES. I WANT TWO TORPEDOES WHEN I GIVE THE SIGNAL, AND THEN TWO MORE FIVE SECONDS AFTER THAT.
REMOTE DETONATE ON MY MARK. FIRST TWO TORPEDOES ONLY.
VVVRRROOOSSHH
PSSHHHH
PSSHHHH

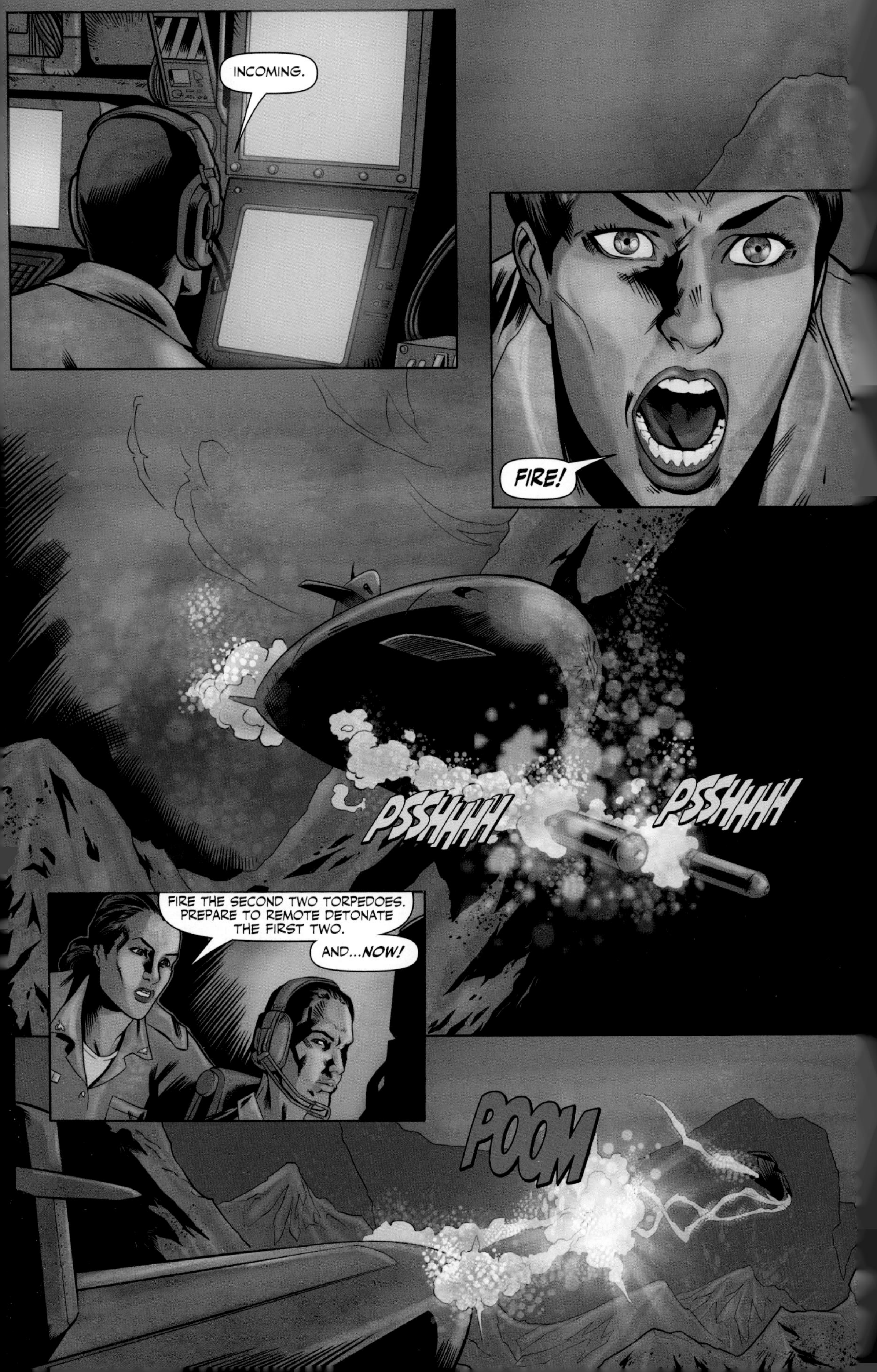
INCOMING.
FIRE!
PSSHHH!
PSSHHH
FIRE THE SECOND TWO TORPEDOES. PREPARE TO REMOTE DETONATE THE FIRST TWO.
AND...NOW!
POOM

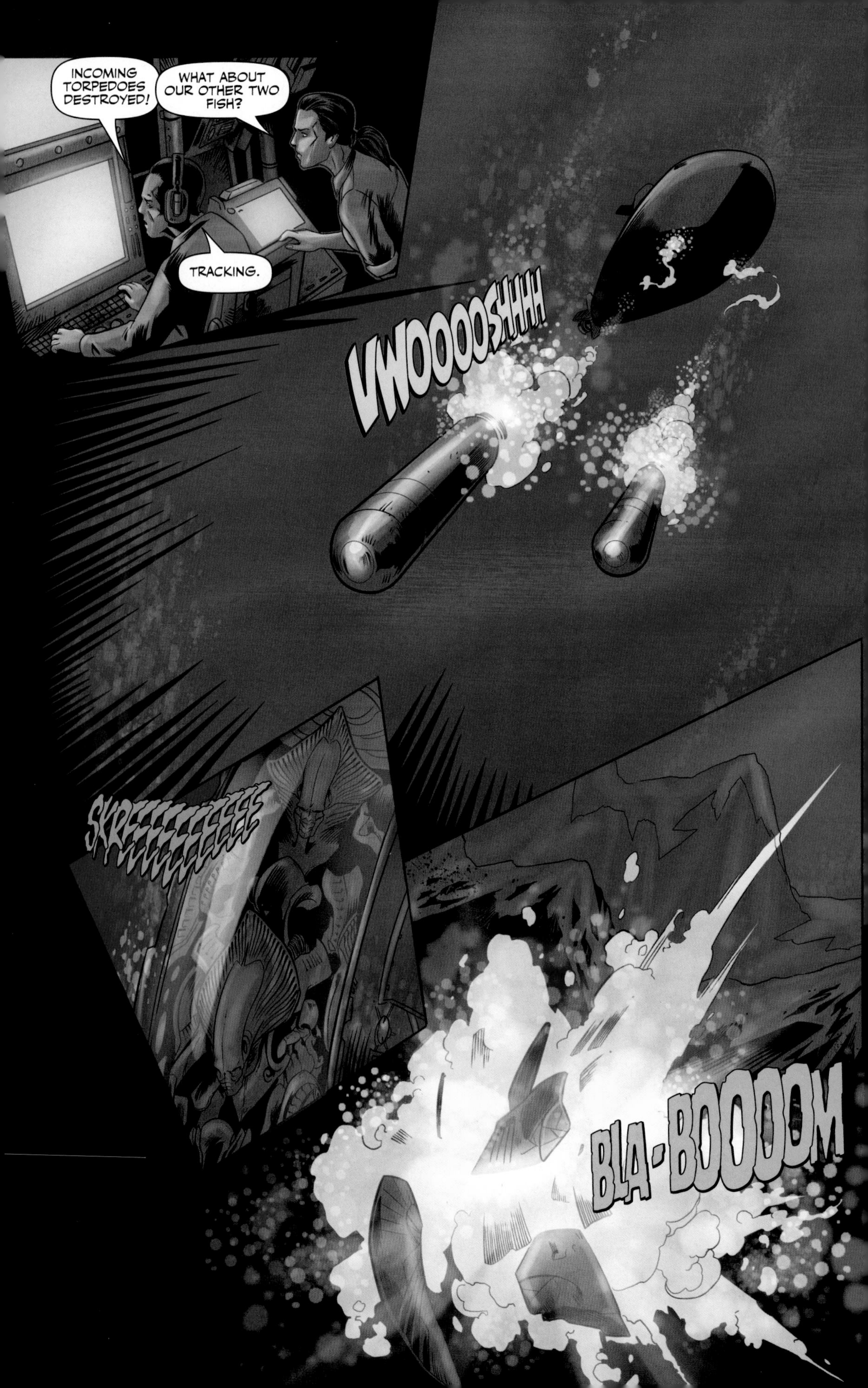

INCOMING TORPEDOES DESTROYED!
WHAT ABOUT OUR OTHER TWO FISH?
TRACKING.
VWOOOOSHHH
SKREEEEEEEEEEE
BLA-BOOOOM

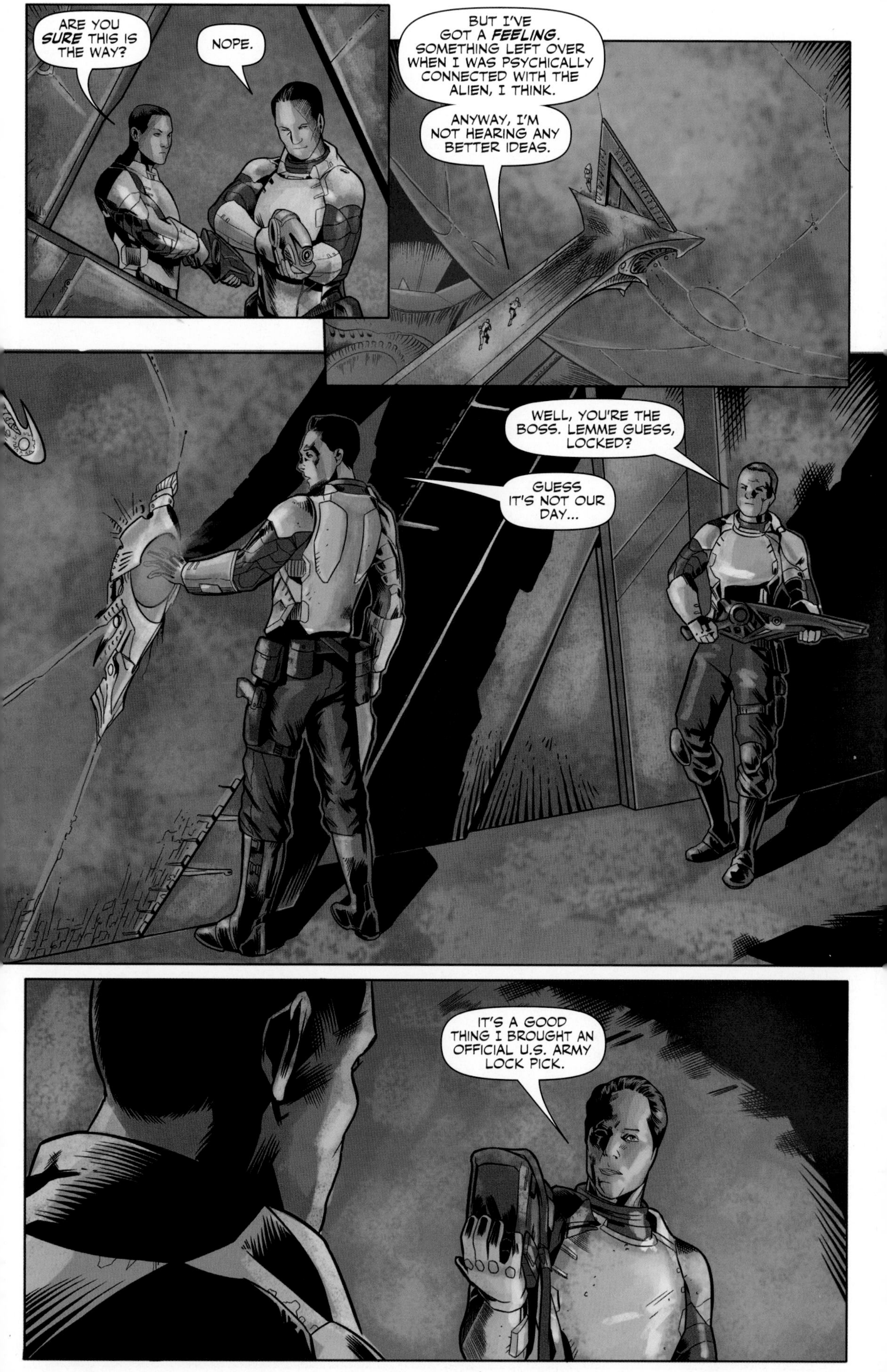
ARE YOU SURE THIS IS THE WAY?
NOPE.
BUT I'VE GOT A FEELING. SOMETHING LEFT OVER WHEN I WAS PSYCHICALLY CONNECTED WITH THE ALIEN, I THINK.
ANYWAY, I'M NOT HEARING ANY BETTER IDEAS.
WELL, YOU'RE THE BOSS. LEMME GUESS, LOCKED?
GUESS IT'S NOT OUR DAY...
IT'S A GOOD THING I BROUGHT AN OFFICIAL U.S. ARMY LOCK PICK.

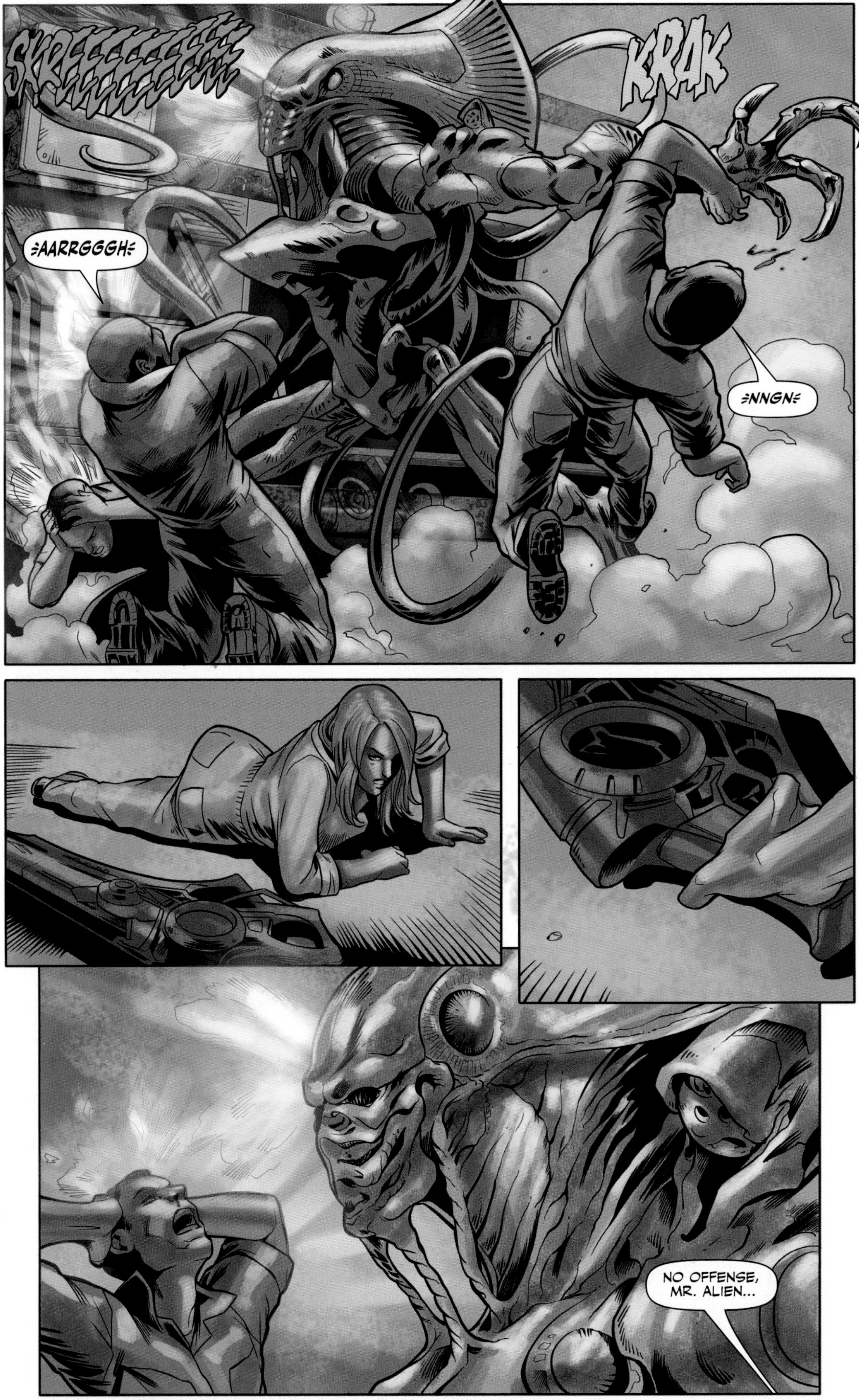
SKREEEEEEEEEEE
KRAK
AARRGGGH
NNGN
NO OFFENSE, MR. ALIEN...

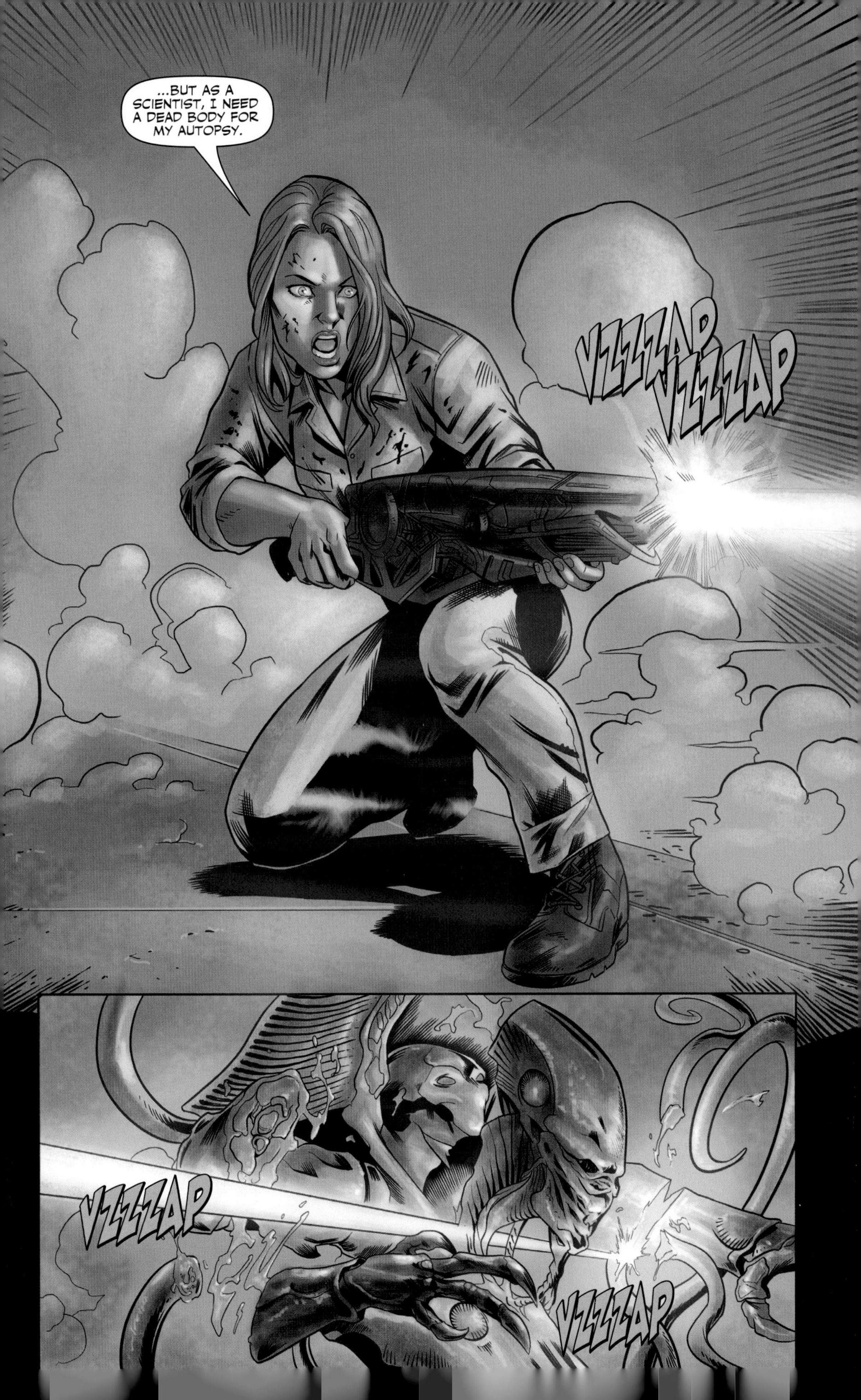
...BUT AS A SCIENTIST, I NEED A DEAD BODY FOR MY AUTOPSY.
VZZZAP
VZZZAP
VZZZAP
VZZZAP

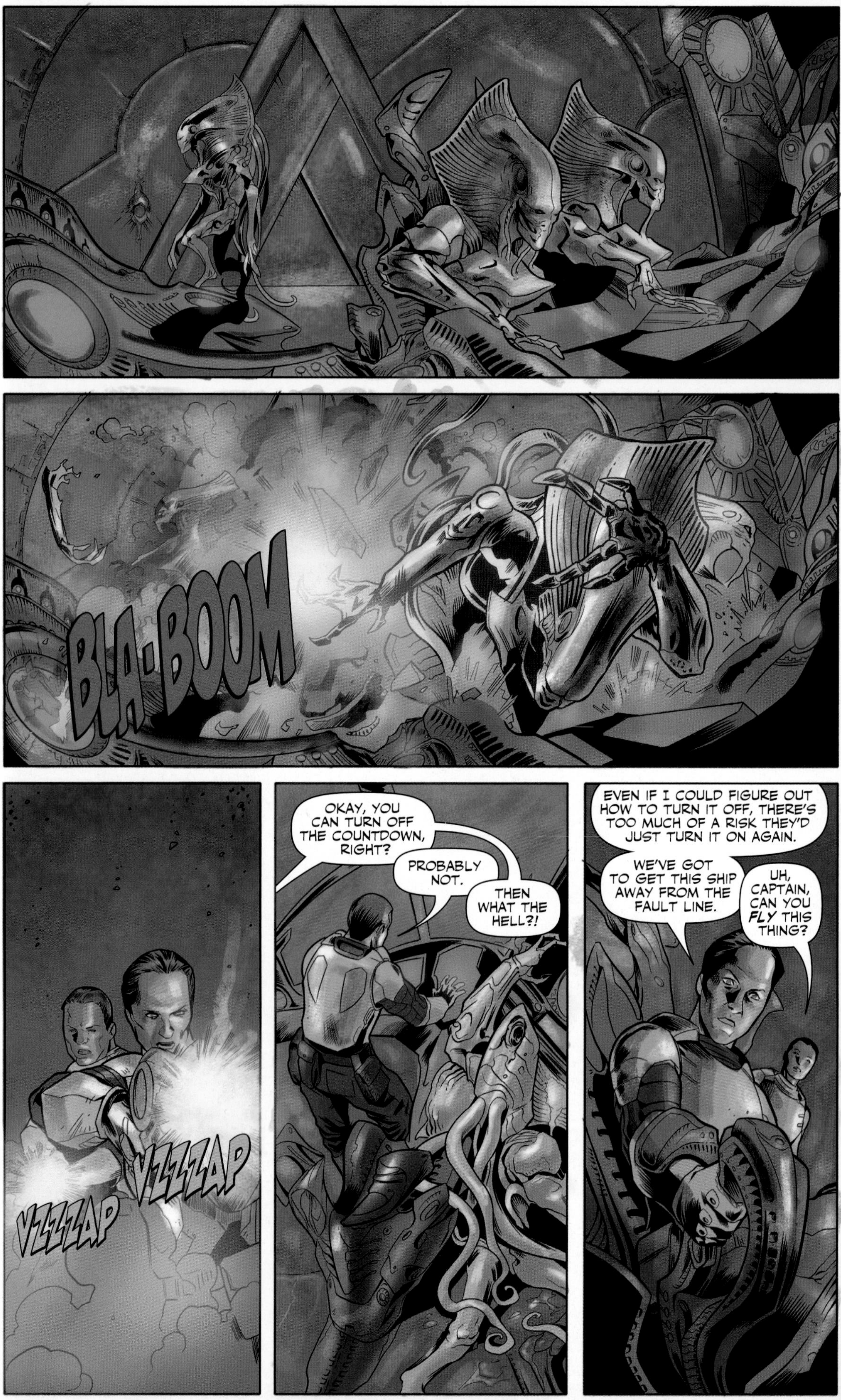
BLA-BOOM
VZZZAP
VZZZAP
OKAY, YOU CAN TURN OFF THE COUNTDOWN, RIGHT?
PROBABLY NOT.
THEN WHAT THE HELL?!
EVEN IF I COULD FIGURE OUT HOW TO TURN IT OFF, THERE'S TOO MUCH OF A RISK THEY'D JUST TURN IT ON AGAIN.
WE'VE GOT TO GET THIS SHIP AWAY FROM THE FAULT LINE.
UH, CAPTAIN, CAN YOU *FLY* THIS THING?

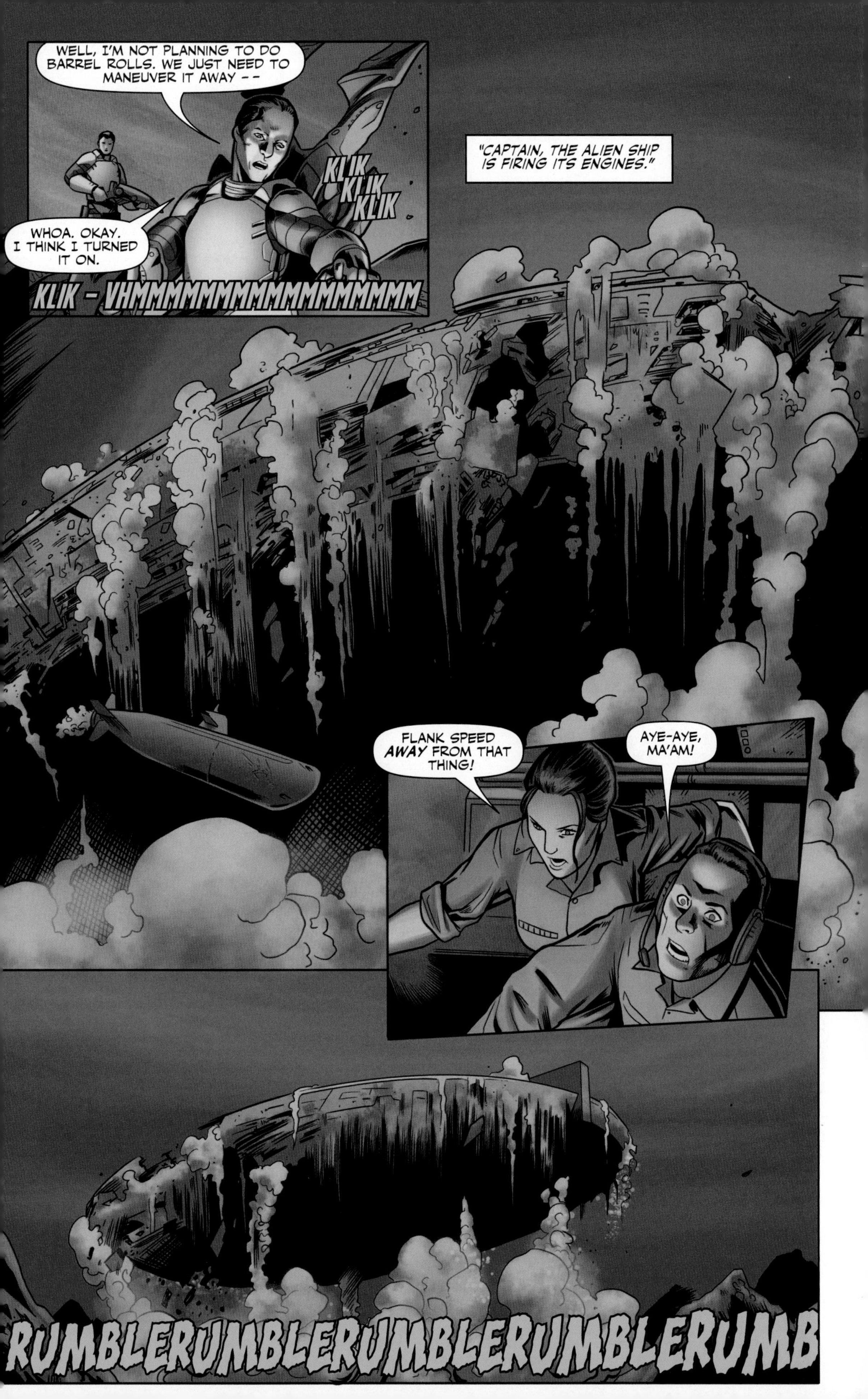
WELL, I'M NOT PLANNING TO DO BARREL ROLLS. WE JUST NEED TO MANEUVER IT AWAY --
KLIK KLIK KLIK
WHOA. OKAY. I THINK I TURNED IT ON.
KLIK - VHMMMMMMMMMMMMMMMM
"CAPTAIN, THE ALIEN SHIP IS FIRING ITS ENGINES."
FLANK SPEED AWAY FROM THAT THING!
AYE-AYE, MA'AM!
RUMBLERUMBLERUMBLERUMBLERUMB

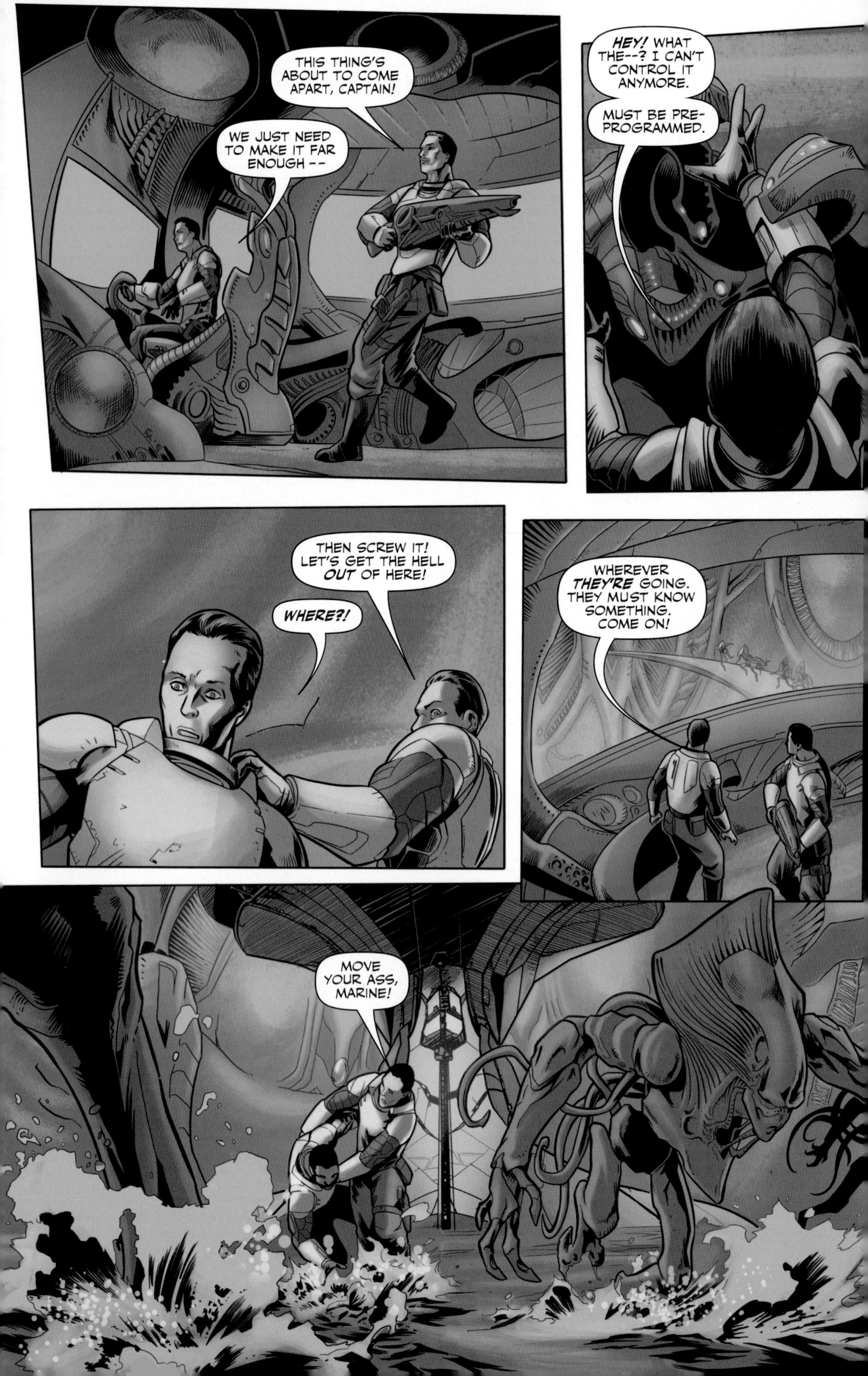
THIS THING'S ABOUT TO COME APART, CAPTAIN!
WE JUST NEED TO MAKE IT FAR ENOUGH --
HEY! WHAT THE--? I CAN'T CONTROL IT ANYMORE.
MUST BE PRE-PROGRAMMED.
THEN SCREW IT! LET'S GET THE HELL OUT OF HERE!
WHERE?!
WHEREVER THEY'RE GOING. THEY MUST KNOW SOMETHING. COME ON!
MOVE YOUR ASS, MARINE!

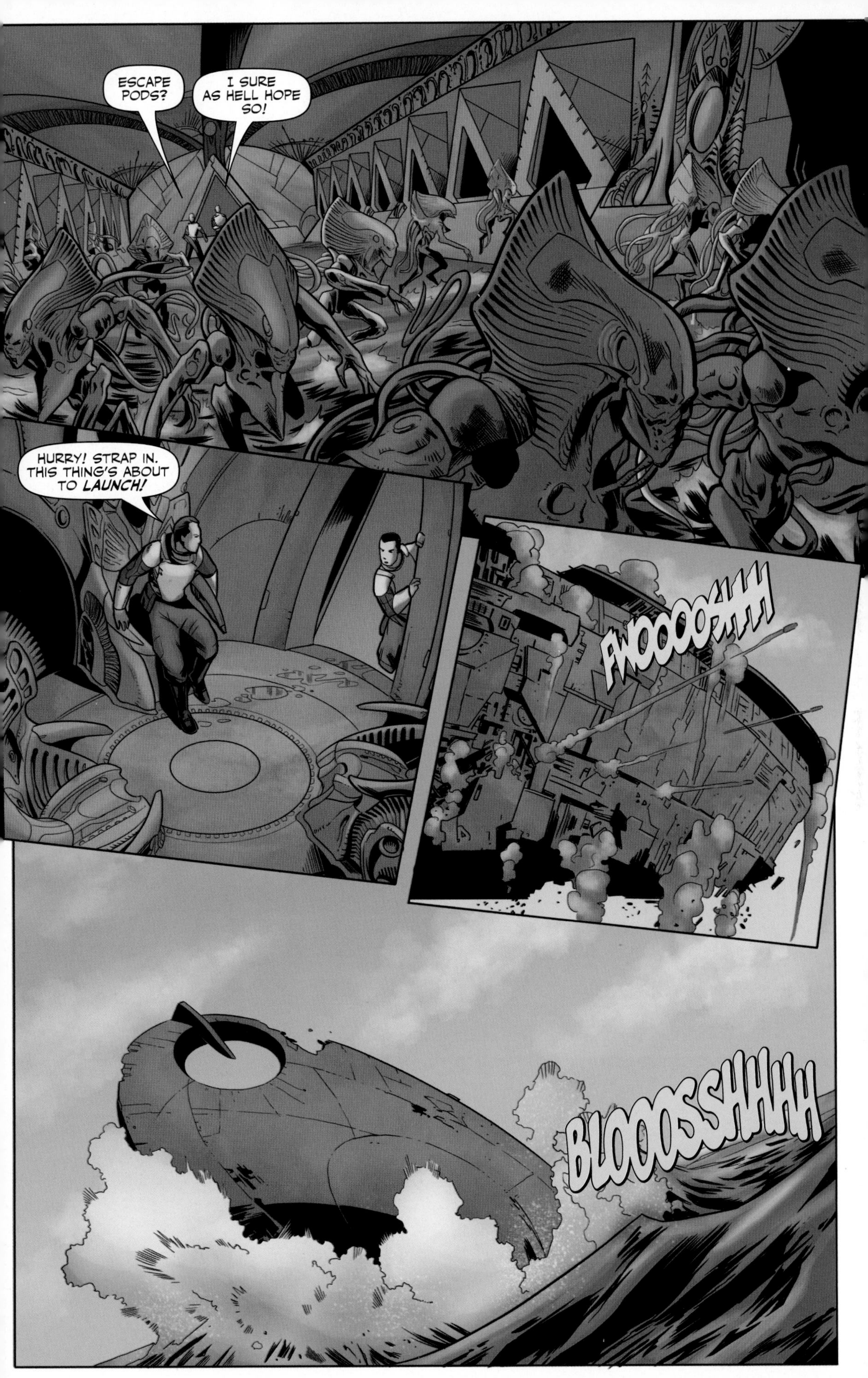
ESCAPE PODS?
I SURE AS HELL HOPE SO!
HURRY! STRAP IN. THIS THING'S ABOUT TO LAUNCH!
FWOOOOSHHH
BLOOOSSHHHH

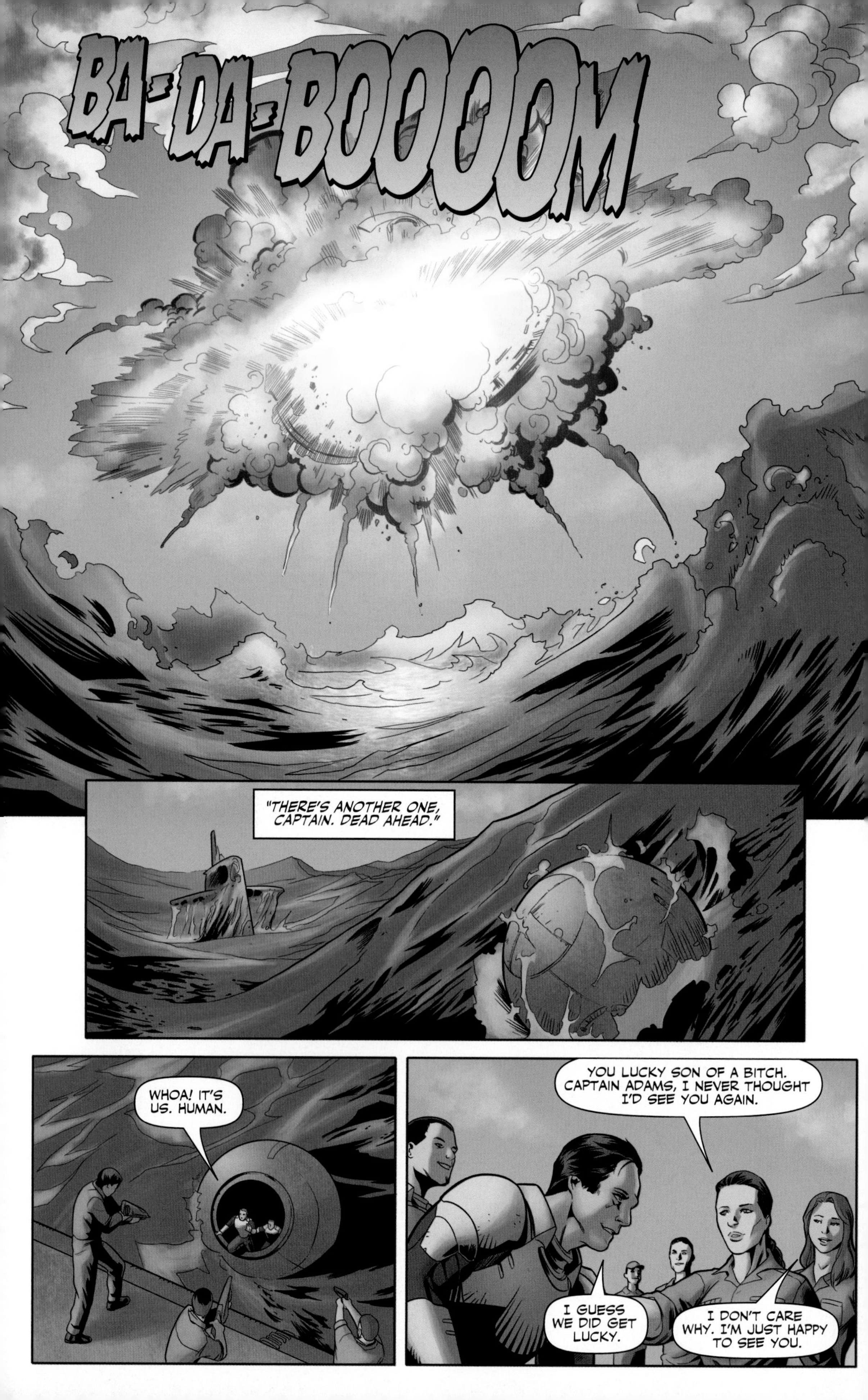
BA-DA-BOOOOM
"THERE'S ANOTHER ONE, CAPTAIN. DEAD AHEAD."
WHOA! IT'S US. HUMAN.
YOU LUCKY SON OF A BITCH. CAPTAIN ADAMS, I NEVER THOUGHT I'D SEE YOU AGAIN.
I GUESS WE DID GET LUCKY.
I DON'T CARE WHY. I'M JUST HAPPY TO SEE YOU.

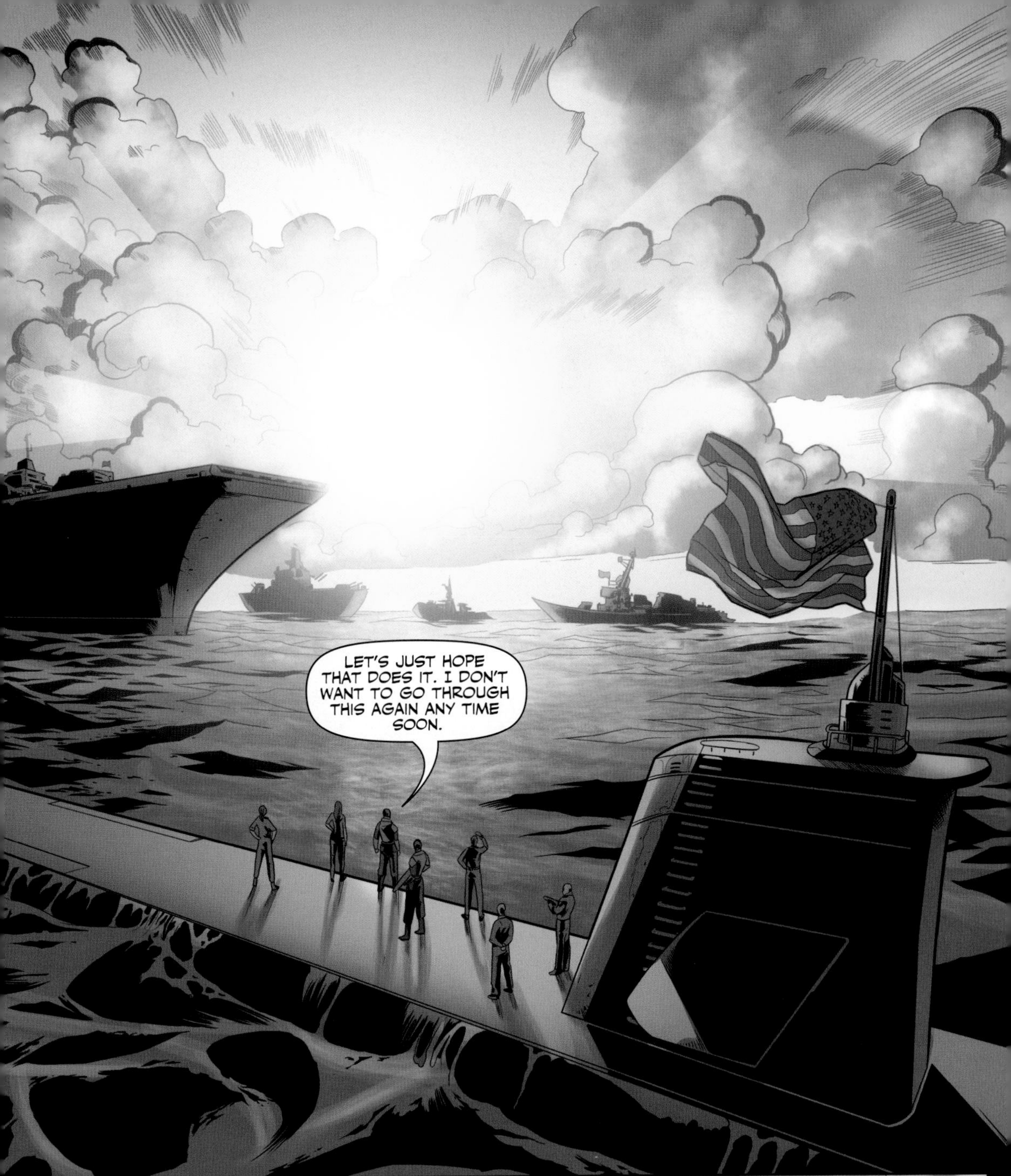
LET'S JUST HOPE THAT DOES IT. I DON'T WANT TO GO THROUGH THIS AGAIN ANY TIME SOON.

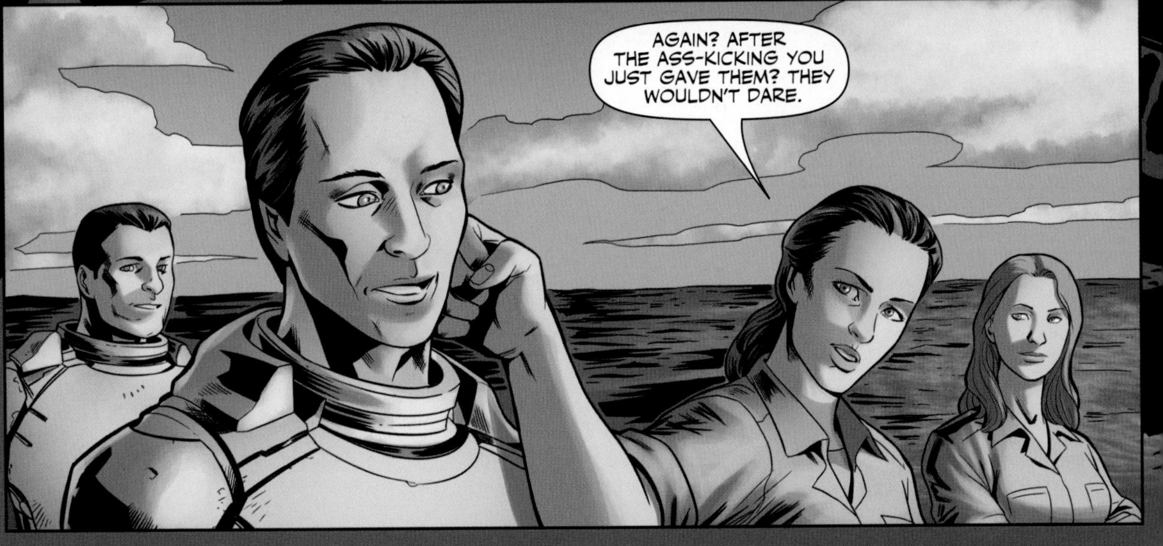
AGAIN? AFTER THE ASS-KICKING YOU JUST GAVE THEM? THEY WOULDN'T DARE.

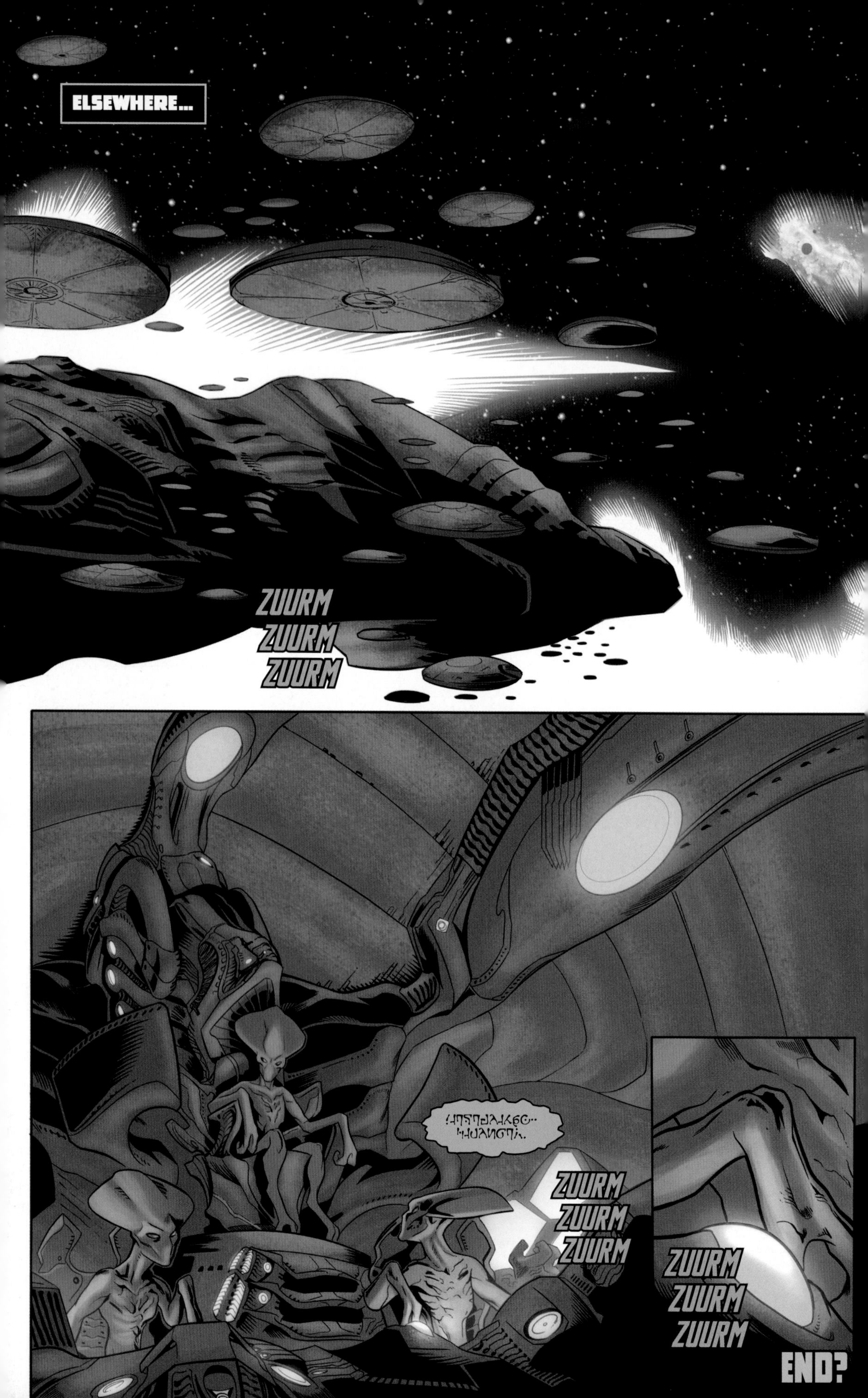
ELSEWHERE...
ZUURM
ZUURM
ZUURM
ZUURM
ZUURM
ZUURM
ZUURM
ZUURM
ZUURM
END?

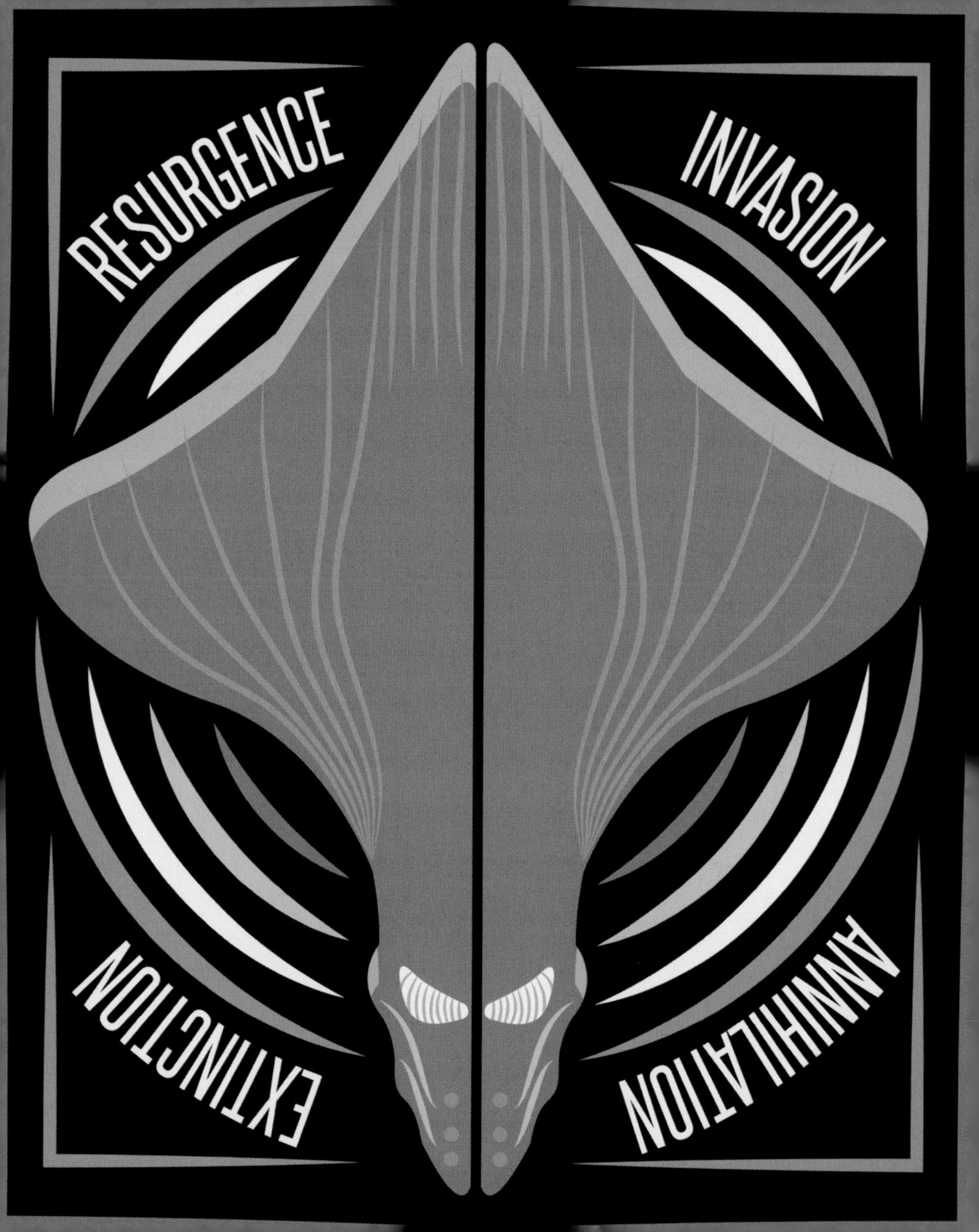
RESURGENCE
INVASION
EXTINCTION
ANNIHILATION

INDEPENDENCE DAY

R E S U R G E N C E

First Contact
1947 - Roswell, New Mexico
An extraterrestrial craft crashlands near a ranch in Roswell, New Mexico. The US military launches an investigation.

World Mourns Col. Steven Hiller
2007 (Area 51, Nevada) - 4/27/07
While test piloting the ESD's first alien hybrid fighter, an unknown malfunction causes the untimely death of Col. Hiller. He is survived by his wife Jasmine and son Dylann.

The World Rebuilds
1997 (London, UK) - 11/30/97
The alien threat has been neutralized - and the world begins to rise from the ashes. Reconstruction starts immediately as the great cities, monuments and landmarks of the world are slowly restored to their former glory.

INDEPENDENCE DAY

WELCOME TO
EARTH

SILENT ZONE
INDEPENDENCE DAY

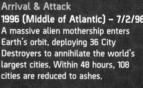

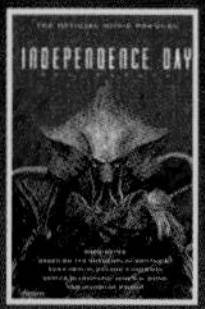

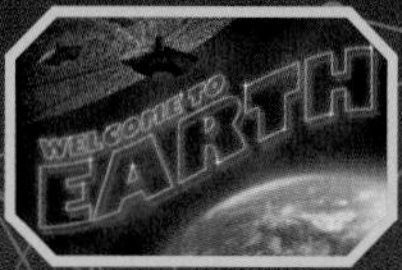

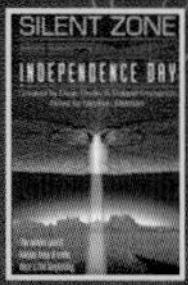

Silent Zone
1970s (Nevada Desert)
Dr. Brackish Okun arrives at Area 51 to work with the NSA and CIA on the study of the New Mexico ship.

Arrival & Attack
1996 (Middle of Atlantic) - 7/2/96
A massive alien mothership enters Earth's orbit, deploying 36 City Destroyers to annihilate the world's largest cities. Within 48 hours, 108 cities are reduced to ashes.

Earth Strikes Back
1996 (Nevada Desert) 7/4/96
Earth's nations launch a globally coordinated counterattack, destroying the alien mothership and eliminating the extraterrestrial threat.

TAKE
THE
TECH

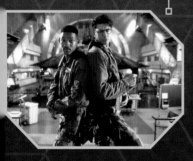

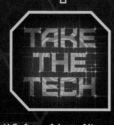

Honoring 20 Years of Global Unity
2016 (Washington D.C.) - 7/4/16
As we remember the last 20 years, we must also look to the future. The world has rebuilt stronger then we ever imagined and we must promise ourselves, as well as future generations, that we're never caught off guard again. We must continue to work together to secure the future of the human race - for as long as we stay united, we will survive.

U.S. Army Adopts Alien Weaponry 2004 (El Paso, Texas) - 10/23/03
Applying new data from recovered alien weaponry, U.S. Army scientists make dramatic advances in applying their findings to military applications.

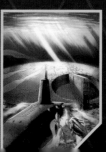

Terror From The Deep
1996 (Atlantic Ocean) 7/5/96
A functioning extraterrestrial craft is discovered beneath the Atlantic Ocean. An investigation - headed by Captain Adams - is implemented by the US military.

PROTECT
THE
PLANET

ESD Moonbase Operational
2009 (Beijing, China) – 2/21/09
The Earth Space Defense Moonbase opens. Designed with both offensive and defensive weapons capabilities, the Moonbase is the first of several planetary bases designed to monitor our solar system for potential alien threats.

Earth Space Defense Formed
1998 (Geneva, Switzerland) – 5/25/98
Following the newly established global peace alliance, the United Nations creates the Earth Space Defense program (ESD) to serve as an early warning system and united global defense unit.

Leaders Unite
1998 (Royal Palace of Naples, Piazza del Plebiscito; Naples, Italy) – 3/17/98
Centuries old conflicts and political distrust are dissolved to create an unprecedented unity among the nations of the world.

HYBRID FIGHTER JET
UNIFIED EARTH

Next Gen Hybrid Fighter Unveiled
2014 (Tokyo, Japan) – 8/19/14
The next generation of hybrid alien vehicles and weapon systems are introduced, after years of research and development from ESD scientists around the world.

War In The Desert
1996 (Saudi Arabia) 7/4/96
Military pilots in the Saudi Arabian desert witness the destruction of Jerusalem and engage in a hand-to-hand assault with extraterrestrial crash survivors.

WAR IN THE DESERT
INDEPENDENCE DAY

Congo Ground War Continues
2002 (Democratic Republic of the Congo, Africa) – 8/10/11
A small faction of aliens continues to hold out in a remote part of the African Congo – the lone survivors of a crashed City Destroyer. The ESD repeatedly offers their support and assistance to the local government, but is met with aggressive refusal.

ESD
EARTH SPACE DEFENSE
PROTECT THE PLANET

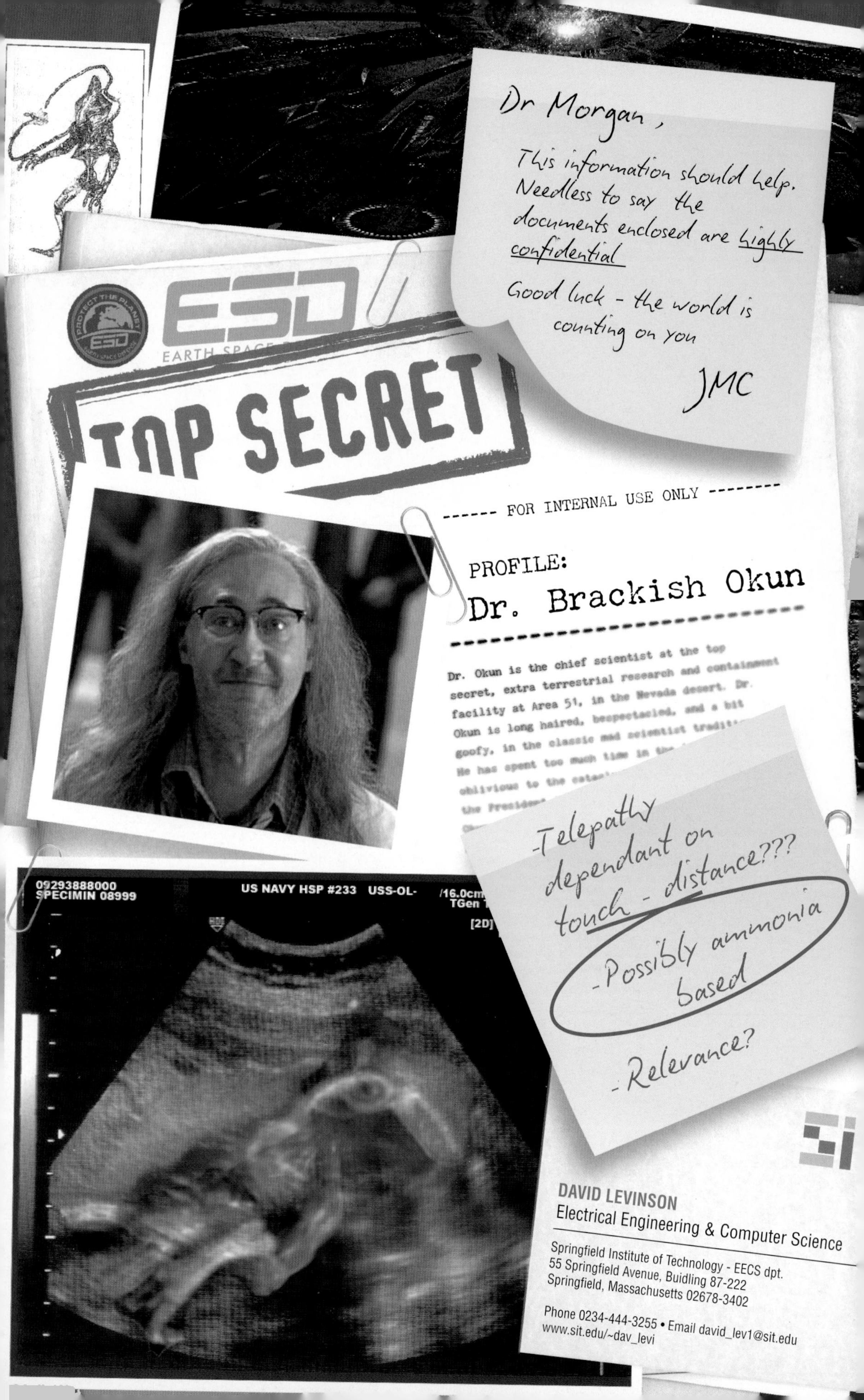

Dr Morgan,
This information should help. Needless to say the documents enclosed are highly confidential
Good luck - the world is counting on you
JMC
PROTECT THE PLANET
ESD
EARTH SPACE DEFENSE
ESD
EARTH SPACE
TOP SECRET
------ FOR INTERNAL USE ONLY --------
PROFILE:
Dr. Brackish Okun
Dr. Okun is the chief scientist at the top
secret, extra terrestrial research and containment
facility at Area 51, in the Nevada desert. Dr.
Okun is long haired, bespectacled, and a bit
goofy, in the classic mad scientist tradit
He has spent too much time in the
oblivious to the
the President
-Telepathy dependant on touch - distance???
-Possibly ammonia based
-Relevance?
09293888000
SPECIMIN 08999
US NAVY HSP #233 USS-OL-
/16.0cm
TGen
[2D]
DAVID LEVINSON
Electrical Engineering & Computer Science
Springfield Institute of Technology - EECS dpt.
55 Springfield Avenue, Buidling 87-222
Springfield, Massachusetts 02678-3402
Phone 0234-444-3255 • Email david_lev1@sit.edu
www.sit.edu/~dav_levi

OFFICE OF THE PRESIDENT'S COUNCIL OF ADVISORS ON SCIENCE & TECHNOLOGY (C25)

AUTOPSY
CASE NO.
0009989'44B

VICTIM'S NAME (LAST, FIRST, MIDDLE)
N/A

SEX	AGE	RACE	WEIGHT	HT
Unknown	Unknown	Unknown	282.67kg	254.4cm

DESCRIPTION OF CORPSE

- Beneath its exoskeleton, the creature appears quasi-humanoid in nature
- although notably diminutive, with slender three-jointed limbs, an enlarged neurocranium and large, pupil-less eyes.
- The suits are themselves are highly durable and appear to be of a biomechanical design – offering the species environmental, as well as physical, protection – with a number of thick, pincered tentacles protruding from the back. These appear to have a prehensile function, though how they are controlled from within is yet unknown...

EXTERNAL INJURIES

- Removed from its embryotic casing (which I believe acts as means of artificial preservation), the creature shows signs moderate signs of trauma to the cranium and lower limbs – consistent with a crushing injury.
- Much of the inital trauma appears to have healed considerably – evidence of new tissue and bone growth suggests regenerative abilities or technologies far greater than our own.

INTERNAL INJURIES

- Due to insufficient medical supplies, I am unable to ascertain what – if any – injuries the creature within has sustained. Without the necessary tools to extract it from its outer casing, I can do little more than speculate as to its condition.
- Diagnostic sonography has proven ~~accurate~~ inconclusive.

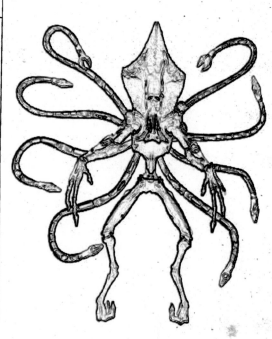

MEDICAL DIAGNOSIS

- Based upon my limited knowledge of the creature's biology and the equippment at my disposal, my diagnosis is naturally subject to conjecture. However, I believe it likely the ~~aliens~~ decedent's injuries and subsequent death are a direct result of the inital impact of its craft.
- All full autopsy will be conducted on transference of the cadaver to a government medical facility.

NOTES

- Further examinations should be conducted with due caution.
- Decontamination is advised as the specimin may present a credible health risk; unknown pathogens, micro-organisms and hazardous contaminants are a distinct possibility.

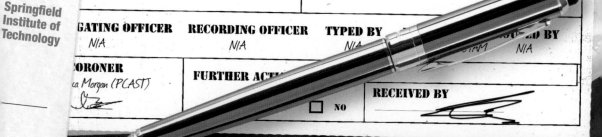

...GATING OFFICER	RECORDING OFFICER	TYPED BY	...ED BY
N/A	N/A	N/A	N/A

...CORONER	FURTHER ACT...		
...ca Morgan (PCAST)		☐ NO	RECEIVED BY

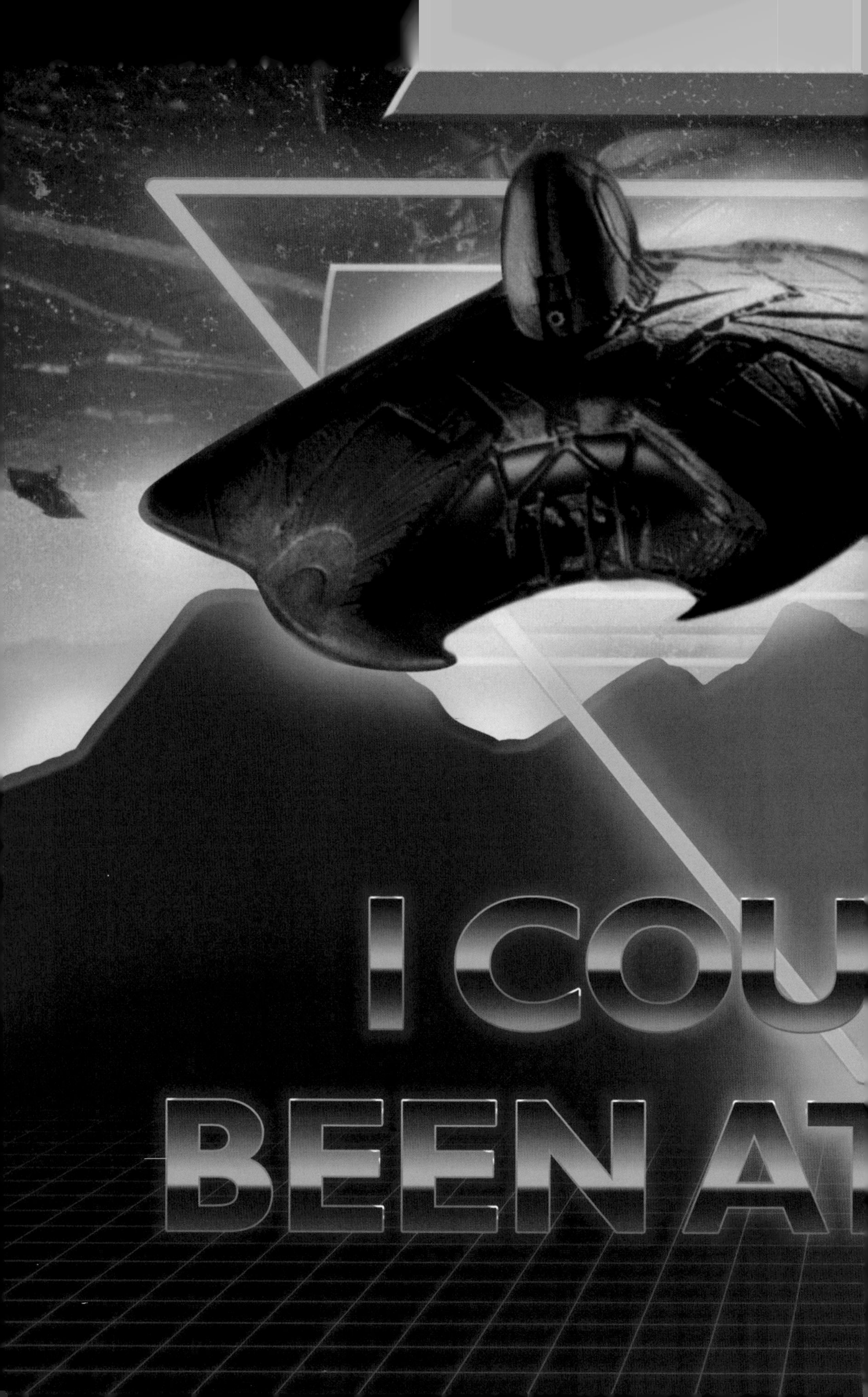
I COU
BEEN A

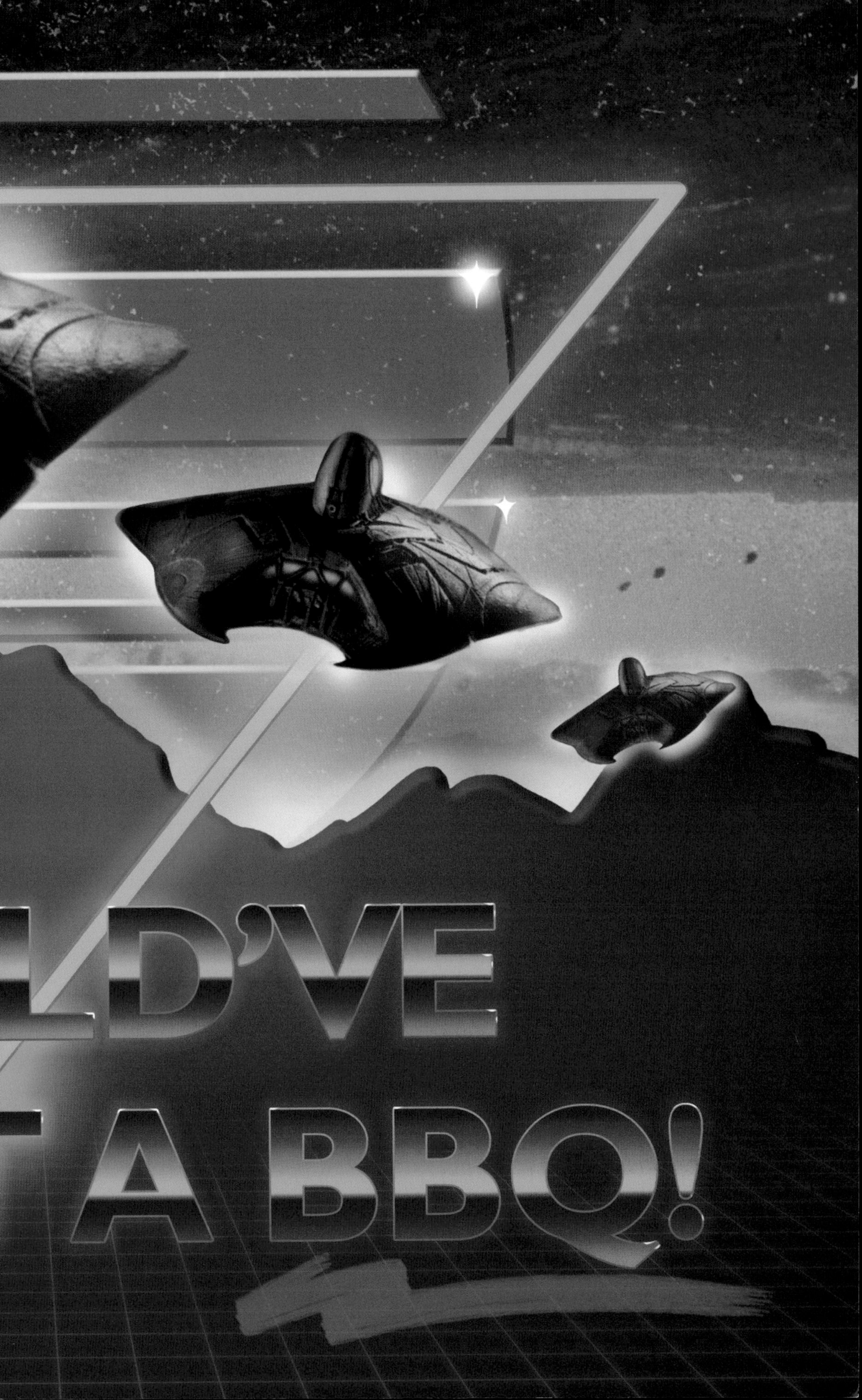
LD'VE
A BBQ!

IDR

★ PROFILE ★★★★★★★★★★★★★★

JOSHUA ADAMS

Born in 1958 to a naval service family in the Midwestern United States, Joshua T Adams' natural aptitude for problem-solving showed at a young age, despite early struggles with his education.

Majoring in mechanical engineering at Ohio State, the young academic's initial interest in a naval career was cut short by the loss of his sister, Erin, who died as a result of a tragic boating accident. The experience left Adams with a lifelong fear of the ocean.

Eventually finding solace and meaning in the US armed forces, Adams received numerous commendations over the course of his career – including the Legion of Merit – for his service in Afghanistan and South Korea. By 1994, he had achieved the rank of Captain.

During the War of 1996, Adams maintained a key position as part of US intelligence, using his expertise in military strategy to help co-ordinate the global assault that would serve as humanity's principal reprieve from the extraterrestrial threat.

With the mothership destroyed, Adams' familiarity with the alien methodology, technology, and mindset marked him as the prime candidate for a military investigation of an additional extraterrestrial craft, newly discovered at the bottom of the Atlantic Ocean.

Eager to serve his country and his planet, but still battling his thalassophobia, Adams has reluctantly assented to this new mission.

ESD
EARTH SPACE DEFENSE
PROTECT THE PLANET

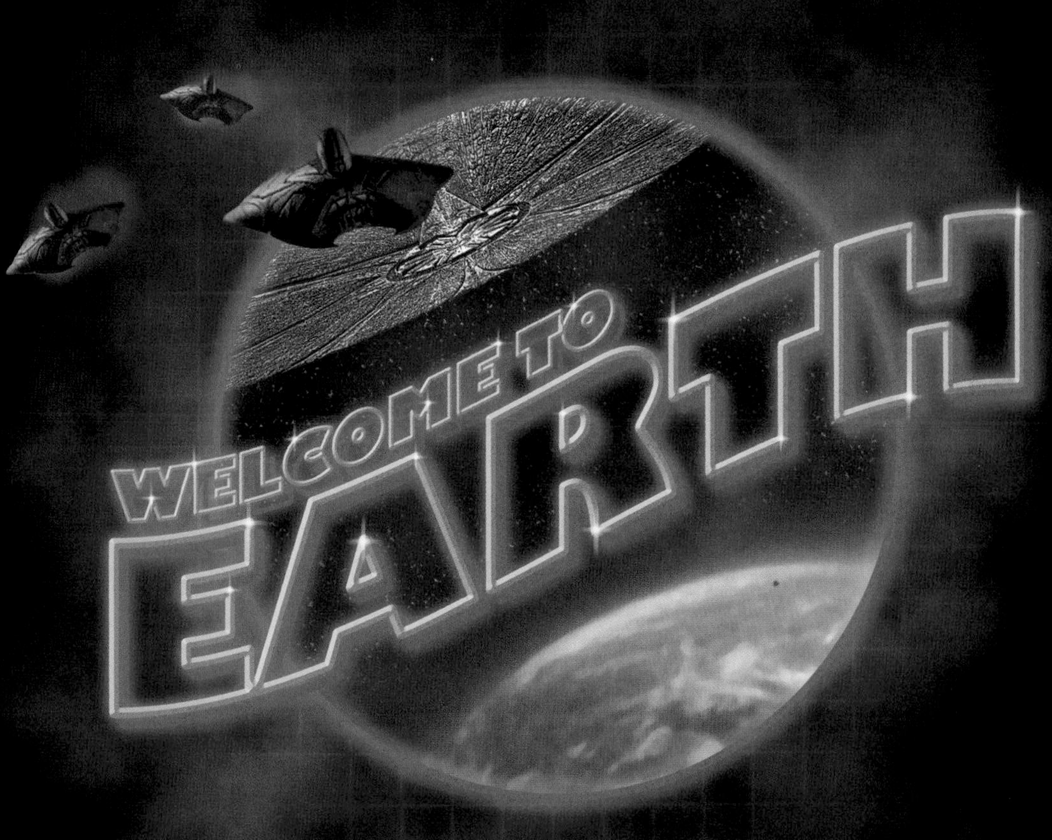
WELCOME TO
EARTH

COVER GALLERY

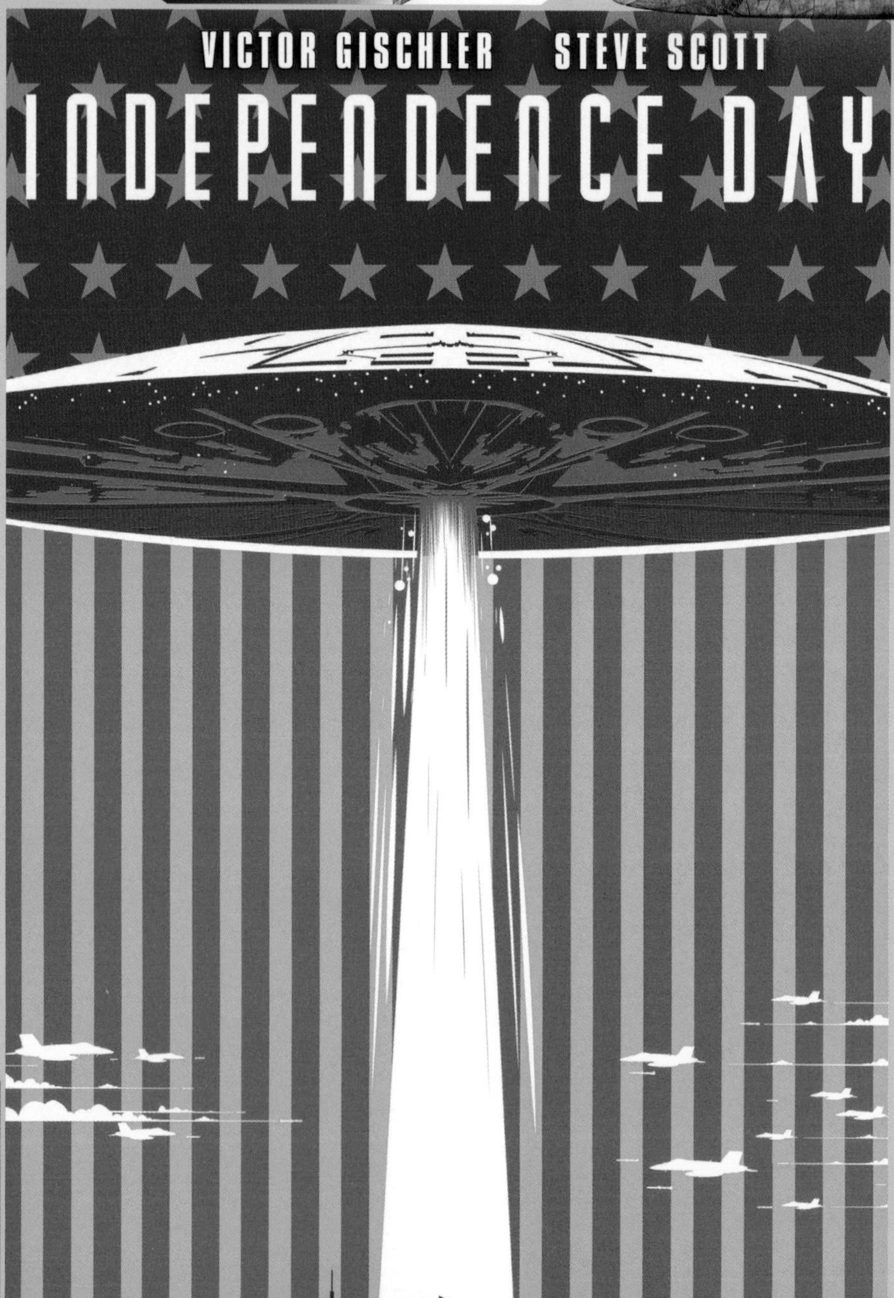
VICTOR GISCHLER
STEVE SCOTT
INDEPENDENCE DAY

ISSUE 1 COVER A MOVIE COVER

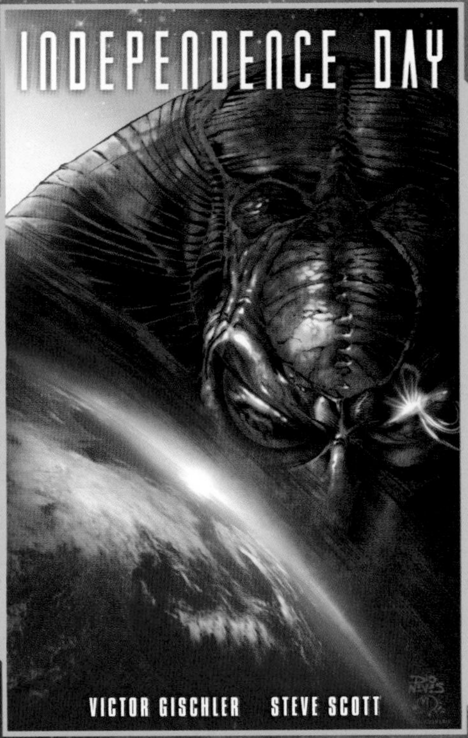
INDEPENDENCE DAY
VICTOR GISCHLER STEVE SCOTT

ISSUE 1 COVER B BY DIO NEVES

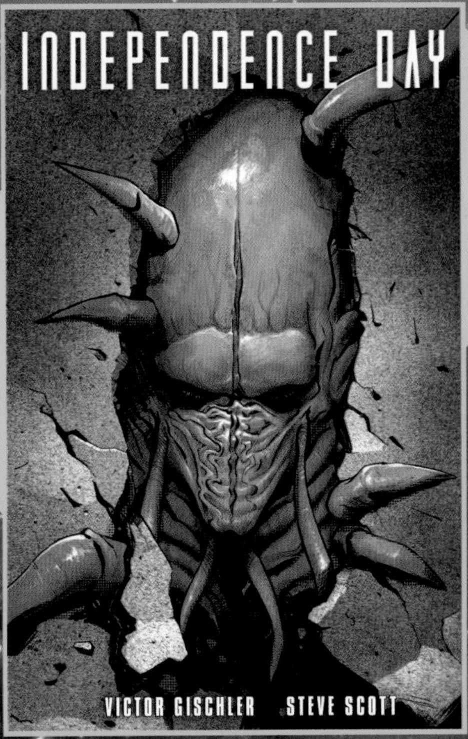
INDEPENDENCE DAY
VICTOR GISCHLER STEVE SCOTT

ISSUE 1 COVER C BY LEE GARBETT

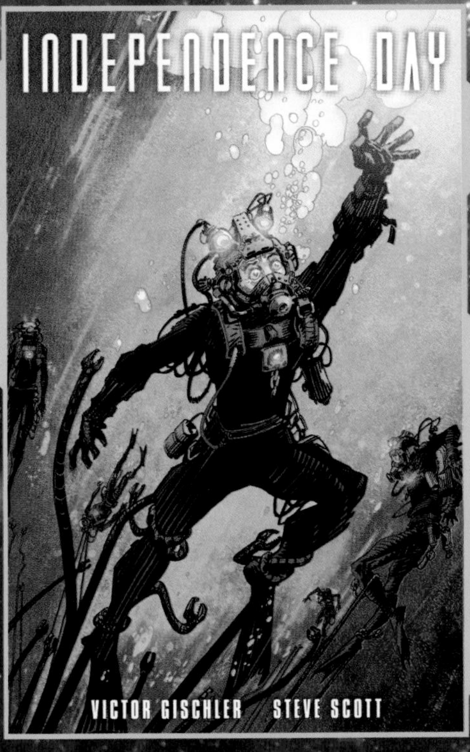
INDEPENDENCE DAY
VICTOR GISCHLER STEVE SCOTT

ISSUE 1 COVER D JOHN MCCREA

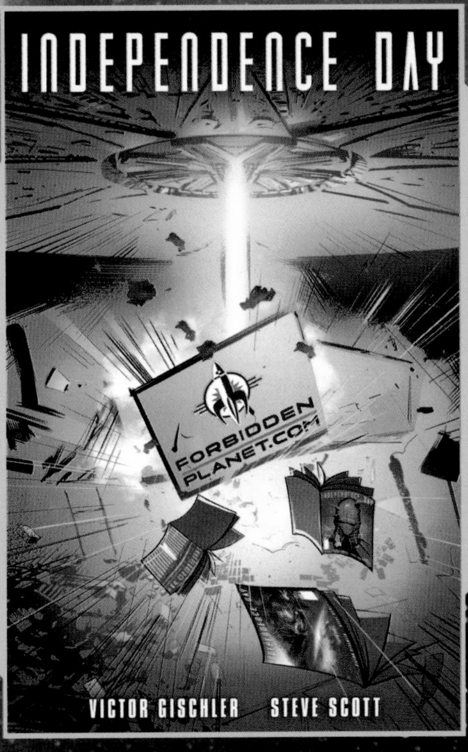
INDEPENDENCE DAY
FORBIDDEN PLANET.COM
VICTOR GISCHLER STEVE SCOTT

CUSTOM COVER – DENNIS CALERO

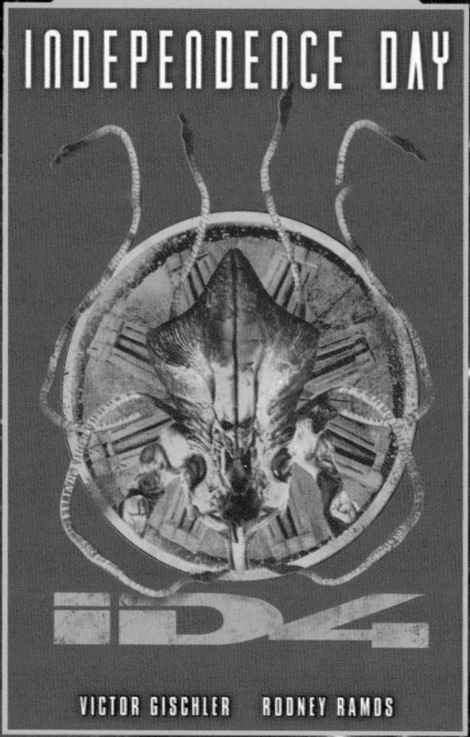
INDEPENDENCE DAY
ID4
VICTOR GISCHLER
RODNEY RAMOS
ISSUE 2 COVER A MOVIE COVER

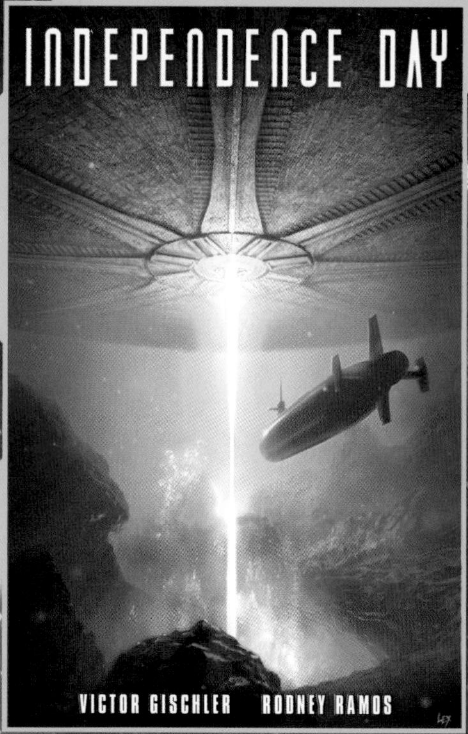
INDEPENDENCE DAY
VICTOR GISCHLER
RODNEY RAMOS
ISSUE 2 COVER B ALEX RONALD

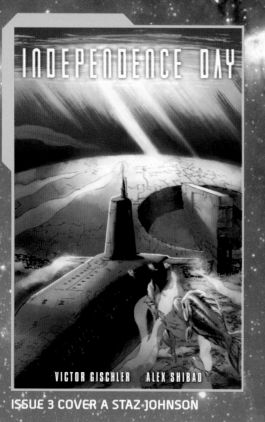

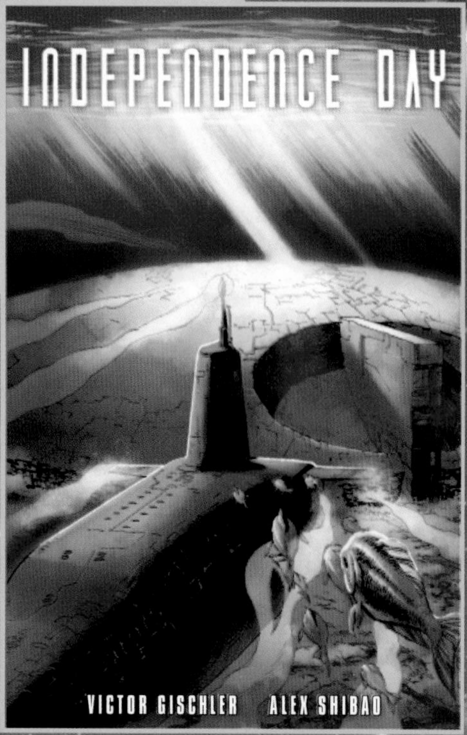
INDEPENDENCE DAY
VICTOR GISCHLER
ALEX SHIBAO
ISSUE 3 COVER A STAZ JOHNSON

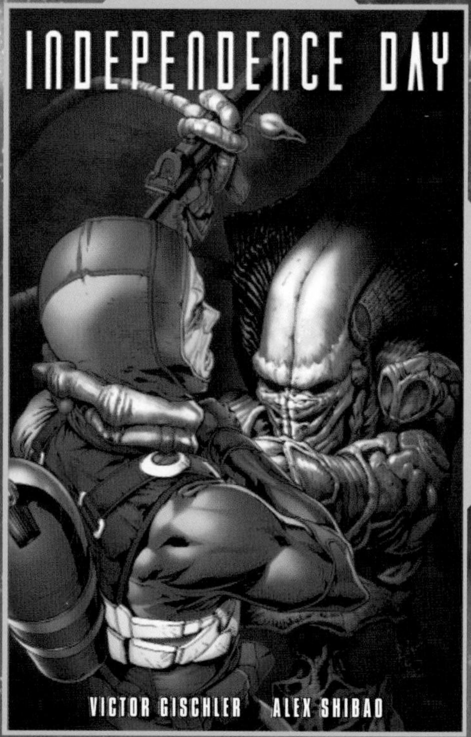
INDEPENDENCE DAY
VICTOR GISCHLER
ALEX SHIBAO
ISSUE 3 COVER B EDGAR SALAZAR

ISSUE 4 COVER A
XERMANCIO

ISSUE 4 COVER B
MIKE RATERA

INDEPENDENCE DAY

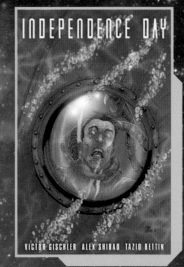

INDEPENDENCE DAY

VICTOR GISCHLER   ALEX SHIBAO   TAZIO BETTIN

VICTOR GISCHLER   ALEX SHIBAO   TAZIO BETTIN

COVER GALLERY

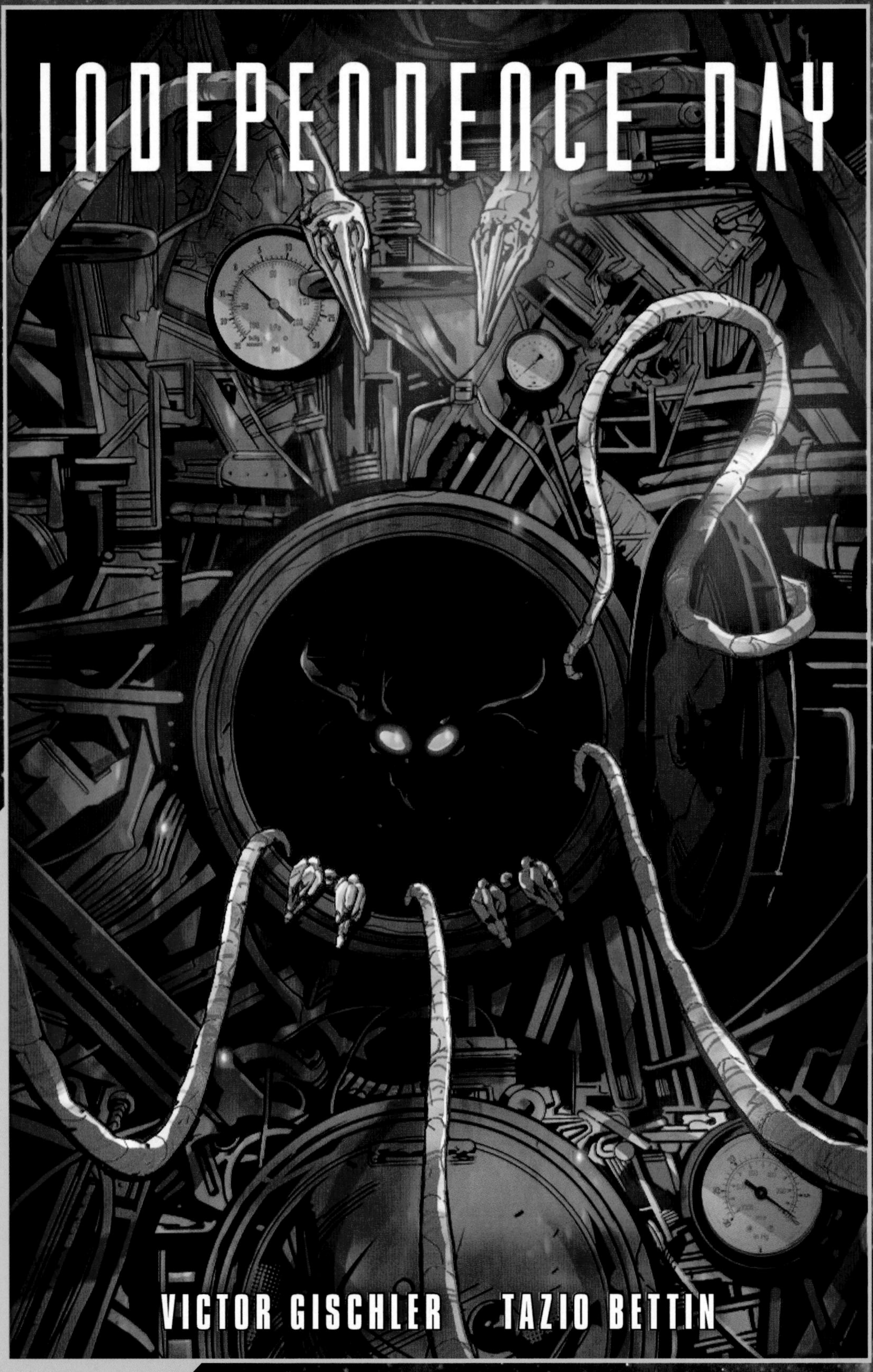
INDEPENDENCE DAY
VICTOR GISCHLER
TAZIO BETTIN

ISSUE 5 COVER A COLIN LORIMER

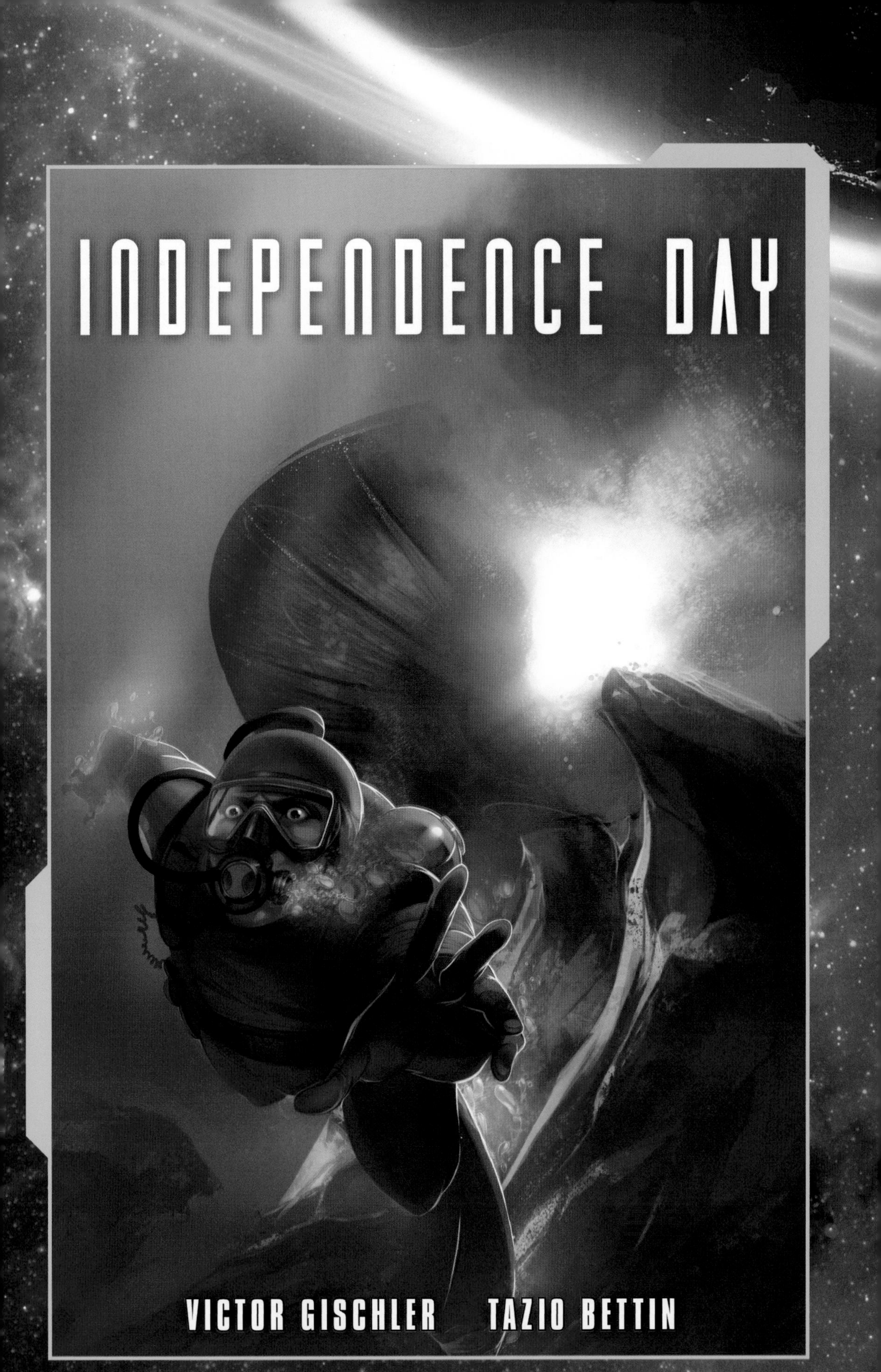
INDEPENDENCE DAY
VICTOR GISCHLER
TAZIO BETTIN

ISSUE 5 COVER B VERITY GLASS

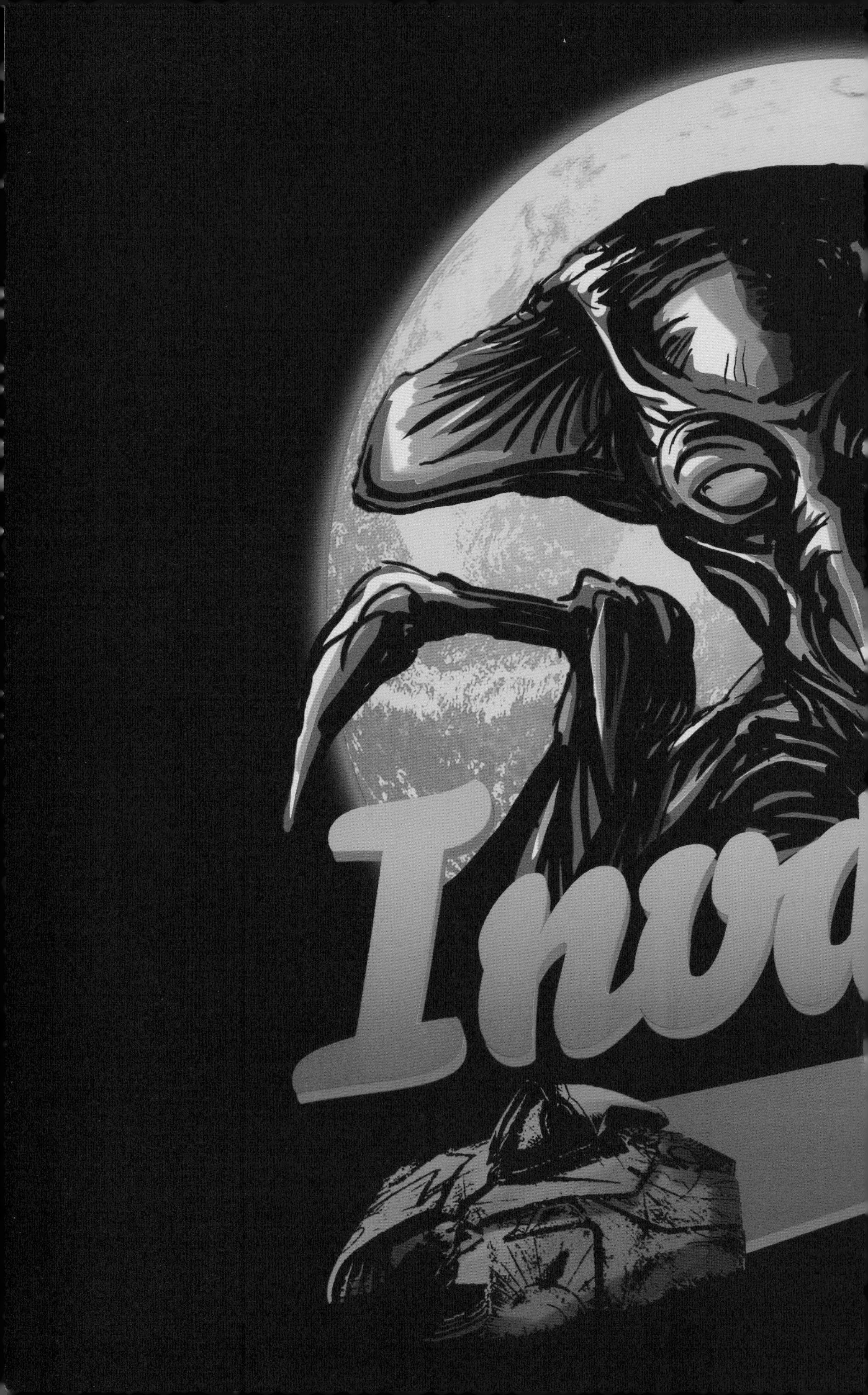
Inva

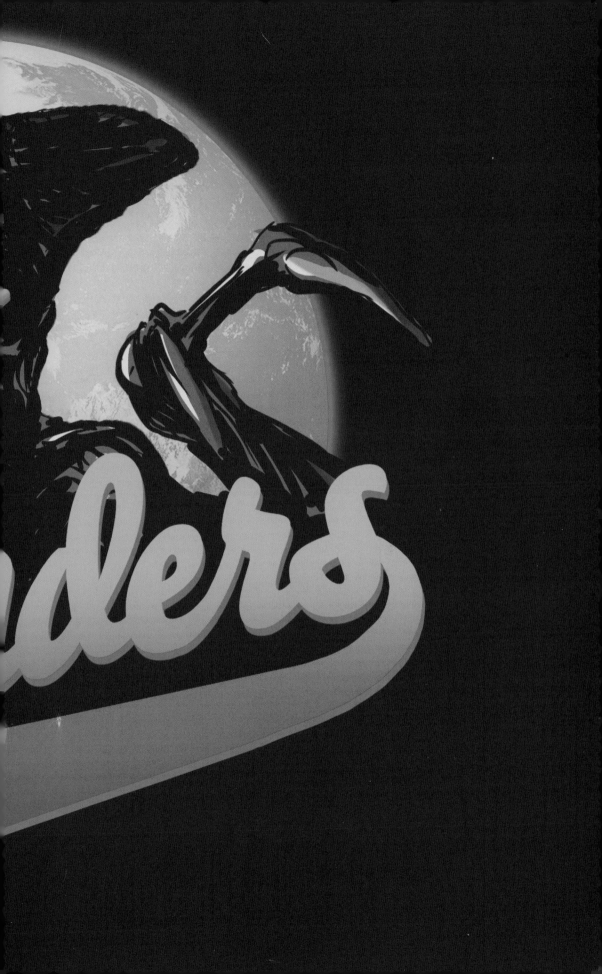

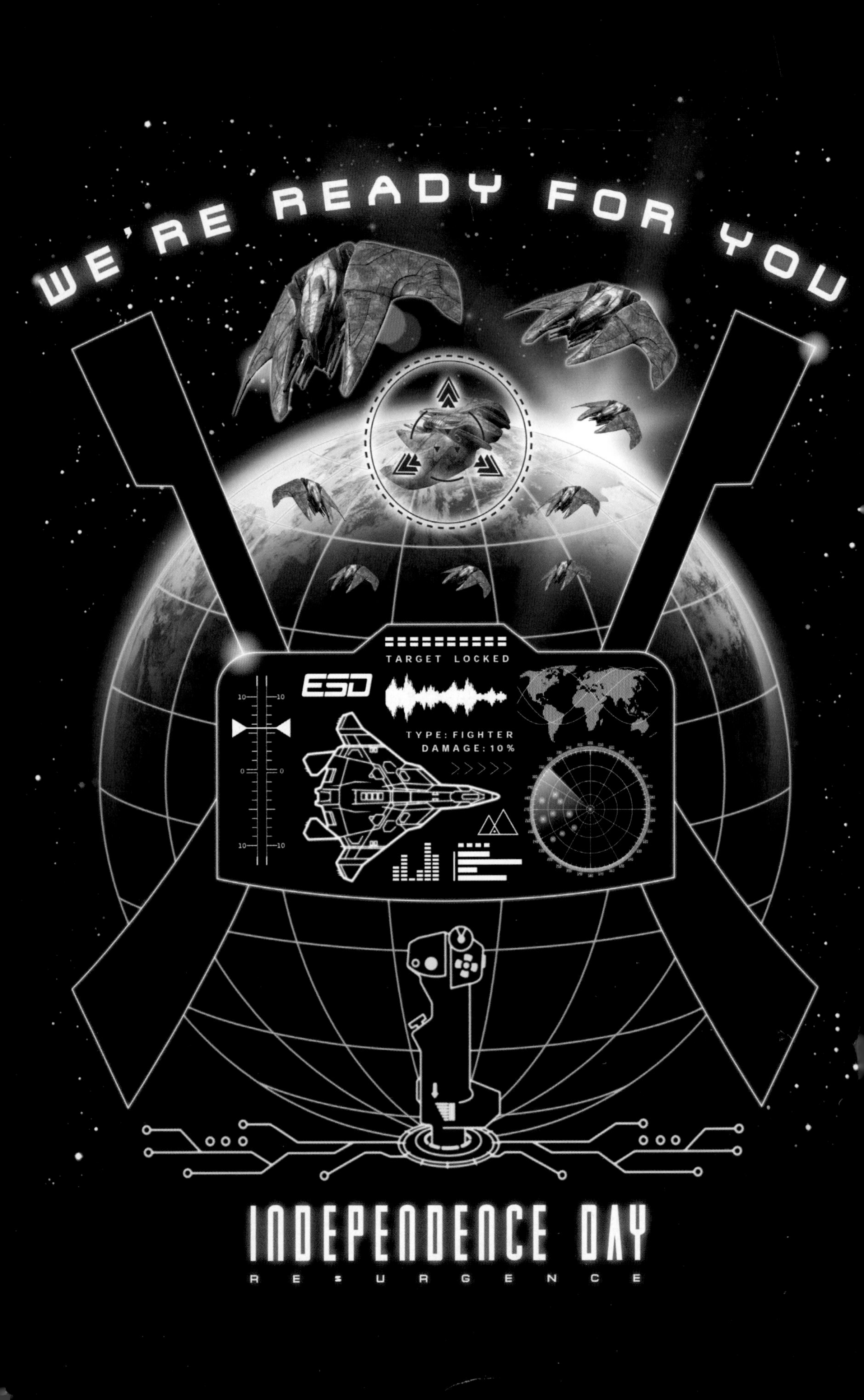
WE'RE READY FOR YOU
TARGET LOCKED
ESD
TYPE: FIGHTER
DAMAGE: 10%
INDEPENDENCE DAY
RESURGENCE

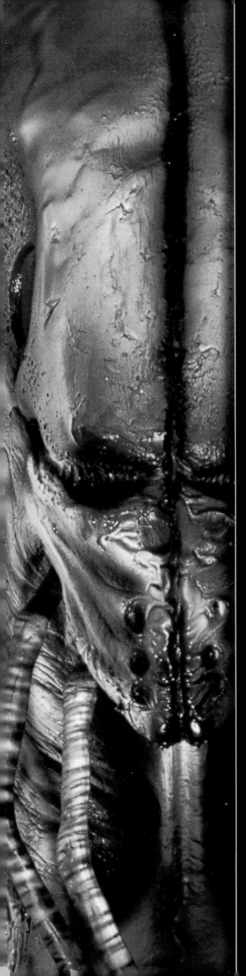

INDEPENDENCE DAY
CREATOR BIOGRAPHIES

Victor Gischler is an American novelist and comic book writer who made his name with a two-year run on *X-Men* for Marvel Comics, and as the writer of Season 10 of *Angel & Faith* for Dark Horse. Other comic credits include *Punisher Max*, *Deadpool: Merc with a Mouth*, *Deadpool Corps*, along with his creator-owned projects *Sally of the Wasteland* and *Clown Fatale*.

Steve Scott is an American comic book artist who has illustrated such titles as *Batman*, *X-Men Forever*, *JLA*, *Batman Confidential*, *Marvel Adventures Hulk* and many more. An industry veteran, his most recent work includes the adaptation of Neil Gaiman's *The Graveyard Book*.

Alex Shibao is a Brazilian comic book illustrator who cut his teeth drawing *Silent Hill* for IDW. He has since worked for numerous publishers on titles as diverse as *Batman/ Superman* and *Vulgaris*.

Ivan Rodriguez is a Brazilian comic book illustrator who has worked regularly for publishers including Dynamite Entertainment and Avatar. He is best know for his work on *Star Wars: Knight Errant*, *The Spider*, and Marvel's *Shadowland*.

Tazio Bettin began his career as a freelance illustrator for roleplaying games such as White Wolf's *Exalted* and Evil Hat Productions' *FATE*.

As a comics artist, he has worked extensively in the Italian indie comic scene, with international credits including Zenescope Entertainment's *Hunters: The Shadowlands*, and Titan Comics' *Sally of the Wasteland*.

Rodney Ramos is an American comic book artist for over 15 years whose career has seen him pencil and ink work for the likes of Marvel, DC Comics, and Valiant. He has worked on such titles as *Batman*, *Green Lantern*, *Wonder Woman*, *52*, *Countdown*, *X-Men*, *Spider-Man*, *Iron Man* and the critically acclaimed *Transmetropolitan*.

Stefani Rennee is a Brazilian comic colorist and illustrator who has worked for a variety of publishers including Image Comics, Dynamite and Zenoscope, His work can be seen on titles such as *Vampirella*, *Ant*, and *The Clockwork Girl*.

Thiago Ribeiro is a Brazilian comic book colorist who has worked on titles including *The Bionic Man* and *Warlord of Mars* Dynamite Enteraiment, and W's *Dead Squad*.

Marcio Myz is a Brazilian comic book colorist who has worked for a range of publishers including BOOM! s and Dynami titles such as *Ven il Ernie*, and *The O Hornet*.

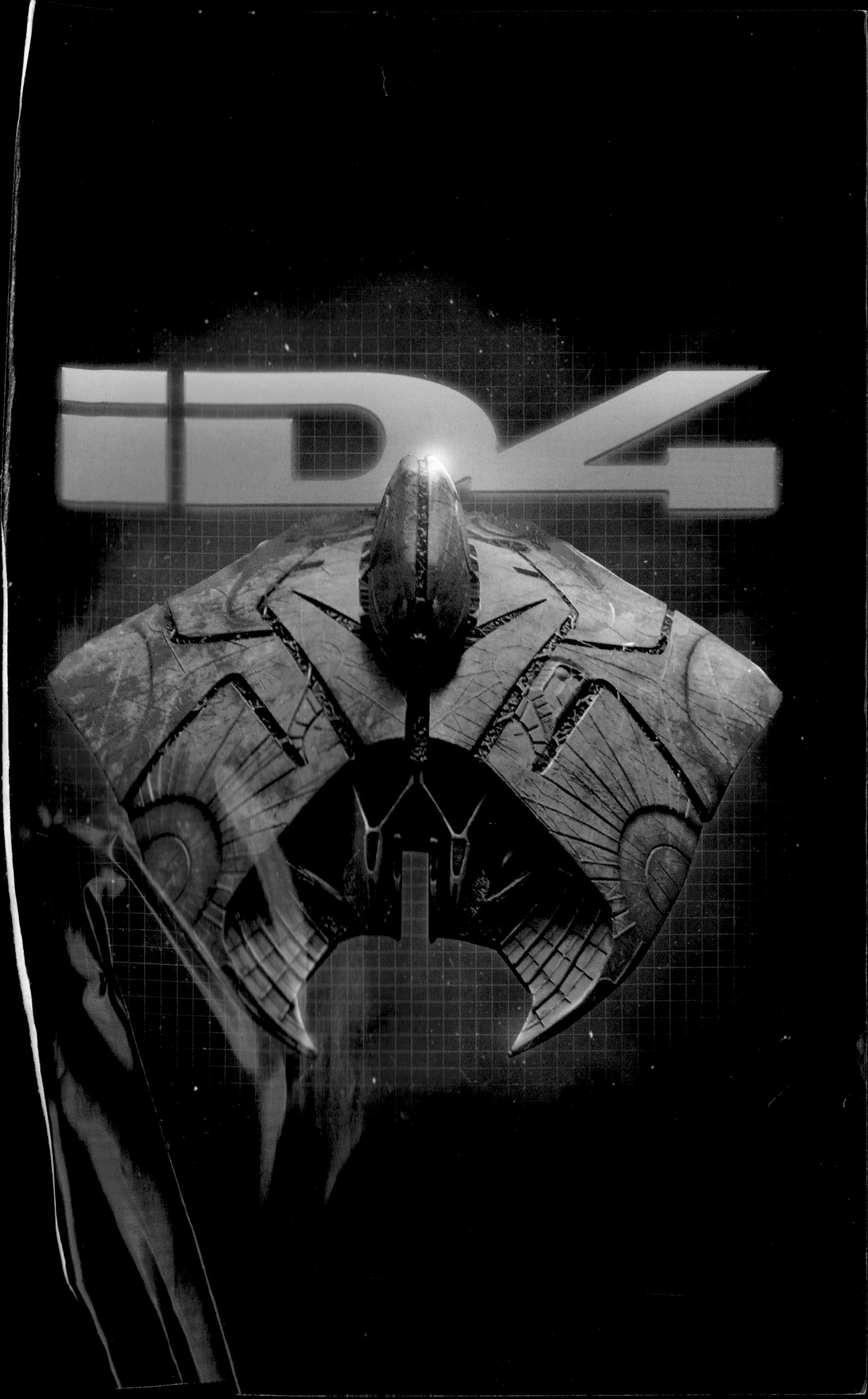
ID4